MAJOR MOMENTS
Life-Changing Lessons of Business Leaders
from the Neeley School of Business at TCU

FOREWORD BY
Robert Bolen

EDITED BY
Rix Quinn and Homer Erekson

TCU Press
Fort Worth, Texas

Library of Congress Cataloging-in-Publication Data

Major moments : life-changing lessons of business leaders from
the Neeley School of Business at TCU / foreword by Robert Bolen ; edited by
Rix Quinn and Homer Erekson.
      p. cm.
  Includes index.
  ISBN 978-0-87565-488-1 (hardcover : alk. paper)
  1. Neeley School of Business--History. 2. Business education--Texas--
Fort Worth--History. 3. Neeley School of Business--Alumni and alumnae--
Biography. I. Quinn, Rix, 1947- II. Erekson, Owen Homer.
   HF1134.N44M34 2012
   650.071'17645--dc23
                              2011048546

TCU Press
P. O. Box 298300
Fort Worth, Texas 76129
817.257.7822
http://www.prs.tcu.edu

To order books: 1.800.826.8911

Book and jacket design by Bill Brammer
www.fusion29.com

We dedicate this book to three inspirational groups:

- to our families, who nurture and support us;

- to the outstanding individuals featured here, who generously shared their stories with us;

- to the Neeley Business School faculty and staff, who strive each day to build the leaders of tomorrow.

Your inspiration reminds us daily that our mission is more than business. It's personal.

CONTENTS

Foreword

Robert (Bob) Bolen served as Mayor of Fort Worth from 1982-1991. He joined the TCU staff as Senior Advisor to the Chancellor in 1991 and serves as a visiting lecturer and advisor to the dean of the Neeley School. He received the TCU Royal Purple Award in 1992 and the Distinguished Alumnus Award from Texas A&M. He was the founder and CEO of Bolen Enterprises before serving as mayor. He has served as president of the Texas Municipal League and the National League of Cities.

Great cities need great universities. And in the best universities is a business school dedicated to preparing its graduates to become leaders in their professions and in their personal and civic lives. The best business education requires not only solid grounding in business principles and applications, but also a commitment to promoting an understanding and practice of ethical behavior.

The Neeley School has a long history of graduating men and women who become leaders in the business world and, in some cases, enter into service to government and nonprofit organizations.

As you read this book, I think you will be amused by many of the stories shared by these very special individuals but even more impressed by their accomplishments and their advice for success in business and in life.

I have always tried to live by the philosophy passed down to me from my father, "to always leave a place a little better than you found it." Clearly the TCU graduates and other successful business leaders highlighted in this book have achieved that objective many times over in their professional, civic, and personal lives.

The men and women profiled herein provide role models who clearly live out the mission of the Neeley School, which is *to develop ethical leaders with a global perspective who help shape the business environment.*

BOB BOLEN

Preface

Nobody knows when business began. It's as old as the first humans who wanted to swap items. "Hey," one cave person might have said to another, "what would you give for this animal skin coat?" Of course neither negotiator could speak English nor write. But each knew the value of trade.

For centuries, while people toiled as farmers, trade was minimal. Eventually a few families banded together in communities for mutual protection.

Village life produced craftsmen who developed special skills. A baker made bread. A barber cut hair — and often performed surgery. A cobbler made shoes. These specialists hired criers to stroll the town announcing what each offered. Those golden-throated narrators took commerce into the marketplace.

INFORMATION SPREADS SEVERAL WAYS

It's speculated that shop signs originated in Babylonia 5,000 years ago. They were probably carved in stone and wood and hung outside the shops. Egyptians get credit for the first road signs, which were stone tablets situated along major wagon paths. These paths served as commercial and military transportation routes, linking Central Asia and Arabia with Egypt and Africa. These routes, called the Via Maris by the Romans and the Horus Road by Egyptians, promoted agricultural trading by land and sea.

The world changed forever with Gutenberg's fifteenth-century invention of the printing press. Now merchants could create and circulate handbills. Next came newspapers, and eventually daily newspapers. The first continuously published newspaper in colonial America was the *Boston News-Letter,* initially published on April 24, 1704. It included items such as political appointments, sermons, lists of ship arrivals, and deaths, along with advertisements for commerce and the lottery. Citizens — especially the ones who could read — could now stay informed about local and national events. Literacy became essential to the world, and commerce embraced it.

BIRTH OF BUSINESS SCHOOLS

Modern universities began around 1100 A.D. as cooperative ventures between teachers and pupils. For early universities, such as the University of Bologna, founded in 1088, campuses didn't exist. The university became any space people gathered to learn, like a house or a church.

Three types of universities emerged: In the first, students paid the teachers; in the second, the church paid teachers; in the third, the government or monarchy paid teachers. Many of those ancient schools stressed seven liberal arts — arithmetic, grammar, logic, rhetoric, geometry, music theory, and astronomy.

In 1759 Lisbon's Aula do Comercio (now the Instituto Superior de Economia e Gestão of the Technical University of Lisbon) became the first institution to teach commerce. This was followed in 1819 by the founding of the Ecole Supérieure de Commerce of Paris, the oldest business school in the world. And in 1881 The Wharton School at the University of Pennsylvania became the first American business school within a university.

TCU's Commercial School began three years later in 1884, offering majors in accounting, business administration, finance, insurance, secretarial sciences, and transportation/public utilities. It became the Department of Business Administration in 1922 and the School of Business in 1938, the first year it offered the master of business administration.

CITIZENS OF THE WORLD

What has been a constant for business education at TCU is the development of great alumni, now numbering more than 17,000, who have made and are making a real difference for business and society literally throughout the world.

This volume celebrates human creativity and entrepreneurship. You hold in your hands the thoughts of some remarkable people, the combined wisdom and experience of an all-star business team. These business executives who are alumni or key partners of the Neeley School tell you about the ideas, innovations, and discoveries that led to career advancement and success.

We have assembled this collection of stories as part of the celebration of the upcoming seventy-fifth anniversary of the permanent founding of the School of Business at TCU. Our plan was to feature at least seventy-five of the leading alumni or supporters of the Neeley School. While we have ultimately included selections for more than eighty persons, we of course know that there are hundreds of other Neeley alumni who could have been chosen. Although it was difficult to finally settle on whom to include, we hope that all friends of the Neeley School will see elements of their own stories here.

We are especially grateful to each person who was willing to voluntarily share his or her story and advice. These people all have very busy and demanding professional lives, along with family and other personal responsibilities. In gratitude for their willingness to be included, a portion of the profits of this book will go to the endowed Neeley Heritage Scholarship. This scholarship honors the many contributions of Neeley alumni, faculty, and staff who have worked together over the years to create a premier educational experience; it will support one or more business students at TCU each year in preparing the next generation of business leaders.

In a letter dated February 5, 1676, Isaac Newton paraphrased an ancient adage, writing, "If I have seen a little further, it is by standing on the shoulders of giants."

We hope this book will help you see further and better.

RIX QUINN AND
HOMER EREKSON

Building the Foundation for
the Neeley School

M.J. Neeley
Our Namesake and
Favorite Aggie

M.J. NEELEY graduated from Texas A&M in 1922 with a degree in textile engineering. He was born in 1898 and passed away in 1996. He was known as a confident entrepreneur, building his wealth from an early start in the transportation industry and expanding into many fields, owning approximately thirty companies. Among his many business accomplishments was the building of Hobbs Manufacturing into a highly successful trailer manufacturer.

Mr. Neeley was elected to the board of trustees in 1947, served as chairman from 1969-72, and was named an honorary trustee in 1975. The business school at TCU proudly represents the name of M.J. Neeley as a leading international business school.

When M.J. Neeley died in March 1996, he left behind not only his family but a legion of friends who'd been mentored by this gentle genius.

One of them, Warren Mackey, says M.J. told him this parable in the Neeley home study:

"A man walks through an orchard looking for a tasty apple. He sees some good ones way up high in a tree but fears he might fall if he climbs to get them.

"So he finds a shady spot to lie down, hoping gravity will cause one to fall in his lap. Finally one falls, but it's rotten and worm-infested. He'd enjoyed the day dreaming about good apples but didn't like what he got.

"Next, he gets up and walks over to a small peach tree, and on a limb within reach hang several beautiful peaches. He shakes that limb, and a basketful of delicious peaches falls to the ground.

"He has a great afternoon gorging himself on the fruits of his labor.

"The moral of this story: When an opportunity comes along, shake the hell out of it!"

EARLY YEARS

M.J. Neeley didn't graduate from TCU. However, he adopted the University whole-heartedly. A graduate of Texas A&M, he played football for the Aggies and received a degree in textile engineering. Neeley's first job was managing a twine mill in Waco. He left that position to come to Fort Worth, where he purchased a house on University Drive and worked as a bookkeeper for Hobbs Manufacturing.

Former chancellor Dr. James M. Moudy recounted Neeley's first major business endeavor. "[Hobbs Manufacturing], as I recall, was struggling. M.J. thought he could turn it around and offered to buy it. The owners were surprised by his offer, because their own views of the business were negative. But M.J. bought the company and built a tremendous business." Today, Hobbs is a part of the trucking manufacturer Terex, a Fortune 500 company.

HELD OWNERSHIP IN THIRTY COMPANIES

"Some very successful entrepreneurs own one or two companies," marveled Stan Block, a Neeley professor and holder of the Stan Block Chair in Finance. "But Mr. Neeley held ownership in some thirty companies over the years. Some of those he helped lift from near-bankruptcy. Mr. Neeley could always spot value in a business. He always looked for opportunity.

"He was a solid Fort Worth citizen," Block continued. "He even encouraged Dean Harrison to get the business school nationally accredited by the American Association of Collegiate Schools of Business."

Mr. Neeley's contributions to the business and civic communities were widely recognized. He received the National Conference of Christians and Jews Brotherhood Award in 1965, the B'nai B'rith Civic Achievement Award in 1966, and the Rotary Bill Todd Award in 1967. TCU recognized his achievements, awarding him an honorary Doctor of Laws degree in 1967.

LIFELONG ASSOCIATION WITH TCU

"M.J. always lived close to the school, in the neighborhood," Dr. Moudy recalled. "His association with the University was life-long. He was elected to the board of trustees in 1947, served as its chairman from 1969 to 1972, and was named an honorary trustee in 1975."

M.J. Neeley epitomized the behavior expected of ethical and moral business leaders. While serving as a trustee, he championed an idea to get more student input into forming TCU's policies. However, he rejected the notion of a student member on the board of trustees because he believed it to be tokenism and that the student might feel overwhelmed and overlooked at a board meeting. Rather, he argued for a student advisory committee with broad representation from the student body.

In recognition of his devotion and dedication to the School of Business and TCU, the school was formally named the M.J. Neeley School of Business in September, 1967.

GROUNDBREAKING
Dean Emeritus Colby Dixon Hall, Chancellor McGruder Ellis Sadler, Trustee M.J. Neeley, and Trustee Granville Walker ('35) officiate at the groundbreaking for Dan Rogers Hall, circa 1956.

Dan Rogers
A Century of Devotion

DANIEL DIXON ROGERS *graduated from what was then known as the Commercial School of TCU in 1909. A lifelong school supporter, he was elected a trustee in 1915 and helped to guide TCU's substantial growth over thirty-seven years. The Neeley School's original business building bears his name.*

Suppose you could actually step inside an old college yearbook and transport yourself back 100 years, to the school Dan Rogers attended. What would you find? One thing you'd discover would be a young university emerging in wide-open spaces on University Drive. The city's population grew from 26,688 in 1900 to 73,312 in 1910.

Dan Rogers came to Fort Worth after graduating from Temple High School in 1905. Two years after his college graduation, he married Lucile Wolford in 1911. They had one daughter, Dorothy.

FROM BUSINESS SUCCESS TO TALL COTTON
In 1925 Rogers joined the Mercantile National Bank and eventually became senior vice president of oil loans. He was with them until 1949, when he became chairman of the board of directors at National City Bank of Texas.

Few know about another of Rogers' achievements. Working with the founder, J. Curtis Sanford, he led the growth of the Cotton Bowl as a national football classic and soon became recognized as "Mr. Cotton Bowl." He led the campaign for the Southwest Conference to adopt the game and pledge its champion as host team. The Cotton Bowl Athletic Association became an official agency on November 23, 1940. Rogers was president and later chairman and held that position until 1952. (Source: AT&T Cotton Bowl Classic, Hall of Fame)

Dan Rogers was a devoted church member. At East Dallas Christian Church, he was an elder and led the famous Slaytor Bible Class in group singing. "My grandfather loved his family, East Dallas Christian Church, and TCU," Sally Holmes said fondly.

"The day before my granddad died," she recalled, "he'd been to Fort Worth for a TCU game. He died of a heart attack in church, right after singing 'God Bless America.'" The date was October 16, 1952.

Rogers generously gave time and money to civic and church causes. Committed to education, he served on the Dallas school board for many years, and in 1955 the Dallas Independent School District opened an elementary school named in his honor.

CHEERING FOR TCU
In *Walking TCU, A Historical Perspective,* Joan Hewatt Swaim wrote: "It would be difficult to find a truer, more loyal and stalwart supporter of TCU than Dan D. Rogers."

While a student at TCU, Rogers was a band member, cheerleader, and class officer. He was instrumental in founding TCU's alumni association and served as its first president in 1913. He avidly supported TCU athletic programs and promoted the building of TCU's first football stadium, old Clark Field. In 1925 he began presenting the Rogers Trophy each year to TCU's outstanding football player.

Because of his many contributions to TCU, Dan D. Rogers Hall — the original building that housed the Neeley School — was completed in the summer of 1957 and named for Mr. Rogers as a lasting reminder to its namesake's devotion.

Charles Tandy
Focus on Simple Processes – and Profit.

John V. Roach — former Tandy Corporation Chairman and now TCU Board of Trustees Emeritus and member of the Neeley International Board of Visitors — spoke at the dedication of Charles Tandy's statue as it was moved from downtown Fort Worth to the Neeley School. At the October 23, 2009, event, he shared these reflections on his friend, the legendary business leader.

After Charles returned from World War II, he joined his father in the leather shoe findings business. They built the Tandy leather store chain with self-manufactured, high-margin leather goods. Store managers were partners with a sharp focus on profits. Every penny counted.

HOW TANDY BUILT STORES BY HAND

For example, one manager related that he and Charles had bought a truck and loaded it with lumber to build fixtures and the store-opening inventory. Then they drove to Boise, the manager in his car and Charles driving the truck. They drove up and down the streets of Boise until they found a store location. They rented it, built the fixtures, moved the inventories into the store, opened the store, and sold the truck. Charles flew back.

The Tandy Leather chain was built, sold, and bought back. It emerged as Tandy Corporation, with a New York stock exchange listing, in 1960.

THE SECRET OF SUCCESS

Charles was a builder. He built Tandy Leather and other handicraft businesses, and in 1963 he bailed out both the First National Bank of Boston and Massachusetts Mutual Insurance Company when he took control of RadioShack. At that time there were nine stores. RadioShack was essentially bankrupt from a mail-order credit program. It had thousands and thousands of stock-keeping units. Charles — with the help of Lew Kornfeld, Bernie Appel, and Dave Beckerman — reduced the number of SKUs and focused on the gross margin.

RadioShack specialty stores grew at an almost unprecedented rate to 1,000 stores, and then to thousands of stores. It was the cash flow from the leather business that built the electronics business.

CHARISMATIC LEADER

Charles was exceptionally charismatic. When you saw him, he always had a group gathered around him. He did most of the talking.

He was a salesman. He pitched his stock to friends and to Wall Street and insisted that executives and store managers buy stock even if they had to borrow to do so. He was quick to point out that if you sold some stock to buy a sofa or a car, you should think twice. That's because it would be the most expensive sofa or car you could possibly buy.

While stock ownership motivated employees and created many millionaires, the Securities and Exchange Commission would not permit his style today. As for friends, many have regretfully lamented to me that they did not follow his sales pitch to buy Tandy stock.

HOW HE DEFINED ENTREPRENEURSHIP

Charles had a sharp business mind. He institutionalized entrepreneurship. The profit-and-loss statement was his bible. In every store and in every business unit, the manager was expected to know the numbers and use the numbers for decision-making. The manager and executive compensation were driven by the numbers.

Here's one personal example of his sharp insight. I started as manager of the data processing department. The accountants had us develop a computerized profit/loss statement — a new edition of the bible — and it became my job to sell the new statements to Charles.

I put on my best sales pitch. It would be more accurate each month to consolidate, and I told him it would permit us to get the P & L out probably three days sooner each month as we continued to grow.

He finally stopped my sales pitch, blew a puff of smoke from his signature cigar, and said, "The store in Bakersfield, California, has been losing money for three months. If the P & L came out three days sooner, I would have known for three months and three days it was losing money. It doesn't make a damn when you get the numbers out. It's what you do with them that makes a difference."

LESSON PLANS
He believed in keeping business processes simple and focusing on profit. He could get extraordinary results out of ordinary people.

Charles was a great teacher and took the time to teach. He would spend hours with an executive or employee to explain a principle. I originally thought that if you had been told something once, it was an insult to have to be told again. Charles' view was different. You got the same lesson over and over to be sure you understood the principle. I'll bet I got a thirty-minute-plus lesson on gross margin thirty or forty times.

ATTENTION TO DETAIL
The sales order office of Tandy Industries was a busy place.

He also taught you to focus on facts, on the numbers. And you'd better know them, because he did. These impromptu teaching sessions might last one to four hours or more.

UNORTHODOX BUSINESS MEETINGS
Charles was unorthodox. Business meetings and teaching sessions would last for hours and were usually unscheduled. He would show up at ten or eleven o'clock in the morning and stay until seven or eight at night or even later. If you happened to be in one of those sessions, you were just late for dinner.

Appointments with Charles were worthless. He might show up late or not at all. It didn't much matter if you were an insider or an outsider. Meetings happened wherever he was working. He always had a headquarters office, but he often held court at his apartment or at a storefront on Throckmorton Street. He managed "by walking around" even before anybody wrote about it!

MAGNIFICENT MOTIVATOR
Charles used his charisma to be highly motivational. While he always pushed in a positive direction, it was sometimes challenging — but people loved it. One phrase he used occasionally was, "You've fought success so long you've nearly won." I remember one day he was talking to the head of store operations, encouraging him to open stores more quickly. The operations guy resisted, probably because it affected his bonus. Charles finally said, "I've drug you up the mountain this far, and I'm going to drag you over the top."

HIS BRAINPOWER GENERATED HEAT.
He would raise the question occasionally as to whether or not you had the sense to get in out of the rain. But it was not mean-spirited. In fact, at that instant you probably agreed with him. If you couldn't stand the heat generated by brainpower, you'd better get out of the kitchen. But as hot as it got, rumor has it that Charles never fired but one person.

Charles had a creative mind. He churned out more ideas in a week than many people produce in a lifetime. Interestingly, even though he had many ideas — often occurring during the marathon sessions — he let his executives think about them when they left and decide to pursue or discard them. Rarely did an idea come with a directive to implement it.

FINANCIAL VISIONARY
Charles was a financial genius. He bought companies like some people buy shoes, because he could always see how they could be successful.

Sometimes management did not have as keen a vision as he did. In the mid-1970s, Charles made a smart move by turning Tandy Corporation into three publicly traded companies: Tandy Corporation, Tandycrafts, and Tandy Brands. It was important because nobody but Charles could have managed the stable of companies we had. Tandy Corporation became an electronics company driven by RadioShack. During this time frame, he baffled Wall Street by buying back stock. This was frowned on by the Street at the time. Charles was simply ahead of his time. He also chuckled at Wall Street when they would trade stock for convertible bonds, then, when the stock went up, he would call the bonds.

At a New York analyst meeting, someone asked how many CB radios he was going to sell. Charles fired back, "Sixty thousand."

The analyst challenged him, "How do you know?"

"Because that's how many we own," Charles said. He was not always the darling of Wall Street, though, because he was probably smarter than most of them!

FORT WORTH SUPPORTER AND FRIEND
What I have attempted to give you today is the essence of Charles Tandy, who was admired by his subjects and friends. For a more complete biography of Charles, read *The Money Machine*.

He made money for his friends, employees, and the investment community. He was a supporter of TCU financially and as a board member. He provided scholarship support at TCU for the lineal descendants of his employees. My daughters benefitted, as well as hundreds of others.

He was a proud citizen of Fort Worth. He gave impetus to the development of downtown Fort Worth when he built the two Tandy towers at a time when downtown was on the decline.

I salute the location of the Tandy statue in front of Tandy Hall. It's a fitting tribute to one of TCU's most outstanding entrepreneurs.

Advice inspired by Charles Tandy
- *Know your business completely. Tandy literally built a few stores with his bare hands.*
- *Find a niche market where you can excel. Tandy created specialty stores that grew at a fast rate.*
- *Keep a tight focus on the specific products that sell best.*
- *Analyze numbers and learn how to use them to make objective decisions.*
- *Educate employees on the most critical numbers to watch.*
- *Keep most management processes simple and easily understandable.*
- *Give company executives the autonomy to make decisions.*

IN HIS HONOR
A statue of Charles Tandy, dedicated October 23, 2009, stands outside Tandy Hall at TCU.

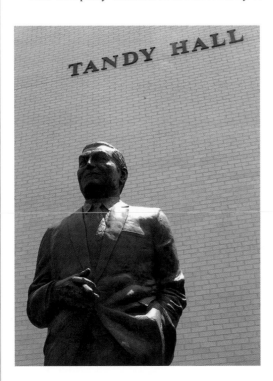

The Neeley School:
It's More Than Business.
It's Personal.®

Homer Erekson,
Dean, Neeley School
(2008-present)

As an alumnus of TCU, I know firsthand the value of a TCU diploma showing that you graduated from the Neeley School. You won't find another business school with such a strong reputation for being personal, connected, and real.

We are very clear about our mission, which is twofold:
- to develop ethical leaders with a global perspective who help shape the business environment; and
- to develop and disseminate leading-edge thought in order to improve the practice of business.

While the study of business has changed dramatically through the years, the focus of the Neeley School, with a commitment to the personal and professional development of our students, has remained constant. We believe that business goes beyond mastering functional business skills to include ethical decisions and motivational leadership. Our niche as a premier private school allows us to provide unique opportunities for our students to learn, grow, and develop their individual strengths.

Our small size and outstanding faculty-to-student ratio enable us to ensure that our undergraduate and graduate students are exposed to challenging business problems, supported in learning to make informed decisions, and positioned to develop premium communication skills to present themselves and their ideas.

HISTORICAL PERSPECTIVES OF THE TCU BUSINESS SCHOOL

The School of Business opened in 1884 as Commercial School. It was renamed the School of Business in 1896 and then the College of Business in 1901. The Department of Business Administration was established in 1922 and became the School of Business in 1938, the first year TCU offered a master of business administration. It is this permanent establishment of the designation as a School that we are celebrating as part of the 75th anniversary in 2013.

In 1938 the undergraduate degree offered by the School of Business was the bachelor of science in commerce, with a major selected from accounting, business administration, finance, insurance, secretarial sciences, and transportation and public utilities.

As director for both the School of Business and the Evening College, A. L. Boeck encouraged the development of evening classes in business subjects. In 1938-39, classes in the Evening College were scheduled in accounting, transportation, advertising, insurance, business administration, and economics. Two years' coursework resulted in certificates in accounting, general business, and secretarial science.

In 1967, the School of Business was named for M.J. Neeley in honor of his twenty-five years of personal service on the TCU Board of Trustees and his financial contributions to TCU.

E. M. Sowell was appointed the first dean in 1944. He has been followed by eight other academic leaders who have attempted to assure that the School of Business at TCU consistently remained on track to become a leading national business program.

RESPONDING TO THE CHANGING DEMANDS OF BUSINESS

A nationally prominent business school requires great faculty and staff, great students, great programs, great facilities, and resources to fuel the vision. At the Neeley School, we believe we have a real advantage nationally in each of these areas. And we have a strong commitment from everyone here to accomplish our best and to prepare students for the changing demands of business.

DEANS, BUSINESS SCHOOL, TCU

E.M. Sowell
(1944-1954)

Ike H. Harrison
(1955-1971)

Joseph L. Steele
(1971-1976)

Gilbert R. Whitaker
(1976-1979)

Edward A. Johnson
(1979-1986)

H. Kirk Downey
(1986-1999)

Robert F. Lusch
(2000-2004)

Daniel G. Short
(2004-2008)

Our programs focus on individual development and emphasize more than strong functional skills. Through a large variety of applied learning experiences, our students learn how to use what they know to make a difference in business organizations. In fact, we want our graduates to be prepared, whether on their first job or later in the boardroom, to stand and deliver.

The opportunities for students to experience the challenges of business during their course of study have changed significantly through the years. In 1939, student organizations included the TCU Chamber of Commerce and the Collegiate Business and Professional Women's Club. By 2000, we had four student clubs and the Educational Investment Fund (EIF). The EIF was founded in 1973 with a $600,000 donation from William C. Conner and was the first completely student-run investment fund in the country, now valued at well over $1 million.

In 2011, undergraduate students in the Neeley School can participate in fourteen different student organizations, and they have the opportunity to be a part of several different special programs including the Educational Investment Fund, the Neeley Fellows, the BNSF Next Generation Leadership program, the Executive Supply Chain program, Neeley Associates, and a Values and Ventures national business plan competition.

Our graduate students have similar opportunities. Our MBA students have the opportunity to work on field-based projects with leading companies through our Neeley and Associates consulting program, to have intimate meetings one-on-one with leading CEOs as part of our C-Level Confidential program, to participate in the EIF program, and — for the last three years —to travel to Omaha for small-group meetings with Warren Buffett.

We are fortunate to have specialized centers that support programming for our students and members of the business community. Our centers include the Tandy Center for Executive Leadership, the Supply and Value Chain Center, the Alcon Career Services Center, the Luther King Capital Management Finance Center, the Professional Development Center, and the Neeley Entrepreneurship Center.

Our proud and active alumni, as well as other prominent business partners, connect Neeley students to a vital business pipeline, and our international programs expand their horizons. Our students have the opportunity to take advantage of more than a dozen different global programs in many different countries.

The key to any great business program is having outstanding faculty committed to high quality education and top-tier research. In the Neeley School, we are fortunate to have twenty-one endowed faculty positions and to have five faculty members who are editors of leading jour-

C-LEVEL CONVERSATION
TCU MBA students have the opportunity to meet and confer with Warren Buffett. Shown here is the fourth-year visit in 2010.

nals in their field. But I am most proud of the dedication of our faculty in assuring high quality learning experiences for our students in and outside the classroom.

There is no question that it's working. We have numerous rankings that testify to the quality of our faculty, staff, and students. For instance, in 2011 the *Bloomberg Business Week* ranking of undergraduate business programs places the Neeley School as twenty-ninth in the country. And it's hard to beat the recognition received by our entrepreneurship program, recognized by the United States Association for Small Business and Entrepreneurship as the Model National Undergraduate Entrepreneurship Program for 2011.

Indeed, as we approach the seventy-fifth anniversary of the School of Business at TCU, the Neeley School can proudly count hundreds of graduates who have become ethical leaders with a global perspective who help shape the business environment every day. I hope you enjoy reading the stories of many of these distinguished graduates included in this book and that you'll be as inspired as I was in learning about their accomplishments and reflecting on their advice.

HOMER EREKSON
John V. Roach Dean
Neeley School of Business

Accounting and Finance

"Listen well, learn to work with others, and communicate clearly."

J. LUTHER KING, JR.

"A good friend once told me this, 'Major in accounting, and you'll always have a job.'"

VERNON WILSON BRYANT, JR.

"Find out what's needed and then do it."

LAURA SHRODE MILLER

There's no doubt that accounting is the language of business. But the accounting and financial industry executives in this section have gone well beyond learning how to use accounting to communicate. They know that value creation involves focusing the mission of any company on value-adding activities that motivate employees to be increasingly productive through appropriate development and rewards. These deliver high returns for investors through revenue growth and attractive profit margins, while providing products and services to customers who respond to their ever-changing demands.

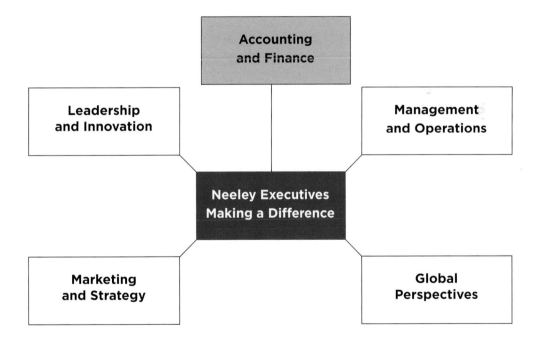

FEATURED ALUMNUS

J. LUTHER KING, JR.
STAYING THE COURSE

J. LUTHER KING, JR. *is president and founder of Luther King Capital Management (LKCM), a registered investment advisory firm in Fort Worth. He attended Fort Worth public schools and graduated from Polytechnic High School. He received B.S.C. (1962) and M.B.A. (1966) degrees from TCU. In 1968, Luther received an honorable discharge from the U.S. Air Force Reserve. He became a CFA (Certified Financial Analyst) charterholder in 1971.*

Luther began his professional career as a credit analyst at First National Bank in 1963. In 1970, he became a senior investment officer, managing mutual fund assets for Los Angeles-based Shareholders Management Co. In 1973 he joined Lionel D. Edie & Company, a New York-based investment firm, and in 1975 he became a director and the manager of the Dallas office.

In 1979, Luther founded Luther King Capital Management. LKCM is one of the largest independent employee-owned investment advisory firms in the Dallas-Fort Worth area.

Luther King is a trustee and was chairman of the board of trustees at TCU from 2005 to 2011, where he received the Distinguished Alumnus Award in 1992. He has been a member of the Neeley School International Board of Visitors since 1991. As a CFA, Luther was recognized in the November/December 2007 issue of CFA Magazine as "Most Inspiring" in the investment advisory profession. He is a founding member of the Strategic Advisory Board of the CFA Society of Dallas/Fort Worth. In May of 2008, Luther was awarded the Daniel J. Forrestal III Leadership Award for Professional Ethics and Standards of Investment Practice by the CFA Institute. He was named the 2010 Executive of the Year for the Fort Worth Business Hall of Fame. And in 2011, Luther and Teresa King received the Royal Purple Award from the TCU Alumni for extraordinary service and support of TCU and to the greater community. Luther King has served on the board of several NYSE-listed companies as well as serving as a board member for several private companies. He is a member of the Investment Advisory Committee for the Trustees of the Employees Retirement System of Texas where he served as chairman. He has served as vice chairman of the University of Texas Investment Management Company, which has responsibil-ities for the Endowment of the University of Texas and a portion of the Endowment for Texas A&M University. Luther served on the board of the Investment Adviser Association in Wash-ington, D.C., where he served as chairman. He also has served as President of the Board of Gov-ernors of the Fort Worth Club, on the board of several philanthropic organizations, and as a former trustee of St. Mark's School of Texas.

The Kings live in Dallas. They have two married sons, both graduates of the TCU Ranch Management Program: Bryan, class of 1994, and Mason, class of 1999.

Two key factors influence our decisions in life:
- *product of age group and environment*
- *mentors for guidance*

Let me elaborate. First, we grow up in a specific time period, graduate with a certain high school and/or college class, and form friendships with contemporaries in our first jobs. These colleagues may be the same age or five-plus years older. Many of these individuals will be important professionally and personally throughout your life.

A factor that influenced me in my early twenties was the military environment. Some people remember the military draft, when most young men were required to serve. I joined the Air Force Reserves as a non-commissioned airman, where I quickly learned to salute everything that moved.

Secondly, mentors are important. Some of my earliest professional guidance came from Paul Mason, then president of First National Bank of Fort Worth. My career began there in 1963 as a credit analyst, supporting the lending function of the bank. Mr. Mason was a mentor who counseled and guided me into the trust investment department, where he believed I would get more analytical experience from an investment perspective. His advice yielded me a wealth of knowledge in security analysis and stock selection. Thanks to his belief in my abilities, I became a security analyst. His positive insight and advice were very important to my career path.

EARLY YEARS

My working memories began early, before the teenage years, when I worked for relatives on their farms in the Texas Hill Country. I repaired fences, combined wheat, and doctored cattle — among other things. It was hot in the summer and cold in the winter. I was paid fifty cents an hour for a total of five dollars a day. These jobs were followed by more urban summer and after-school jobs while in high school. Working taught me to be organized and to strive for balance.

I began college at Arlington State College, now the University of Texas at Arlington. As a sophomore, I transferred to TCU. The tuition was higher, but it was a great choice and the right school for me. I worked seven of eight semesters in order to offset a portion of the cost.

After active duty as a reservist in the Air Force, I returned to Fort Worth and received job offers from two banks. The decision was simple: I chose First National Bank because it paid $25 more a month.

My soon-to-be wife, Teresa, obtained a job teaching math at Rosemont Junior High. After we were married in 1964, we settled into our furnished apartment. During this period, life was basic and simple — going to school at night, being at Carswell Air Force Base on the weekends, and building investment analytical skills as an assistant investment officer at the bank.

From First National I then went to work for Shareholders Management, a large mutual fund company based in Los Angeles that had a Dallas office. There I worked with Bill Sams, an excellent investor, and continued to refine my investment skills and generate good returns.

In the summer of 1973, I joined Lionel D. Edie & Company, a New York-based investment counseling firm that focused on shares of growth companies — "one-decision growth stocks." While working there, I learned the importance of valuation in controlling risks. The manager of the Edie Dallas office was Bill Custard, who wisely guided me in the nuances of client relations in the private wealth sector. His mentorship continues today to be very important to me.

In the 1970s, several career advancement positions were offered. In 1973, Shareholders asked me to move to Los Angeles, and in 1977, Lionel D. Edie asked me to move to New York to be chief investment officer and in 1978 to be president. I turned down these opportunities because I wanted to stay in Texas. At the end of 1978, we sold Edie to a New York bank.

In 1979, I established Luther King Capital Management with the support of a local family as our first client. My new company initially occupied about 400 square feet as a subtenant of Dee Kelly's law firm. I hired one employee to handle operations, got two card tables and some folding chairs, and we began LKCM. Thanks to great clients and their support and good returns, we have grown.

LKCM is now into our third decade as a private, independent, and founder-managed investment firm. We have been fortunate to be able to give something back to the community and profession that have been so good to me.

LEARN FROM YOUR MENTORS
AND TEACH OTHERS, TOO.

Your best chance of being successful in a career is to identify what you enjoy. If you enjoy your work, then several things happen. First, you can pursue your career for a long period of time, and the risk of burnout is greatly diminished. If you're pursuing a career only because of the financial rewards, the risk you run is that by the time you're forty, especially in a competitive environment, you are toast. Identify a career path that you can enjoy, because this path will yield longevity at a high level. Consequently, you will have a fuller professional life, and your fulfillment will be greater.

There are no shortcuts in the investment business. One needs to know the fundamentals and realize that good investors are patient and disciplined. That's one of the reasons we established the Luther King Capital Management Center for Financial Studies at TCU, which provides study stipends for Certified Financial Analyst (CFA) candidates. We also offer student scholarships and provide subscriptions to information platforms.

Since the inception of our firm in 1979, I have been very pleased that, through our LKCM intern program, we have been able to guide, advise, support, and champion hundreds of Neeley School students. Our interns get right into the office flow — they are not here to file. Often they come in early and stay late. Each year our interns go to New York to visit Wall Street firms and to visit the floor at the New York Stock Exchange.

Our LKCM interns are young, bright, and inquisitive. They bring high energy to the firm — an important component in any organization. They ask questions and don't take "That's the way we've always done it" as a good answer. To be able to make an impact on those young people's lives is something that is lasting. An LKCM internship is one way to give back to bright people.

Individuals like Paul Mason and Bill Custard advised and counseled me. They believed in me, gave me a start in my career, and offered advice along the way. These men could hit the ball, and they didn't mind telling me how to hit the ball. That's the kind of mentor and adviser I strive to be.

SUMMARY
- Do a good job, and a mentor will find you.
- Stay at least two years in your first job.
- Develop the ability to focus.
- Listen well, learn to work with others, and communicate clearly.
- Demonstrate consistent determination, integrity, and professionalism.
- Identify what you enjoy to further improve chances for professional success. The cornerstone of pursuit is passion. If you have passion for your work, you can continue longer at a higher level.

BIG APPLE ADVENTURE
Neeley undergraduates traveled to New York City in 2009 to meet with leading executives.

Ann Dully Borowiec
The College Class
I'll Always Remember

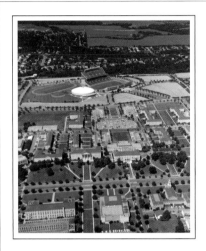

FROM ABOVE
This aerial view of the TCU campus was photographed in 1966.

ANN DULLY BOROWIEC *is managing director and chairman for J.P. Morgan Private Bank New Jersey, which serves high-net-worth clients. Operating in 25 states and 11 countries, the private banking division of J.P. Morgan manages more than $250 billion in client assets.*

Ann graduated from TCU in 1982 with a bachelor of business administration in accounting and finance, followed by a CPA designation and a Harvard MBA. She joined J.P. Morgan in 1987 and worked with corporate clients in the firm's investment bank. She joined the private bank four years later, working with clients in New York and Philadelphia.

For a few years she rotated through the firm's different divisions, taking on increasing levels of responsibility before returning to the private bank in 2006 to run the New Jersey operations.

I sat in my TCU Honors English course and felt out of place. Accounting was my forte; English was not.

But my professor — Dr. Bob Frye — took a real interest in me. I was different. I was from the East Coast. I was a little older.

For our final paper, he asked us to write something about ourselves. I chose to write about my grandmother. She had graduated from Smith College back in the 1920s and believed education was critically important. In my paper, I quoted lyrics from the song "Time" by Pink Floyd:

"You are young and life is long, and there is time to kill today," the song said. "And then one day you find ten years have got behind you. No one told you when to run, you missed the starting gun."

My grandmother made the most of her time. I was determined to do the same. At TCU, I participated in student government and many other activities and kept a 4.0 GPA.

For all of us, time passes quickly. How we spend our time defines our lives.

FROM MARYLAND TO FORT WORTH
I grew up outside Washington, D.C., in Maryland. TCU came on my radar after my sister decided to attend. She found the school in a college fair, and she loved horses and the West. So her personal interests drew both of us.

At that time, I was putting myself through college by attending the University of Maryland at night and working full time as a bookkeeper at a medical clinic. It took me three years to finish freshman year.

Since my sister was already at TCU, I decided to go there as a full-time student. The school was wonderful with financial aid, and the business school was excellent.

I became an accounting-finance major. Dr. Geraldine F. Dominiak was a terrific accounting professor, and I loved the challenges she gave the class.

My first job after graduating from TCU was as a tax accountant at Arthur Young. While there, I worked with some great people, learned the foundation of the U.S. tax system, and learned to do tax research.

After two years of accounting and receiving CPA certification, I applied for an MBA at Harvard Business School.

HARVARD AND CAREER

When I was accepted at Harvard, I also got a letter asking whether I had the financial means to afford it. I'd put myself through TCU and had about $6,000 in student loans.

The letter was discouraging. I asked my grandmother to write to Harvard saying she would pay my tuition if I couldn't find other means.

I had absolutely no intention of having her pay! So I worked diligently to find scholarships and take on loans as required.

I was determined to get the education I needed to open doors to my career interests. Having your dream ahead of you and then being told you can't have it is a terrific motivator! Someone once told me, "When you want to get from Point A to Point B, first look for the door. If there's not one, make it."

At Harvard I met amazing students, including Olympic medalists and already-successful entrepreneurs. I spent the first six months wondering how I got there!

I worked hard and graduated with distinction, in the top 10 percent. And I met people who've become wonderful life-long friends. I would be remiss if I did not mention that I met my husband at Harvard Business School.

Upon graduation, I started with Goldman Sachs in mortgage finance and later joined the investment bank group at J.P. Morgan and have been here for twenty-five years. I have been able to have both a challenging career and a family. We have three wonderful daughters.

Don't let be boundaries scare you or keep you from accomplishing what needs to be done. You have to bring a lot of people with you, however. That's a consensus style of leadership that results in more buy-in at the end of the process. As part of that, it's important to take the time to motivate, mentor, and develop others.

ADVICE

- Because I put myself through college, I'm extremely appreciative of the learning opportunities provided at TCU, both inside and outside the classroom. I worked very hard at everything, and this drive and dedication to excellence are part of who I am. I operate this way and expect the same from others.
- Your reputation is established early in your career. Always over-deliver and do more than what is expected from you.
- While in college, take every liberal arts course you can, even if you are a business major.
- The head of the tax department at Arthur Young took an interest in me as a young professional. I remember how this helped me, and I try to slow down and do the same for younger professionals today.

Vernon Wilson Bryant, Jr.
Community Banks
Help Regions Grow.

VERNON WILSON BRYANT, JR. *is chairman and CEO of Southwest Bank, the largest locally owned independent commercial bank in Tarrant County. He graduated from the Neeley School in 1968. After serving as CEO of TexasBank, he bought CommunityBank of Texas, N.A., bought Southwest Bank, and combined its operations under the Southwest Bank name, now operating in eight locations — seven in Tarrant County and one in Dallas.*

Selected as Fort Worth's 2009 Business Executive of the Year, Vernon has been a leader in the Texas banking community for more than 26 years. He was named in 2007 as one of the "50 Most Powerful People In Town" by Fort Worth, Texas *magazine.*

Have you ever heard that phrase, "Sink or swim"?

That's what happened to me my first day as a lifeguard at my hometown pool. Somebody began to struggle, and I had to jump right in and rescue him.

I've had many jobs over the years, and I've learned something from each. Actually, I've enjoyed most of the jobs I've had. I just don't want some of them back.

My first job was in junior high. I worked on a farm driving a tractor and chopping cotton. I figured there had to be something better. Next I sacked groceries. Once I got the lifeguard job, I kept it for five years.

Thinking back, a lifeguard and a banker share several traits. Both must respond quickly. Both must be alert to a customer's needs and challenges.

And we provide a community service. We offer our experience and our skills to our communities. We sink or swim by the service we provide.

Today, as a community banker, I still want to serve my customers, make sure this region grows, and help opportunities continue to develop.

COLLEGE LIFE

I graduated from Lamesa High School in West Texas. I looked at a few other universities, but several Lamesa students told me they enjoyed TCU. And I liked Fort Worth.

Once I got to campus, I couldn't figure out what I wanted to do. Math and accounting were my best subjects. Several people told me, "You're really good at accounting. Maybe you should make it a career." That convinced me to major in business.

I also remember taking an English class my senior year that required me to memorize poetry each week. I was not a big fan.

The professor asked me why I had signed up for the class, and in turn I asked him, "Did you ever take an accounting course?"

"I didn't want to," he replied.

"Well," I told him, "I don't want to take English either, but I need it to graduate."

In 1967, the year before I graduated, I started working at Haskins and Sells. I got my CPA while I was there and stayed with them until 1972.

ACCOUNTING AND BANKING

I moved to Dalhart in 1972 and practiced public accountancy for several years. It was a great background for banking. And we started raising our family there. My wife Nancy — who also has a business degree — and I have two sons and four grandchildren. It's a very supportive family.

In 1982 I joined Citizens State Bank in Dalhart as executive vice president. I also got involved in several organizations, like the United Way, the Chamber of Commerce, and Central United Methodist Church, and served two terms on the city council.

We moved to Cleburne in 1987, where I was president and COO of First State Bank. In 1989, I became president of TexasBank in Weatherford. In 2006 TexasBank merged with Compass Bank.

Obviously, there are lots of changes and acquisitions in banking, but I knew there was a demand for a strong local community bank. In 2006 I founded First Texas BHC, Inc. We raised in excess of $94 million in capital from 350 investors with almost no investor turning us down. We purchased Community Bank of Texas, N.A., in Grand Prairie and Southwest Bank in Fort Worth. We sell service and relationships, as community banks can't make it on price alone. I still enjoy this business every day.

Fort Worth is a big relationship town, more so than Dallas. Loyalty is really important, as lending is more about loaning to the right people, rather than collateral.

ADVICE
- Work hard and be fair and honest with everyone.
- A good friend once told me this: "Major in accounting, and you'll always have a job."
- Usually, a town's just as friendly as you are. I've always tried to blend in.
- As a banker, you need to keep up with economic trends, know what your competitors are doing, and study how new legislation affects your business. That helps you become a more informed person.

David Corbin
Invest in Companies You Thoroughly Understand.

DAVID A. CORBIN *is president and CEO of Corbin & Company, founded in 1992, and is a nationally recognized mid-cap and small cap funds manager. The company is recognized for its "value style" investments and praised for being conservative and risk-averse. It specializes in the management of assets for individuals, trusts, pension plans, endowments, and foundations.*

David graduated from TCU with a bachelor of science in economics in 1989 and is a Chartered Financial Analyst. He is a member of the board of trustees of the William C. Conner Foundation and the advisory board for the Neeley Entrepreneurship Center. His life story and investment strategies have been featured in a number of publications, including The Wall Street Journal, BusinessWeek, *and* Forbes. *He has received numerous accolades, including being featured earlier in his career as one of the* Fort Worth Business Press' "40 Under 40."

I was president of my high school class at Glenbard South High School in Glen Ellyn, Illinois. My interests were like most teenage boys: sports and women.

But I had one other interest: investments. And by the time I was ready for college, I'd decided to pursue a finance career.

I got a paper route quite early. I bought stock for the first time when I was eight. I didn't do very well with it — and that's when I realized that if I didn't invest wisely, I could lose hard-earned dollars.

When I turned 12, I bought a subscription to *Value Line Investment Survey*. My grandmother also let me manage some of her money.

By the time I was 15, I'd had enough experience to begin offering advice about the pension plan to the publishing company run by my grandfather.

COLLEGE INTERESTS
At TCU, three professors greatly influenced me.

Dr. Bob Frye in English expected my best when it came to the written language. I took several English courses … about 18 hours. Dr. Chuck Becker in economics was a great mentor and encourager and always made time to talk about investments, security analysis, and history. And Dr. Stan Block in finance made me realize I could be a great investments person.

Perhaps my best experience in the university was serving as the portfolio manager for the Educational Investment Fund (EIF) of the William C. Conner Foundation. The EIF was the oldest student-managed fund in the country and the reason I had chosen TCU. It gave me an environment where I could show that I could do the job.

INVESTING IN THE FUTURE
Professor Stan Block founded the Educational Investment Fund in 1973 with a $600,000 donation from William C. Conner, co-founder of Alcon Laboratories.

A LIFELONG CAREER

After graduation, I started as a trust officer and investment manager for MTRUST. The guy who recommended me for that job was a grad student teaching a course I was taking!

I worked there for three years, then opened Corbin & Company in 1992. I was very pleased that two years later Nelson's Directory of Investment Managers ranked 258 companies, and we were rated No. 8 among investment managers.

My investment philosophy? We're primarily known as a multi-cap value manager. We look for stocks that offer the most value at the current time. Mostly, I buy companies involved in basic things like burgers and bug shields. I like to understand what a product is, what a business does, and how the business operates.

OTHER ACTIVITIES

After spending many years researching the investment market, it's fun to tell others about it too. For a long time I wrote a weekly investment column for the *Fort Worth Business Press,* and I've been a guest on Bloomberg Radio and Television and CNBC. I talk about the market and about various stocks.

If I weren't able to do this, I think I might want to be in politics. It's fun and emotionally rewarding to help people set financial objectives and achieve them.

ADVICE

- I get up every day to go to work, and I ask the Lord to make me the best boss, friend, brother, son, boyfriend, investment manager — and a bunch of other things — that I can be. People see the big deals, awards, and other good things that happen; they do not realize that those are the high points resulting from showing up every day and working.
- Because one spends so much time at work, it's important to be excited about the work one does.
- While growing up, I spent a considerable amount of time talking to older people, many of whom experienced the Great Depression. This had a profound effect on their investment views, and their perspectives made a huge impact on me.
- Make your life worth something to society through work, responsibility, and generosity of time, money, and spirit.

J. Philip Ferguson
Gather Your Thoughts and Keep a Journal.

J. PHILIP FERGUSON *is on the board of directors of ABM Industries and serves as vice chairman of the University of Texas Investment Management Company. After graduating with a BBA in finance from the Neeley School in 1967, he received a law degree from the University of Texas and a certificate in international law from City of London College.*

He is the former chairman, president, and chief investment officer of AIM Capital Management, serving as a senior investment professional from 2000 to 2007. As chief investment officer of AIM from 2005 to 2007, he led a team of roughly ninety investment professionals responsible for almost $100 billion in equity and fixed income assets under management.

Before that, Philip held senior roles at several investment management firms, including managing partner at Beutel, Goodman & Company; senior vice president at Lehman Brothers, Inc.; and vice president of Goldman, Sachs & Company. He serves or has served on many investment and civic boards, including the Chancellor's Advisory Council at TCU, the Houston Ballet, the Memorial Hermann Foundation, and as chair of the UT School of Nursing at Houston Advisory Council.

My most eye-opening college job was the night shift at a funeral home. I rode "shotgun seat" in an ambulance during TCU summer school and attended class during the day. I studied or slept at night between emergency calls.

These were the days before municipal control of EMS services. Each funeral home had its own ambulances (read: sunk cost) and raced the other funeral homes to be first to the scene of an accident. Once on site, the driver would triage the scene and determine which of the injured parties to transport to the hospital.

I soon learned that the most desirable "pick-ups" were those with very little chance of survival, since the funeral home that got the body was generally hired for the funeral (read: fat profit margins). Other critically injured people in need of immediate treatment were often left for subsequent ambulances to retrieve.

The lesson: There are some functions that should — and must — be strictly controlled and regulated monopolies of a central governmental body ... not left to the unbridled profit motive of the free enterprise system.

SCHOOL YEARS

I was raised in a middle-class family in Fort Worth. My father did government accounting work most of his life but joined a start-up company late in his career. He was responsible for marketing and found that he was good at it.

In high school, I was a B student, ran track, had a part-time job, and spent a lot of time thinking about girls and cars … all in all, a pretty normal background.

TCU had a lot of appeal for me. I had researched the business school and knew they had a serious program. Going to TCU would also allow me to continue with a part-time job at a local sporting goods store.

My best job in college gave me my first big break. I was working part-time in a dead-end job at the First National Bank of Fort Worth and was somehow lucky enough to be hired away as Luther King's first investment clerk in the trust investment department.

Luther was fresh out of TCU's MBA program, and it was under his tutelage that I developed my interest in the investment business and chose to devote my career to it. I learned from his example how to treat people and interact with them and how to approach the business. Luther has since had scores of student interns. He no doubt influenced them as strongly as he did me.

I wanted to pursue a career in the investments business but was advised by those I trusted that a law degree might broaden my educational background. At the University of Texas law school, I focused on the courses germane to a business career: tax, international law, securities regulation, contracts, oil and gas, and property.

TCU gave me a great foundation in the business basics, and the law training advanced my skills in thinking through and analyzing fact situations, seeing the other side of an argument, and oral advocacy.

CAREER

My first full-time job out of law school was as a security analyst at the Teacher Retirement System of Texas. There I learned the importance of fulfilling your responsibilities when you are part of a team effort and that others depend on you to do your part.

As I noted earlier, Luther King introduced me to the investments business. He had a quiet competence about him and a way of dealing with people that I wanted to emulate. Some of his traits that had an impact on me include these:

- Gather your thoughts, and codify them before speaking.
- Never extemporize about things you don't know about.
- Speak directly and avoid clichés.
- Treat people honestly and fairly.
- There is almost never a good reason to raise your voice in a business setting. Let the clarity of your thinking speak for itself without the need for volume.

ADVICE

- *Never* compromise your integrity. Warren Buffett insightfully noted that it takes twenty years to build a reputation and five minutes to ruin it. If your chosen field is as small and tight-knit as the investment business was during my time in it, you will become known for your cumulative actions over decades. You will see many of the same people over and over as they resurface in different roles. If you play on the edge or bend rules, the world will know it.
- You will have many opportunities to violate or to avoid the rules of good conduct; it might make you more money, but it is not worth it.
- In your business dealings, never be gratuitously rude to anyone, for you are quite likely to deal with that person again down the road. There are occasions when abruptness or rudeness is appropriate, but never go there unless you are absolutely compelled by circumstance.

- Learn to delay gratification. Do the hard things first and get them out of the way. If you know you are going to have to swallow a frog, you don't want to look at it for very long.
- No matter what the company dress code says, dress like the people on the management tier just above yours.
- One of my favorite credos is, "If you always tell the truth, you never have to remember what you said." These are always good words to live by, but they are especially valuable when you get older and can't remember everything you said.
- The key to effective presentations and public speaking engagements is: "Prepare, prepare, prepare." If you don't know the subject cold, the audience will see right through you and tune you out. Preparation and dry-run practices will give you the confidence to be at your best. Winging a presentation is almost never effective.
- Keep a journal of your thoughts and decisions at crucial junctures in your career and revisit it from time to time to help you honestly learn from your mistakes.
- Our minds are hardwired to "self-cleanse," and we use hindsight bias to subconsciously mis-remember how we came to certain decisions. It's OK to make every mistake in the book, but you want to make each one only once.

And a few notes about meetings:
- If you are chairing the meeting, distribute an agenda, start on time, make sure everyone understands the mission of the meeting, and end on time. When attending a meeting, be on time, prepare, and always make sure you have something meaningful to contribute.
- It is not acceptable behavior to continuously check your cell phone or otherwise multi-task during a meeting. It's rude — don't try to convince yourself otherwise.

James Hille
From Marine Officer to Endowment Officer

JAMES R. HILLE *is the first chief investment officer for the Texas Christian University Endowment, which manages the long-term assets of the University. Formerly he was the chief investment officer of the Teacher Retirement System of Texas, a $100 billion public pension plan, and served as a portfolio analyst with the Employees Retirement System of Texas.*

A native Texan, Jim graduated with a degree in engineering from the U.S. Naval Academy in 1983 and served six years as a U.S. Marine officer before going on to earning his MBA from TCU in 1992. He is a Chartered Financial Analyst and Chartered Alternative Investment Analyst and serves on the advisory board for the Luther King Capital Management Center for Financial Studies in the Neeley School.

I made my first mutual fund investment a long time ago in a place far from Texas. I was a young Marine Corps first lieutenant aboard an aircraft carrier. That was in the summer of 1987, and the market cratered that October. But I had developed an interest for investments and knew I wanted to learn more.

DRESSING THE PART
This group of Neeley students gathered for a photograph in 1977.

MARINE AND ENGINEER

I grew up in Austin and received a scholarship to the U.S. Naval Academy, graduating with an engineering degree. I chose the Marine Corps for my service; I wanted to be part of their elite team.

With this choice, I also gained a global perspective. I got to go around the world on an aircraft carrier and learned much about leadership.

The engineering and math fields are populated with people who are very good at what they do, and I enjoy that association. I also wanted to acquire the leadership component the Marines could provide.

After completing my tour of duty, I worked briefly at Texas Instruments but set my sights on getting an MBA in a full-time program.

I naturally looked at all the Texas universities while also applying to a number of top-tier national programs. I ultimately chose TCU's MBA program because of its small size, strong and growing stature, geography, and scholarship package. This was a great experience for me. With legendary professors like Stan Block, Chris Barry, and Rob Rhodes, coupled with an internship experience, I was very well grounded in securities analysis and prepared for a senior analyst position upon graduation. These professors drew from formidable real-world research and consulting backgrounds to bring the class to life, as opposed to focusing on outdated and irrelevant Harvard business cases.

CHARTING A COURSE FOR A CAREER

My MBA internship at the Bass Brothers Trust was extraordinarily helpful. I was surrounded by many brilliant people, and the exposure to all angles of capital markets helps me to this day. And frankly, at times I felt lost, surrounded by so many brilliant type-As.

After MBA graduation, I became an analyst for the Employees Retirement System of Texas. This was a lean and growing staff. The few who were there had to do a lot more than just their job descriptions. I quickly and eagerly learned to be a portfolio manager.

I have been blessed to have mentors like John Young and John Peavy, previous CIOs for the Teacher Retirement System, as they taught me how to navigate board governance.

These experiences prepared me to return to TCU, where I am the investment officer for the long-term investment assets of the University. These assets are invested in perpetuity. Hundreds of donors have contributed, creating endowment funds that support scholarships, professorships, and other University programs. Every day is different and exciting, especially during the last couple of years. And it's a privilege to work for an alma mater that I love.

ADVICE

- Cast a wide net. There are many areas of investment specialization to learn.
- Many things taught in school actually work! A business degree can provide you with sound analytical training to cope with volatile market shifts.
- Though it might be difficult to be selective in this particular job market, try to go with a small but stable and growing shop that will give you a chance (or force you) to work on many things, rather than a narrow focus.

Michael B. Hobbs
Every Opportunity Is a Building Block.

MICHAEL B. HOBBS *is president of Guaranty Bank and Trust in Denver, Colorado. Prior to assuming this role in July 2011, he was a managing director at St. Charles Capital, a firm providing expert investment banking services regarding sell-side and buy-side M&A transactions, recapitalizations, fairness opinions, take-private transactions, private placements of debt and equity, and general financial advisory services for middle-market companies in Denver, the Rocky Mountain region, and throughout the United States.*

Michael Hobbs has nearly twenty years of experience with financial institutions, including five as manager of KeyCorp's Denver and Seattle investment banking offices. Before joining St. Charles Capital, he served as regional president of KeyBank's Rocky Mountain region, comprised of Idaho, Utah, and Colorado.

After earning a bachelor of business administration in marketing from TCU in 1984, he went on to an MBA from TCU in 1992, concentrating in finance. He serves on the Chancellor's Advisory Council at TCU.

I made a big discovery before completing my MBA: The world is very big — but the world is also very small.

Along with MBA classmates Jim Hille and Paul Lauritano, I participated in an international travel summer program offered by TCU. We attended the program in Cologne, Germany, and visited manufacturers, government agencies, unions, and professional advisors.

My colleagues and I also researched a German institution: beer halls. Of course, you should understand that this was strictly a scholarly exercise. Here's what we found:

- Every region brews its beer differently and serves it in different receptacles. Brewing styles determine how they serve it.
- In Cologne, for instance, we got the brew in exaggerated shot glasses. And they kept serving until you told them to stop.
- We also discovered regional pride. Bavaria reminded me of Texas. They're proud of their location and its products and are glad to tell you why.

This overseas experience far from home convinced me that people are the same worldwide and that we share more similarities than differences.

LESSONS FROM THE FAMILY BUSINESS

I grew up in Oklahoma City in a family that valued education. Both my parents received college degrees, as did all five of their children. I was active in high school sports and the social life of a teenager.

Our family owned a small distribution company, and I worked there every summer and spring break. From age seven on, I accompanied my father and grandfather to the office on Saturdays, where I swept floors, emptied trashcans, and things like that. Over the years I worked every facet of the job, including warehouse stocking, customer delivery, and client interfacing activities.

I chose TCU because of its size, academic reputation, distance from home, ratio of out-of-state students — and truthfully, because of its affiliation with the Southwest Conference and the ratio of beautiful women to male students. It served me well, because I married my college sweetheart.

During my undergraduate studies, I majored in marketing. I'm not one to sit behind a desk and crunch numbers but would rather be in front of clients, analyzing situations and offering solutions or innovative ideas.

CAREER DECISIONS

After completing the BBA, I joined a small privately owned manufacturer in sales and marketing. While I honed many skills and traveled North America in this role, I quickly learned to appreciate the impact — or lack thereof — of focus and dedication in the classroom. This fed my desire to enroll in TCU's MBA program and to earn a position with NationsBank (now Bank of America).

I started TCU's MBA program on a full-time basis six years after graduating the first time. Although I loved college life, I felt I'd been unfocused as an undergraduate student. I was determined to improve myself. I essentially doubled my GPA and was MBA class president, a consistent Neeley Scholar, and a member of the Educational Investment Fund.

One major thing I learned at NationsBank — which recruited almost exclusively at top-ten business schools — was that TCU's program prepared its students to successfully compete with anyone from any program.

ADVICE

- Two lessons from my grandfathers: First, do an exceptional job in every role. It's critical to success. Second, lead from the front in any job. Others will mimic the behavior, both good and bad.
- The glass is always half full. Focus on the positive and look for solutions.
- If presented with an opportunity, seize it, whatever it is, no matter how large or small. Every opportunity is a building block to what you will become.

Jenny Jeter
Match Your Personality with Your Profession.

JENNY JETER *is a wealth management advisor with Merrill Lynch in Dallas and a Certified Investment Management Analyst (CIMA) professional.*

Jenny graduated from TCU in 1991 with a BBA in finance. She is a member of the TCU Dallas Alumni Network, Junior League of Dallas, Kappa Kappa Gamma Dallas Alumnae Association, Leadership Dallas Alumni, and Leadership University Park Alumni.

When Dad died suddenly, my world changed overnight.

I was 29 years old and running my own residential real estate appraisal business. Dad owned and operated several businesses, including home health-care agencies in Fort Worth and Amarillo. After his death, my mother was forced to consider closing the doors.

Our family met with an attorney and decided that — since I was the person with financial skills — I should run the businesses. The attorney suggested that I get involved immediately, hit the ground running, and rescue the companies.

I accepted this challenge. I immediately became guardian of Dad's estate, obtained a loan to keep the businesses going, cut costs where possible, and hired some very capable nurses to run the health agencies.

Within a year, the companies were restored to profitability, and Mom eventually sold the businesses.

ROOM FOR INNOVATION
The Steve Smith and Sarah Hales Smith Entrepreneurs Hall opened in 2003 and houses the Neeley Entrepreneurship Center and the Luther King Capital Management Center for Financial Studies, along with state-of-the-art classrooms, conference spaces, and team rooms for students.

CHOOSING A SCHOOL

I grew up in Dalhart, in the Texas Panhandle, and was one of four sisters. I knew about TCU because several Dalhart families had sent their children there.

During my high school senior year, I worked at Dalhart Federal Savings & Loan reviewing mortgage loan escrow accounts. I learned I had the ability to quickly and accurately assess technical financial reports.

I really enjoyed my college experience. TCU was the ideal size for me … about the population of my hometown. The professors had high expectations and were committed to their students' success. I especially appreciated Roger Pfaffenberger, a professor of operations research, who encouraged me to develop and hone my analytical skills. These skills are, I believe, one of my strong suits.

I joined Kappa Kappa Gamma sorority, as did several other girls from Dalhart. The organization fostered the development of my leadership skills. I majored in finance, which laid a broad foundation for me to start my own business.

MATCHING APTITUDES WITH A CAREER

After graduation in 1991, I started a residential real estate appraisal business in the midst of a recession. I rode along with the refinance boom and built a successful practice. The most important thing I learned about myself is that I could trust my natural instincts for initiating and building productive relationships with clients, supervisors, and co-workers. This became a critical component that helped me rebuild our family's companies after Dad's death. I'm very grateful to Vernon Bryant, Jr. of Southwest Bank (also a TCU grad). He expressed confidence in my financial savvy and provided financial backing for rebuilding our businesses.

When I joined Merrill Lynch, Director David Oberman took time to mentor me and to help develop unique tools and strategies so that I could be successful in a highly competitive industry. He taught me how to market myself based on my personality. He told me I was a people person and should develop my public-speaking skills.

As an investment advisor, you must remember that the business is not about you. It's about your clients. You must have genuine concern for others' well-being, taking time to listen and understand their needs. You must develop strategies to help clients navigate financial challenges and achieve their financial goals. You must be honest and reliable; it's imperative to demonstrate integrity and the ability/desire to stay current in an ever-changing financial environment.

ADVICE

- As soon as possible — perhaps during or right after high school — take an aptitude test to determine your natural abilities. Then look for a college major or career that pairs your aptitudes with something you enjoy.
- Before you enter a business, meet and spend a day with someone in that field. See what that person does and what his or her job requires. Determine if it's something that fits your personality and interests.
- Learn to listen … to mentors, clients, and supervisors. That's how you learn.
- Learn to speak comfortably to both individuals and groups. Some technical skills require more education and specific training. Interpersonal skills require experience.
- Trust yourself and never give up.

Urbin McKeever
Life Is Too Short
to Tread Water.

URBIN McKEEVER *is a senior vice president with the Frost Bank Financial Management Group. His responsibilities include financial planning and investment portfolios for both individuals and organizations. Earlier in his career, Urbin was senior vice president of Overton Bank and manager of their investment services division.*

Urbin graduated with two degrees from the Neeley School, a bachelor of business administration with a major in accounting in 1975 and an MBA in 1976.

In 1993 I was managing bond underwriting for Bank One Securities in Dallas when the company decided to close the Dallas bond trading office. That put me at a real career crossroads.

I'd always wanted to get into the full services brokerage securities business. So I approached Overton Bank & Trust in Fort Worth about starting a securities division. David Tapp and Denny Alexander asked me to develop a business plan for it. I created a 40-page document and acted like I knew what I was doing, even though I had a lot to learn!

They liked it and hired me — as well as two other people whom I brought along from Bank One Securities — to start the division.

Suddenly I went from Mr. Inside, as a bond analyst and underwriter, to Mr. Outside, offering investment advice to individuals and businesses.

The Overton executives' confidence in me gave me a great opportunity. And after about a year, they asked me to start managing the bank's portfolio, too.

EARLY MEMORIES

My dad told me he first came to TCU right after World War II to attend a summer business program on bookkeeping. Soon after that, he reopened McKeever Chevrolet Co. in Ferris, Texas, twenty miles south of Dallas. The business had closed in 1942 due to the war. Dad became a Frog fan after his Fort Worth experience. I started coming to football games with him when I was eight or nine and never really considered going anywhere else when it came time for college.

I started school in Ferris but went to high school in Waxahachie. I particularly remember my high school literature teacher and how much she influenced me. She had dignity; she was demanding and thought-provoking. She taught us how to write clearly and to think about what we were writing. I always looked forward to her challenging class. When my mom died in 2000, that teacher came to the funeral home. I hadn't seen her in twenty-five years and much appreciated her thoughtfulness.

At TCU I received a BBA in accounting and an MBA in finance. While there, I received great exposure to the markets and learned much from the Educational Investment Fund, which was new at that time.

That's one of the main reasons that I became interested in the financial services industry.

CAREER GROWTH

My first real job was as a teller at University Bank while working on my MBA. This experience had a great influence on my interest in the financial services industry.

After graduation, I worked in leasing and corporate sales at Jack Williams Chevrolet. I really enjoyed growing up around a dealership and thought for years that was what I wanted to do.

However, the eighteen months that I spent in this field — along with my MBA experience at TCU — pointed me toward the financial services industry. I learned so much from my dad about serving clients. I remember the respect and care he showed employees and customers. He was a positive person, and people seemed to have a good time when they were around him. He was serious about his profession and almost always in a good humor. He was also very involved in civic activities; he served as both mayor and president of the school board. One can't underestimate these positive traits of service to clients and community.

Serving as a financial planning advisor will always be important, but the burnout rate in this field is high. Some people burn out because they start as investment advisors too early and just don't have the experience. I recommend serving in a support role to an advisor for a few years, learning the business, and observing investment goals and market fluctuations. Pursuing the Certified Financial Planner certificate requires intense study in both estate and tax planning. It's beneficial if you're working on either the research or advisory side while preparing for the examination.

ADVICE
- Develop the ability to communicate well and connect quickly with people.
- Find a career you're passionate about. Life is too short to tread water.
- Look for an industry you enjoy. The earlier you find it, the earlier you may discover a specialty within the industry that appeals to you.

FIT AND FUN
Urbin McKeever ('75, '76), left, shown here with TCU parent Phillip Stephenson, is an avid bicyclist.

Thomas Meagher
From Government Service Sector to Investments

THOMAS F. MEAGHER, JR. *is managing director of Grosvenor Capital Management, L.P., a leader in the alternative investments industry. Since its inception in 1971, Grosvenor has provided its clients with attractive risk-adjusted returns and client services. Grosvenor employs more than 200 people in Chicago, Tokyo, and London. The firm invests on behalf of its global client base across a broad range of investment strategies.*

Tom graduated in 1982 from the Neeley School with a bachelor of business administration in management and marketing, has served on the Chancellor's Advisory Council at TCU, and now serves on the Neeley School's International Board of Visitors. In 2010, he was named by Irish America magazine as one of the leading Irish Americans in the financial world in their 13th Annual Wall Street 50 edition.

This wasn't exactly the career start I'd dreamed about. The economy was terrible in the fall of 1982. After months of interviewing, I took a job I swore I would never do: I worked for my dad.

I was back in Chicago with a small child and another on the way. I drove a parts truck from location to location from 4 p.m. to midnight. I was paid $17,000. The president of the company — my dad's partner — did not want me there, nor did I want to be there.

I stayed two years, doing different jobs, including parts delivery, and working in the parts department and accounts receivable.

I learned that while I respected my dad tremendously, I loved him too much to work for him.

FROM ILLINOIS TO TEXAS

TCU offered a "big-time" school atmosphere. It had a great campus, Greeks, athletics, and a nationally ranked business school. I also liked the size of Fort Worth and wanted a different experience than that of the Midwest offered by metropolitan Chicago.

My father was a successful businessman. He was an entrepreneur and a director on a number of large boards. I liked the potential for financial success and the possibility to build and run something of my own.

My undergraduate degree in management and marketing provided the tools I needed to help me forge real opportunities and experiences at a very young age. I really enjoyed learning from John Thompson, who offered a very proactive approach to business problems and opportunities. Former Dean Ed Johnson, who'd worked with Blue Cross/Blue Shield in New York, was also a great listener and advisor.

CAREER

From 1985 through 1988, I served as the Illinois Governor's Assistant for Economic Affairs. I got the opportunity to open economic development offices internationally, including London, Moscow, Toronto, Warsaw, Brussels, Sao Paulo, Osaka, and several other places. One of my peak professional experiences occurred when I was the deputy director of the Illinois Housing Development Authority in 1988. My first bond issue was $350 million, with Bear Stearns as the lead banker on the deal. I was enamored with the process — its structure and the legal and financial aspects. I knew at some point I wanted to be around the financial services business.

I've been fortunate to have fine mentors, including Jay Hedges, former director of the Illinois Department of Commerce and Community Affairs; Tom Stobbe, Monitor Manufacturing Company president; Tom Dooney, First Union Securities managing director; along with Michael Sacks, chief executive officer, and Paul Meister, chief operating officer, of Grosvenor Capital Management, L.P. All of these gentlemen are good numbers people and are hardworking and focused, strong leaders and good communicators.

ADVICE

- Strong leadership and communication skills — whether up the chain or down the chain — are critical to be able to direct, communicate, and execute effectively.
- Be prepared and keep your options open. You never know when a door will open and another will close.

Laura Shrode Miller
A Major Change—
A Major Success

LAURA SHRODE MILLER *graduated magna cum laude from TCU in 1979 with a bachelor of business administration in marketing. During college years, she served as vice president and president of the student body and was also elected homecoming queen.*

She served as marketing director at Rattikin Title, commercial lender at Fort Worth National Bank, president and chief marketing officer at Summit Bank, and a market president of Frost Bank (after it purchased Summit) before becoming a market president and chief marketing officer for Liberty Bank.

She and her husband Tod, also a bank executive, and son Jay (BBA 2008 and MBA 2011) are alumni of the Neeley School. Son Scott graduated from the Neeley School in 2011. Jay's wife Emily is also a TCU grad. Laura has served on the board of trustees of TCU and as president of the National Alumni Association.

I grew up in Houston and came to TCU for several reasons — one being that I'm a fourth-generation member of the Disciples of Christ Church. My freshman year, I picked English and history as my majors.

I came home for summer vacation. "Laura, you should change your major," my dad advised. "Go to the business school. It's the best background for any career."

I returned to TCU that fall and followed his suggestion. This life-changing decision was his idea, not mine. But it's been absolutely the right one for me.

THE MARKETING PATH

Once I changed majors, I was drawn to marketing. I viewed it as a combination of both science and art. I still do.

After graduation, I joined Rattikin Title Company as director of marketing. Jack Rattikin taught me many things. I began to understand the difference between line and staff functions. And I discovered why it's so important to know how a business makes money.

At Fort Worth National and later at Summit Bank, I worked with commercial loans, a wonderful way to learn about how various businesses function.

Throughout my career, I've been able to work in some phase of marketing.

THE COMMUNITY

Two role models for me — Jim Murray and Ben Gunn, founders of Summit Bank — are long-time Fort Worth residents and local bankers. They understand this community well. Over the years, they've made a commitment to community service and support.

I've also tried to do the same. I've worked in leadership of the Junior League, YWCA, National Conference of Community and Justice, and as a trustee of Trinity Valley School and many of TCU's constituency groups. I'm an elder at University Christian Church. Nationally, I'm treasurer of my sorority, Chi Omega.

I think we should devote time and talent to groups we believe in.

ADVICE
- Go to work for people who share your values.
- I've spent my career working for honest people, and I've tried to be worthy of their respect.
- Find out what's needed and then do it.
- If you've got bad news, deliver it in person.

THAT WAS THEN...
An early home of the business school, shown here in the 1950s, was the barracks known as Splinter Village.

...AND LATER
Construction on the Dan Rogers Hall was completed in summer of 1957 at a cost of $825,000.

Maribess Miller
It's Better to Lead the Parade.

MARIBESS MILLER *recently retired from PricewaterhouseCoopers as the North Texas market managing partner, leading eighty-five partners and more than 1,000 employees. She joined the firm — then Coopers & Lybrand — just after college graduation in 1975. She rose quickly in the company and during her tenure became a nationally known expert on health-care issues.*

A certified public accountant, Maribess graduated cum laude from the Neeley School with a degree in accounting. She and her husband Jerry live in Dallas, where she's active on a number of boards, including the Texas State Board of CPAs, the International Women's Forum, and the Texas Health Institute, where she served two terms as chair. In 2010, she chaired the 35th reunion of her TCU graduation class. She serves on the Neeley School International Board of Visitors.

I grew up in the Texas Hill Country in Kerrville. I enjoyed sports — loved the competition — and played on the tennis team. Dad was an Aggie, and my older sister went to the University of Texas at Austin. But after a visit to TCU's friendly, welcoming campus, I knew where I wanted to be.

I started as a math and computer science major but couldn't connect with the career options, so I switched to accounting. Changing my major was a practical decision. Business graduates had higher incomes than most majors. I was getting an education for a career, so why not go into business?

At the Neeley School, Professor Geraldine Dominiak challenged and motivated me. Why? I think that because I was in a sorority and played on the tennis team, she initially dismissed my seriousness. That bothered me, so I was determined to be one of her top students.

My grandfather and dad were business people. Pops owned a group of five-and-ten variety stores called Lehmann's. My father sold the stores and went on to develop the Inn of the Hills resort in Kerrville. He developed property and built unique homes. He loved adventure. He jumped out of an airplane at age 80. And Dad was a true entrepreneur — he taught his five children how to spell the word!

CAREER PATH

My plan was to work in accounting for a few years and then go to law school. If I started my career again, I'd focus even more heavily on health care and preventive medicine. That's the wave of the future. It's no secret that my favorite magazine is *Prevention*.

But once I started advancing in the firm, I never looked back. I started out doing audits for big companies. Over the years I've worked with many wonderful people, including my mentor, Ronald Clinkscale, also a TCU grad.

When I had the opportunity to transfer from the Fort Worth office to be a manager in Dallas, the Fort Worth managing partner suggested I talk it over with my dad. But I had already accepted based on my gut. Throughout my career, my instincts have guided me. If you socialize a decision too long, the window closes or you lose sight of your goals. I constantly had windows of opportunity throughout my career that interested and motivated me and kept me learning and advancing.

Accounting is much more of a people business than most might think. I found that if I performed at a high energy level and provided professional expertise and service, I was given more responsibility and more opportunity. Clients expect you to give them sound financial advice.

I became a PwC partner in 1984. In the last twenty-five years, the industry has changed tremendously. Technology completely changed the way we keep records. And because of international commerce and trade, the latest challenge is adopting new international accounting standards.

ADVICE
- Speaking of goals, set long-term and short-term ones. I've always got some specific goal in front of me.
- Take advantage of both big and small opportunities. How do you know which is which? If you worry whether you can handle it, it's a big opportunity.
- Take charge of your life, and welcome new responsibilities. If somebody doesn't like it, they'll tell you about it. When you're in a parade, it's more fun to be leading it.

ON THE COURT
Maribess (Lehmann) Miller ('75), as a TCU student-athlete in 1973, shows how a tennis ace performs.

Phillip Norwood
Long-Term Business Relationships Are Critical.

PHILLIP E. NORWOOD *is regional president of Frost Bank. Before Fort Worth's Summit National Bank acquisition by Frost in 2006, he was chairman and CEO of Summit. He had been with them since 1980, when he was president of their affiliate Altamesa National Bank.*

A lifelong Fort Worth resident, he was named 2005 Banker of the Year by the Tarrant County Bankers Association. He graduated from the Neeley School with a bachelor of business administration in 1973 and serves on the Neeley School International Board of Visitors.

From the time I was eight or nine years old, I had all sorts of part-time jobs, like working in a gas station after school. But my favorite was working for my brother-in-law in the car business.

I learned not only how to prepare vehicles for sale and manage a sales lot, but also how to sell cars. And the sales training classes offered tips on how to "read" people. For instance, they told me that if a pipe smoker came onto the lot, he was contemplative and would not buy anything that day.

Before this, the thought of selling anything terrified me. The main things I learned from this job were how to deal with rejection and how to overcome potential buyers' objections.

The experience also gave me the ability to talk to people face to face without being afraid. It taught me that one must develop a relationship with a customer. It's important that people know and trust you before they buy anything.

FORT WORTH NATIVE

I was born in Fort Worth and graduated from Eastern Hills High School in 1968. My freshman year I went to Tarleton State on a football scholarship and got injured in spring training. While rehabbing with a couple of good friends who were on football scholarship at TCU, they convinced me to enroll at TCU to see if I could walk on and try to earn a scholarship there.

I needed enough money to pay for my first year of tuition. So I worked for my brother-in-law and discovered I could earn enough money to pay my way through TCU and gain valuable experience along the way.

The two best decisions I made early in my life: Go to TCU and work throughout college.

A BANKING CAREER

I earned a BBA at TCU. While in college I began working part-time for the local City National Bank in 1970, which turned into a full-time position in late 1971.

The business classes — including accounting, finance, statistics, and marketing — were more meaningful to me than they probably would have been otherwise. The class work and employment taught me discipline, time management, and how to multi-task at a fairly early age. Murray Rohman taught business law and was the hardest professor I had at TCU, but he also provided one of the best learning experiences of my college career. He definitely taught me about being prepared before walking into class.

These important lessons were vital as career preparation as I was hired as president and CEO of the new Altamesa National Bank when I was only 30 years old. The organizers of the original Summit National Bank obtained a charter for the new bank. After interviewing more than twenty potential candidates for this job, they settled on me. At a very young age, I was expected to raise capital, contract for data processing, hire an entire staff, and build a facility for the bank.

Fortunately, many people have invested in my success. My brother-in-law, Garry McKinney, gave me the opportunity to work for him while I was in school, enabling me to earn enough money to pay for a large part of my college expenses during my first two years. And Bob Walker hired me into the banking business in 1970, giving me significant responsibilities at an early age and allowing me to learn from my mistakes.

Barclay Ryall hired me as a commercial lender at Bank of Fort Worth in 1977, even though I had no experience at that job. While supporting me through mistakes, he made sure I learned accountability and even introduced me to the organizers of Summit Bank.

And Ben Gunn and Jim Murray — co-organizers of Summit National Bank — supported me thorough the banking crisis of the late 1980s and early 1990s and encouraged my independence in running a bank.

Ultimately, banking involves common sense and people skills. If you would like to understand how other businesses operate, if you have good analytical ability, if you like helping people, then banking may be for you. But remember that everyone needs some understanding of finance and accounting. No matter what your career, it's helpful to understand how the business world works. And remember the value in "spheres of influence." Use those connections to get interviews. Sometimes getting an interview is the hardest part.

ADVICE
- Regardless of the job you're in, you must sell something — your product, your work, or yourself.
- Never pass up the opportunity to learn from experience, regardless of how menial that experience may seem to be.
- Eliminate assumptions when evaluating risks and be willing to take on and manage risk.
- Develop effective communication skills beyond e-mails, texts, and other nonpersonal types of communication.
- People need passion for what they do. One way to think about this: Ask yourself, "Am I building a career or just getting a paycheck?"

Mike Pavell
From Junior Achievement
to Major Achievements

MIKE PAVELL has two major professional responsibilities: He is president of Bank of America Tarrant County and heads a team within U.S. Trust, Bank of America Private Wealth Management in downtown Fort Worth. An Abilene native, he began his career as a credit analyst for NationsBank after receiving his bachelor's degree in finance from TCU in 1993 and his MBA from TCU in 1999.

Mike takes on many civic leadership responsibilities, most recently serving on the Slant 45 Action Team as well as the host committee's Sponsorship Development Team for Super Bowl XLV. He is president-elect of the Neeley School Alumni Executive Board.

My business awareness began as a sophomore in high school economics. Our class project involved setting up a company through a Junior Achievement program. We went to a local firm and bought candy at wholesale. We planned to make a profit by selling it at school. Each of us put a little money into this project, buying shares of the company.

I became either president or treasurer, I can't recall which. And pretty soon I became the largest shareholder. I bought everyone else's share because they believed we couldn't make money!

But things worked out well. I got my first management experience and decided I wanted to learn more about business.

ACADEMICS
TCU wasn't on my "radar screen" until my senior year. I went along with a friend for a high school visit. That week there was a TCU vs. Texas football game.

I watched that contest on Saturday and began to root for TCU like a lifelong fan. The school was the right fit for me: all of the elements of a big-time university experience, plus the friendly, hometown environment of Fort Worth.

I majored in finance, an excellent preparation for a business career. It seemed to me that no matter what the industry, the ability to attract capital and provide a return on that capital was the cornerstone of a company's success.

I was fortunate to have a number of fantastic professors at TCU, but a couple stood out as exemplary. Chris Barry took the theories of finance and applied them in real-world scenarios and his own professional experiences, while Bob Vigeland in accounting had a way of bringing "debits and credits" to life.

My experience at TCU provided me not only the academic tools to succeed, but also the contacts to launch my career.

CAREER DECISIONS
A few years into my banking career, I decided to go back to TCU for my MBA. It was the right time: before starting a family and getting too entrenched in my career. I wanted to further my education, add credibility to my skill set/resumé, and build a broader network of connections.

School is the perfect place to hone these skills. The stakes are low, and you have nearly unlimited opportunities to experiment and determine your style.

The banking environment is a great place to begin any business career. The training can take you in many directions. Actually, I never set out to be a career banker, but it gave me such a broad perspective on so many industries. As credit analyst, I got to see companies from the inside out and learn about many industries.

It's always helpful if you can find an experienced mentor. That person for me was Luther King. I worked as an intern at Luther King Capital Management during the last year and a half of my undergraduate career and was able to observe how he handled business in an honorable and ethical way. He connected personally with his clients and employees in a style that I've tried to emulate as my career has progressed.

ADVICE
- Place a heavy emphasis on relationships. No matter what the business situation, relationships always come into play.
- The strongest and most valuable relationships are those based on integrity and consistency, something that I try to keep top of mind in all personal interactions.
- Focus on communication skills, negotiation skills, and being able to tell your story.

RETURN ON CAPITAL
Chris Barry, Emeritus Professor of Finance and former Robert and Maria Lowdon Chair in Business Administration, makes a point in a 2006 MBA class.

Robert J. (Bob) Schumacher and Frank Kyle
Find a Mentor and Make a Difference.

BOB SCHUMACHER *will be remembered not only for his corporate success, but even more so for the many ways he made a difference in the lives of his family and friends and even those who never had the opportunity to meet him. He was chairman and director of Texland Petroleum, a privately held oil and gas company based in Fort Worth. He was born on March 7, 1929, and passed away on May 4, 2010.*

Bob lived in Fort Worth with his wife, Edith. They celebrated fifty-nine years together and had three children and five grandchildren. He was a generous supporter of TCU through funding a scholarship and endowing the Robert and Edith Schumacher Executive Faculty Fellow in Innovation and Technology.

Bob Schumacher graduated from the Neeley School in 1950 with a bachelor's degree in accounting, then went on to earn a master's degree in professional accounting from the University of Texas in 1952. His days at TCU were interrupted while he served for three years in the service during World War II. After completing his degrees in accounting, Bob worked with Sproles Woodward as a CPA and then joined Sojourner Drilling Company as CFO in 1953. Bob often referred to the importance of his training in accounting as key to his success in business — or any business, for that matter. He once said, "When you ask a person about their business, they answer you in accounting. It's a language."

In 1973, he and W.E. "Bill" Rector co-founded Texland Petroleum, which operates primarily in the Permian Basin of West Texas. In those rare moments when you didn't find Bob working, you might have found him in his plane, as he was a pilot for over fifty years.

MAKING A DIFFERENCE
Bob Schumacher was known for getting things done the right way, or as one of his business partners, Don Paige, once said, "Bob likes things done his way, but his way is usually the right way."

And part of the right way for Bob was the love and support he gave to his children and grandchildren. He loved to hunt and fish with his family, but most of all he wanted to make sure they received a high-quality education. Bob recognized the importance of education for his family members and also ensured that many others would have the opportunity to pursue college education by means of the accounting scholarship at TCU that he endowed.

Bob was about making a difference in the lives of others. You saw that in his church activities and support of community groups.

TCU THROUGH GENERATIONS
Frank Kyle ('81), Kathy Kyle ('83), Corey Kyle ('08, '09), Ryan Millett ('09), and Edith and Bob Schumacher ('50) are loyal to their university.

FRANK KYLE *is an executive director and CFO of Texland Petroleum and former president of Frost Insurance. He is a 1981 graduate of the Neeley School, where he was a member of the golf team, and he serves on the Chancellor's Council for the Clark Society at TCU.*

I was born in Fort Worth and attended Southwest High School. I was always a TCU fan, as my father was a graduate of TCU and had season football tickets all his life. We attended every home game. While I love hunting and fly-fishing, I played golf in high school and wanted to play in college. TCU gave me that opportunity and was the only school I considered.

My first job in high school was working at a driving range. The most important aspect of that job was to make sure there were enough golf balls cleaned and ready for the next member. Never have a member wait. That was the rule.

My first job after graduation was working for an insurance agency in Fort Worth. Each Monday I was given a list of people to contact to discuss the value of supplemental insurance. I had to learn all aspects of the coverage, how to call on someone I had never met to schedule an appointment, how to explain the coverage and gain their confidence so they would find value in the benefits of the policy.

This attention to detail was nurtured by two real estate classes I took at the Neeley School from John Staples, who was in the commercial real estate business in Fort Worth. I found his classes to be valuable because he would bring actual real estate projects to class, take us through deal points, have a class discussion on whether the property should be purchased, and if so, what the offer should be and the expected return on investment. Learning from real situations involving real local property, rather than from a textbook, taught me valuable lessons I have used my entire adult life.

VALUE OF A MENTOR
The most significant mentor is my life was my father-in-law, Bob Schumacher. He was a true master of how to build and grow a business. He was a CPA and was co-founder of Texland Petroleum. I was so fortunate to have a mentor with such vast business experience, as he had interests in oil and gas exploration, refining, drilling, banking, the automobile industry, and real estate. He was so easy to approach, and for twenty-five years we discussed how to grow the many companies in which he was involved.

His philosophy was simple: Have a strong work ethic, know every aspect of the business before you get involved, and make sure you can live with the downside, as the upside will take care of itself. Whatever success I may have achieved, or will achieve, in my career is a result of his mentorship.

ADVICE
- Experience is a key factor for success. You can reduce the time it takes to have the experience necessary for success by finding a strong mentor.
- Don't assume anything; find the information that will provide you with the correct answer.
- For those who knew Bob well, he would be most likely to have given the following advice: Work hard; make a difference in life for your family, your profession, and your community. And when you make a difference, remember it's for those you are helping, not to honor yourself.

Robert (Bob) Semple
Nothing Beats a Strong Work Ethic.

ROBERT SEMPLE *is Tarrant County Chairman of the Bank of Texas. He came to TCU directly from high school in Midland, Texas. He graduated with a degree in management from the Neeley School in 1972. Bob and his family are die-hard TCU fans, as his older brother and wife both graduated from TCU.*

He is a member of the Neeley School International Board of Visitors, and you are sure to find him at most TCU athletic events. He has been an active volunteer for TCU through the years, having served on the Chancellor's Advisory Council and the National Alumni Board.

My first job at age 12 was working on our family farm, where we planted one of the first commercial pecan orchards in West Texas, utilizing drip irrigation techniques and structuring a rotational grazing program. I learned that there is a high risk to innovation, as not all of our projects resulted in financial returns justifying the cost regardless of how good it looked initially. I also had the opportunity to manage legal Mexican immigrant workers, learning the importance of treating all employees with respect and dignity.

ACADEMICS

My first class at TCU was Accounting 101 at 8 a.m. on Mondays, Wednesdays, and Fridays. As an 18-year-old freshman, I knew absolutely nothing about accounting (and obviously nothing about scheduling my classes).

But my professor, Sanoa Hensley, was great. She was a tough teacher, and you had to be prepared in class or she could make you look foolish. That course gave me the basics for understanding accounting as I know it today.

BUILDING CONNECTIONS
The Neeley School sponsored Fort Worth Business Week in 1972, providing opportunities for students and faculty to meet with business leaders.

CAREER

I cultivated my interest in banking by majoring in management with a concentration in finance. But I also used electives to take additional finance and accounting courses, read extensively about the industry, and visited with bankers and regulators, including an overseas economics course in Europe with Dr. Ken Herrick. And I landed a summer job in a bank in my hometown.

I took advantage of my opportunities to develop my expertise and interest in commercial lending, balance sheet management, and commodity lending by attending banking schools at Texas A&M and the University of Oklahoma. I also had important on-the-job training learning about the importance of having a strong work ethic and client relationship-building from my industry mentor, James B. Gardner, current chairman of Commerce Street Capital. He was a senior executive for the first bank I worked for after leaving the FDIC and was instrumental in expanding my creativity and knowledge of corporate finance and investment banking. He gave me more corporate and management responsibility than I deserved at an early age, but he also gave me the support I needed to do the job.

I remember driving all night without any sleep for an early morning meeting with a prospective client in the Texas Panhandle to assist him with an emergency credit need. We obtained a significant new customer, not only because we provided the credit needed but also because of the extraordinary effort I made to put in the time and effort to get the job done.

ADVICE

- Find an industry or occupation that you enjoy. Success comes so much easier when you enjoy your work.
- Nothing beats a strong work ethic; make sure you work harder than your peers and supervisors.

Leadership and Innovation

"If you want to be an entrepreneur, start sooner rather than later."

ADAM BLAKE

"Don't hang onto failures or successes too long. Both of these happened yesterday. Focus on the challenge of today."

JOHN F. DAVIS III

"Entrepreneurship is about sales. It's about finding business needs and creating a way to fulfill those needs. Roll your sleeves up, explore, and make it fun."

ASH HUZENLAUB

In the introduction to his book, *A Whole New Mind,* Daniel H. Pink argues that "We are moving from an economy and a society built on the logical, linear, computerlike capabilities of the Information Age to an economy and a society built on the inventive, empathic, big-picture capabilities of what's rising in its place, the Conceptual Age." In this section, we find Neeley alumni who have embraced leadership and innovation with entrepreneurial ideas and approaches across many different industry segments.

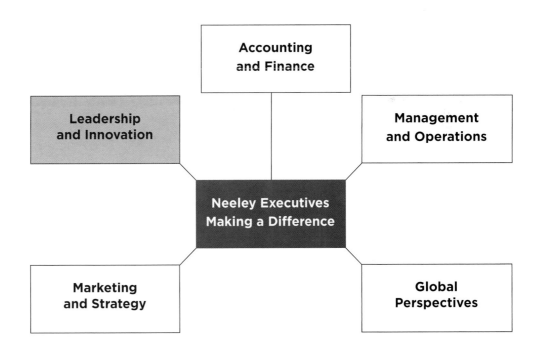

ROBERT J. McCANN
CHARTING A PATH
FOR COLLEGE

ROBERT J. MCCANN *is chief executive officer of UBS Wealth Management Americas and a member of the group executive board of UBS AG. Bob McCann graduated with an MBA from the Neeley School in 1982 and spent twenty-six years at Merrill Lynch, eventually becoming vice chairman of Merrill Lynch & Co., Inc., and president of Global Wealth Management. He was recognized in* Irish America *magazine as one of the 2011 Top 100 Irish Americans. He is on the board of directors of The American Ireland Fund and is a member of the President's Circle of No Greater Sacrifice, the latter dedicated to funding the education of children of military personnel who have been wounded or killed in the line of duty.*

I was an undergrad at Bethany College, TCU's sister school, when I first learned of the University. At the time, the president of Bethany was a guy named Bill Tucker. Bill was a very charismatic leader. He was smart, down to earth, and I was lucky enough to get to know him during my first three years.

The summer after my junior year, I lived at Bethany and worked at the school. One afternoon I saw Dr. Tucker on campus. He asked what I was going to do after I graduated next year, and I told him my plan was to go to business school and get my MBA. Dr. Tucker had just accepted a position as the chancellor of TCU and suggested I pay a visit. I said I would.

A year later, I graduated and was accepted at five good schools. My plan was to attend Duke, and then one afternoon the phone rang in my fraternity house, and it was Dr. Tucker. He had heard that I'd been accepted to TCU and was wondering why I hadn't come down to visit the school. For the price of an airline ticket, he said, I should really come and take a look. So I went. I saw the campus, met the dean of the business school, and was introduced to a wonderful professor named Stanley Block. From the people to the programs to the vibrant Texas culture, I knew right away that this was a special place. About a week after I returned from my visit, I got a letter from TCU indicating that I had been awarded a Sid Richardson Fellowship. I mailed my acceptance form the very next day.

MENTORS LEAD THE WAY.
Professor Stanley Block, who ran TCU's Finance Department, was a wonderful professor, a good man, and a great mentor. I took a course called the Educational Investment Fund (EIF), became the lead portfolio manager, and it was that experience that motivated me to come to Wall Street. In fact, I ended up starting a similar EIF program at my alma mater, Bethany College.

One of my good friends and classmates was Mike Berry, and I got to know his father, Sam Berry. Mr. Berry was a stockbroker, now called Financial Advisor, at Rotan Mosle (ironically, Rotan was eventually acquired by PaineWebber, which was acquired by UBS, my current company).

Mr. Berry was one of the nicest, most caring individuals I had ever met, and he really took me under his wing. When I told him that I wanted to work on Wall Street, he arranged for me to meet with Richard Rainwater and Tom Taylor from Bass Brothers. The Bass family is very influential, and they were doing the most exciting things in Texas at the time. So I went over there, and at the end of our conversation, they decided to give me a chance. I was the first intern they had ever hired at the firm.

I learned two important lessons as an intern for Bass Brothers. The first concerns the value of relationships. I was one of six people in a tiny, one-room trading floor, and business was done on speakerphones, so I could hear both sides of the conversation. I remember Tom Taylor talking with Stanley Shopkorn at Solomon Brothers, Bob Mnuchin at Goldman Sachs, and Luther King of Luther King Capital Management. I was in the room as Bass acquired their big position in Disney and talked about Michael Eisner, a guy they thought would be great to run the company some day. It was like a seminar right in front of me. The relationships they had with industry leaders, the opportunities to bounce ideas off of some of the best minds in the business, and the networking that took place because this person knew someone at that company, and so on — it was incredible. I realized quickly that in business, it's not just what you know, but who you know, and if I was going to be successful, I had to start building relationships.

The second lesson is that nothing happens without hard work. As a young man watching Richard Rainwater and Tom Taylor, I saw how hard they worked and how committed they were to getting every little detail right. I also saw how much they cared and how they truly believed in what they were doing. It instilled in me a tremendous work ethic that I carry with me to this day. There may be people in this world who are more accomplished than I am, but I've never been outworked. That was true when I was 23, and it's true at 53.

GETTING STARTED IN A CAREER

After graduating from TCU, I started my first job as an analyst at Merrill Lynch on July 6 of 1982. I believe the Dow Jones Industrial Average was at about 800, and trading volume on the NYSE was averaging from 35 to 40 million shares a day. The prime rate was 16 percent, and we were in a deep recession. There was very little hiring being done at the time, so I was pretty fortunate to get a job on Wall Street. And then, almost overnight, the world changed. On August 12, 1982, Paul Volcker announced that inflation was no longer a concern and that he was going to ease up on monetary policy. The markets exploded. The Dow was going up 90 points a day, and the volume on the NYSE jumped to 100 million shares a day. I still have some old pins at home that say "100 Million Share Days — A Breed Apart."

So we had this big rally, and there I was: intelligent, hardworking, and relatively cheap. It was just what Merrill Lynch needed. With very few individuals with two, three, or even five years experience above me, I had an opportunity to work directly with senior managers and leaders. It was a huge learning curve, but it was exciting and fascinating. I was extremely fortunate to enter the business during a time of such explosive growth.

A huge turning point in my career was meeting David Komansky, now former chairman and CEO of Merrill Lynch. It was November of 1990, and I was the head trader of the listed equity-trading desk, covering all stocks on the NYSE & the American Stock Exchange.

One day I lost my temper on the trading floor. Dave was my manager's boss at the time, and he saw the entire episode. Yet he didn't say a thing. He waited a few days, then called me in my office. He said to me, in a very calm voice, "You don't need to be the loudest person in the room to be heard." It was from that point forward that I began my journey from manager to executive.

Over the next two years, Dave mentored and coached me. At times, when I needed it, he would put me in my place, and other times he would pat me on the back. Most importantly

FINANCIAL WIZARDS
Professor Stan Block chats with EIF alumni Mike Berry ('82) and Bob McCann ('82) at an alumni gathering of the Educational Investment Fund in 2006.

though, he helped me understand what it really means to lead someone. He used to say that instead of scoring the touchdowns myself, it was important that I help and encourage others on my team to make the score. That's how, he told me, you will define the next part of your career. It sounds simple, but I'll admit it wasn't easy — I was used to doing things myself. But as time went on, I became more and more comfortable sharing the responsibility. I also found it much more rewarding. To be able to share the experiences and knowledge I had gained over the years but also to listen to new ideas and perspectives from individuals who were approaching the business from different points of view — it was a tremendous learning experience. And our business thrived because of it.

I've been very fortunate in my life and my career, and a lot of that is the result of hard work and determination. But I think it's fair to say that I would not be where I am today if it weren't for the great mentors and coaches who have helped me along the way.

FINDING OUT ABOUT IMPORTANT THINGS IN LIFE

The events of September 11 had a profound impact on me, as was true for many New Yorkers and Americans. If you had met me before September 11 and asked what I thought about New York, I probably would have said, "It's fine. I love my work, and to do what I do, I need to be in the city." But the truth was, I really still considered myself a Pittsburgher. I just happen to work in New York and live in New Jersey. What happened on September 11 changed all that.

For the first time, I saw a city that was tough and tenacious and a community of people who were unrelenting in their determination to rebuild and restore. I remember coming together with business, community, and policy leaders in the hours and days following the attacks to figure out how to get our exchanges and markets back up and running. We had a clear mission: to keep New York open for business. And the overwhelming show of solidarity and partnership that resulted is something I will never forget. It made me love New York. It also heightened my sense of personal responsibility for others. I couldn't stop thinking about the individuals who got up and went to work at the World Trade Center that day, not realizing that they would never return. It reminded me how short life is, and it got me thinking about life beyond my office walls. I asked myself how I was making a difference outside of work, and at the time, I didn't really have an answer. So it started me on the path of getting involved in things like the American Ireland Fund; educational initiatives; my alma mater, Bethany College; and most recently, No Greater Sacrifice. It was a huge wake-up call.

ADVICE

- First and foremost, I am convinced that now, more than ever, the global community needs young, bright students. We have a long road ahead of us as we help turn our industry and our economy around, and we need the talent and innovation of the next generation of leaders to help us do it.
- The time to focus on your reputation is before you have one. When you establish a good reputation, it precedes you into every room you enter. Unfortunately, a bad reputation does the same thing. Some students may think that when they get to a big city like Chicago, New York, Tokyo, or London that somehow things change, that people don't know about individual reputations. But they're wrong. Your reputation is everything — in business and in life. And it is as much about who you are and how you do things as it is about what you do.
- I encourage our young people to think about who they want to be and what they want to stand for and then go out and lead in a principled way. As Abraham Lincoln used to say, "Whatever you are, be a good one."

D.D. Alexander
The World Wants Performance, Not Excuses.

D.D. ALEXANDER *is president and CEO of Englewood, Colorado-based Global Gas, Inc., a propane supplier with customers from the Rocky Mountains to the East Coast. The company contracts with a vast number of product sources in each market area to ensure dependable propane delivery to customers.*

D.D. is the third generation of her family to be involved in the propane industry, with thirty years of experience in wholesale, trading, and retail operations. She received her bachelor of business administration degree in marketing from TCU in 1982 and returned to the Neeley School for her MBA with concentrations in accounting and finance, graduating in 1985. She joined the Neeley School International Board of Visitors in 2011.

In seventh grade, I bought a building. My dad had me bike to the bank to ask for a loan to buy it. Not knowing he had already agreed to sign for my loan, I had to "convince" the banker to lend me the money. I then had to paint the building for my tenant, a Volkswagen repair shop.

I hired my brothers and sister to help me. They got into a paint fight and ended up splashing paint all over the cars that were there to get repaired — my tenant's customers.

I got really disgusted and fired them on the spot! I knew from there forward I wanted to have my own company, be in charge, and make decisions to make the business successful.

EARLY LESSONS

Both of my parents had their own companies; my mom owned travel agencies, and Dad was in the propane industry. It was our lives growing up: listening to our parents talk about business at the dinner table.

It became my goal while still in elementary school to own my own business. This goal seemed normal to me; everyone I looked up to did it. That's how my seventh-grade building purchase came about.

There were many factors that landed me at TCU, but I recall one specific event very clearly. I grew up in Kansas playing tennis. Every summer I went to tennis camp at Lakeway Resort near Austin. One year I met Janet George, a TCU admissions counselor, who was attending the adult tennis program there. I talked to her about TCU and the opportunities the school offered. I came home from camp and announced to my parents that I was going to go to TCU; from that moment on, my mind was made up.

During undergrad, I had a sobering situation with one professor that helped toughen me up for the real world. I broke my right arm the night before an accounting final. I went in to explain my situation to Professor Sanoa Hensley and asked if I could have a non-business major or someone else write the answers for me during my final. She just laughed — I took that as a no. Instead, she had me sit in the front row, and I took the exam trying to write left-handed. I didn't finish the final and had to repeat the class in summer school.

However, this taught me a valuable lesson: The real world doesn't want to hear excuses; just get things done! And as result, my associates tell me my best traits are dedication and determination. I totally dedicate myself to my customers, vendors, and employees. I'm determined to do whatever it takes to make the company successful.

SALES TRAINING

After graduation, I worked for my dad's propane business. He was by far my biggest mentor and taught me so much about business in general and especially the propane industry. He had me open up an entirely new sales territory. I called on customers who had never heard of his company. Because of the extra work I put into this new territory, it turned out to be a great experience.

I had to go somewhere that I couldn't rely on his company's image or name recognition and sell people for the first time. I learned much about sales — and myself — from doing that.

After working a few years, I went to Kansas State University for the MBA. I thought I needed to go somewhere else to get a diversified educational experience. The first thing I realized was how big the classrooms were. I decided having a more one-on-one student-professor experience was what I wanted, so I transferred back to TCU and concentrated on finance and accounting. I realized during the two years I had been out of school and working that it was the things you didn't know that could hurt you in business. And clearly, a strong accounting and finance background are helpful to anyone running a business.

ADVICE

- Find an occupation you have passion for, something you love to do. Work should be challenging, yet rewarding in more ways than financial.
- Persevere in life no matter what the odds are or what people think you can do.

Justin Avery Anderson
A Success Story
to Chew On

SNACK TIME
Justin Avery Anderson ('09)
displays the product he developed —
Anderson Trail granola — in 2010.

JUSTIN AVERY ANDERSON *is founder and CEO of Anderson Trail, which produces and distributes The Original Premium Soft Granola. Justin has been running the business full time since finishing college and reports revenues in 2010 were three times that of 2009.*

Justin has been featured in several media articles, and his uniquely soft granola —sold in major food retailers like Whole Foods, Central Market, and Costco — has also been spotlighted on the Home Shopping Network.

Justin received his bachelor of arts in English with a business minor from TCU in 2009. He was a winner of the TCU Texas Youth Entrepreneurship Award and was actively involved with the Neeley School CEO (Collegiate Entrepreneurs Organization), the largest CEO chapter in the country and top-ranked national chapter in 2009.

It's weird, but sometimes a negative event leads to a positive outcome. That's what happened for me.

Back in 2001, when I was a high school freshman, I went on a vacation to New Mexico with my best friend Spencer and his mom Nancy. We stayed in a bed-and-breakfast inn far up in the mountains.

I wore braces, and just before the trip I broke a bracket off my teeth from eating crunchy granola. I was fascinated by that inn's soft granola, which tasted wonderful.

On the way back, we started discussing food, and Nancy remarked, "If somebody were to market a soft granola to specialty food stores, they'd be rich." As soon as I got home, I started trying to recreate the recipe.

I gathered a bunch of ingredients in Mom's kitchen. It took several attempts and thousands of oats scattered across the kitchen floor, but I finally came up with something that tasted even better than what I remembered from that inn.

I loaded the mixture into one of those gallon zip bags and brought it along on a Boy Scout camp-out. My fellow Scouts loved it and finished the bag the night before its intended use at breakfast the next morning.

In 2003, I produced a big batch and gave it as Christmas presents to family and teachers. The consensus was: "It's healthy and has the consistency of a crumbled-up oatmeal cookie."

Then, when I went to see an aunt in Colorado, she drove me around Denver to look for competition. There wasn't much — and slowly I began to build the business.

And this all started when I broke a bracket on my braces!

YOUTHFUL ENTREPRENEUR
I grew up in southwest Houston in an area called Sharpstown and was raised by my mom and maternal grandparents.

As an only child, I had to keep myself entertained. Playing make-believe teacher and pilot were favorites, and I had my share of lemonade stands growing up.

We didn't have much money, but I don't think it really mattered. I created my own adventures.

I chose TCU after applying for the TCU Texas Youth Entrepreneur of the Year award and being chosen as a winner. I got to live life like a Horned Frog for two days and fell in love with the people and the University.

I came to TCU thinking that I had to be a business major since I came in through the entrepreneur scholarship. I was always terrible at math and was deathly afraid of Neeley's applied calculus requirement.

I sat through the calculus class two and a half times. I dropped it the first time and failed it twice. I had a tutor and went to my professor's office hours for extra help. It didn't work.

When I knew I was going to fail the second time, I asked to meet with two great mentors: Neeley Entrepreneurship Center director David Minor and Dean Dan Short.

Both recommended that I focus my studies where I was passionate. I was always great at English and loved to read and do research, so I switched majors to pursue a B.A. in English and a minor in business.

The business minor helped give me the solid foundation I needed to grow Anderson Trail, and the English degree fueled my passion for the arts. And special thanks to Professor Bonnie Blackwell, who taught me to love Jane Austen.

FINDING THE RECIPE FOR COMPANY GROWTH

Another serendipitous moment occurred back in 2006. I volunteered to be at a TCU parking lot at 7 a.m. to show the business executives on the Neeley School International Board of Visitors how to get to their board meeting. The first person to arrive was Scott Ward, co-president of Russell Stover Candies.

When I told him about my young company, he asked several specific questions. Then he asked me to eat lunch with him and the rest of the board. Later, he generously invited me to Russell Stover's Corsicana plant, where he gave us a full-day tour. I loved it. I felt like Willy Wonka in the chocolate factory!

I'm also grateful to Evan MacMillan, who founded The Chocolate Farm with his sister Elise. I met him when I was brainstorming Anderson Trail in Denver, and he was the first person outside my family to really encourage me.

Clayton Christopher and David Smith founded Sweet Leaf Tea. Clayton told me about mistakes he'd made early on, and this advice has saved Anderson Trail lots of money.

When we first started, I got a commercial kitchen to produce the recipe, and Mom packaged it! Now we contract out those tasks and concentrate on spreading the word about my uniquely soft granola.

ADVICE
- Patience and unbridled determination will create success.
- If what you are doing is your true passion, you will never feel like you are working.
- Meet as many people from as many different industries as you can. New contacts provide new learning opportunities.

Adam Blake
Advantages of House Hunting

BUILDING A SOLID FUTURE
Neeley Entrepreneurship Center Founder Emeritus David Minor ('80) congratulates Adam Blake ('07), the 2005 Global Student Entrepreneur of the Year.

ADAM BLAKE *began to invest in real estate while a TCU freshman. His remarkable story is one of youth, energy, intellect, persistence, and attention to detail.*

This 2007 Neeley School cum laude graduate with degrees in entrepreneurial management, accounting, and finance has already made a big impact on the national scene. His company, Atlas Properties, owns mineral rights on land in Appalachia and property in Texas, Missouri, Louisiana, and New York. In 2009, Atlas Properties was named as the 123rd fastest-growing private company in the U.S. by Inc. Magazine. *Adam has been named as one of the top "Forty Under Forty" by* The Fort Worth Business Press *and was recognized as the 2005 Global Student Entrepreneur of the Year.*

In commercial real estate, his company has made major urban purchases, including the Historic Electric Building in Fort Worth and the Pabst-Pendergast Building and the Liberty Lofts condos in Kansas City.

In 2003, when I was a freshman, a fraternity brother and I made an interesting discovery: Several students in dorms wanted to move into off-campus houses — but there was a shortage of inventory and finding the housing was difficult.

We quickly identified a strong market demand for providing rental housing and assisting students in finding off-campus housing. We decided to purchase an investment property that spring semester and found tenants before we closed on the property. We advertised availability in a student newsletter called *TCU Announce.* We were overwhelmed with around fifty responses and knew there was a business opportunity.

Later that summer we bought a few more houses, and by my junior year I had started a property management group primarily focused on rental housing in the TCU area. By 2008, one year after graduation, I had bought and sold about 200 units in the Fort Worth-Dallas area. After that, I got into larger commercial real estate projects.

CAREER PREPARATION

I grew up in Kansas City and attended Rockhurst High School, an all-male Jesuit preparatory school. Rockhurst fostered a very competitive environment where I learned values of hard work, integrity, and pride.

I was attracted to TCU's beautiful campus, warm weather, and impressive business school. I also received a significant scholarship that made the decision much easier.

I took several advanced placement courses in high school and tested out of a few courses, so I started college with about fifty semester hours. This afforded me the time to triple-major in entrepreneurial management, finance, and accounting. Since I was also running a business in college, the entrepreneurial management courses were extra valuable since I could relate to a lot of the curriculum. The finance and accounting courses were also crucial in helping me understand the financial complexities of my business.

At the beginning of my sophomore year, I interviewed for an internship with a commercial real estate company. During this process, I talked about the business I was running, and the interviewer asked why I wanted a job. I thought about it and realized she was right! Ever since then I have focused 100 percent on growing my business and never considered taking a job.

Because I am young, and most of my competitors are twice my age, a lot of people assume things. For example, they'll ask, "Who do you work for?" or "Is your family in real estate?"

This business takes lots of energy. In college I worked very hard and didn't sleep much. I didn't spend time playing video games, watching movies, or taking part in many non-productive activities.

IDENTIFYING BUSINESS OPPORTUNITIES

My parents are extremely supportive and did a great job instilling confidence in me. My dad was an executive at a telecommunications company that went bankrupt during the dot.com bust. After seeing the effect it had on him and my family, I was determined I would never work in a corporate environment where I was financially dependent on someone else.

At TCU, David Minor, Director of the Neeley Entrepreneurship Center, introduced me to several real estate guys, bankers, and CPAs who were very helpful. I met Doug Rippeto through the Entrepreneurs' Organization and mentorship program. He's a very successful real estate veteran and wise businessman. I meet with him regularly, and we talk primarily about strategy, goals, situations, and the vision for my business.

I think it's very important to do something you feel good about. As for me, I am very passionate about sustainability and have aligned my business interests with my beliefs. In real estate, for example, I like higher density, mixed-use developments because they are more practical and sustainable than urban sprawl. As such, nearly all of my real estate investments involve projects near urban cores.

ADVICE
- If you want to be an entrepreneur, start sooner rather than later.
- Develop confidence; find something you can be the best or at least very good at.

Eddie Clark
Surviving Tough Times

EDDIE CLARK *is president and CEO of Professional Turf Products, the Toro distributor of golf equipment and irrigation in the south-central United States. A Philadelphia native, Eddie was a highly recruited high school footballer and says he chose TCU for many reasons. He graduated from TCU in 1982 with a bachelor of business administration and management major.*

I worked at Goldthwaite's Distributing during college and upon graduation joined them as sales coordinator. They sent me to New Mexico to fix a customer's irrigation system. I dug down about ten feet and started repairing a water line coupler. Suddenly the line exploded, flooding the hole. Underground water in New Mexico is a lot colder than in Texas.

That's the day I learned to swim really fast. I discovered that ice water is a really cool motivator.

EARLY LESSONS
I was fourth-born in a family of eight children. I started a paper route when I was 12 and learned one thing immediately: There are two ways to fold a newspaper. If you fold it wrong, it flies apart when you throw it. I paid to replace several customers' papers before I learned the right way.

I had other jobs, like cleaning restaurant tables and mowing grass. But I put every ounce of effort into football because I wanted to play in the NFL. Any academic effort I made was to improve my college choices.

COLLEGE DECISIONS
Several schools recruited me, but I really liked Fort Worth's climate, hospitality, and eating my first Mexican food at Joe T. Garcia's. Sports and business school taught me that team effort is important. Everyone has different strengths, and we can learn from others' perspectives.

I never really considered another major besides business. I majored in management to give me the fundamentals for accounting, marketing, management, and finance. This gave me confidence to sit in on any meeting regarding any business specialty.

Summers at Goldthwaite's taught me so much. I worked on forecasts, projections, and inventory. One summer I unloaded carloads of fertilizer, one bag at a time, in the July heat. It didn't take me long to decide I wanted a cooler, cleaner, more fragrant desk job.

What started out as a summer paycheck turned into a year-round interest. After graduation, they gave me my first full-time job as sales coordinator.

BUILDING A LIFE
I met my wife Pam on the student center steps. Twice I said hello, but she ignored me. I finally approached her and asked her why she didn't speak, and she said she was shy. But I knew she was going to be important in my life, so I persisted until I got a date. That worked out great, because she had a car, and I didn't.

She was also a business major and the best college teacher I had. She believed in me and helped me survive some tough academic challenges. She went to all my football games and took notes on every play.

Marrying Pam was the best decision I ever made. Today we work together too; she's human resources manager for ProTurf. My children, Graham, Hannah, and Hayden, teach me something new every day and remind me how blessed I am.

Life-long friends really influenced my early years here. Coach Bubba Thornton, head track

DISTINGUISHED LEADERS
M.J. Neeley pauses for a photograph with Dean Ike Harrison in 1959.

coach at the time, always welcomed conversations. He knew that as a Philadelphia boy, I was a square in a round hole walking on the TCU campus.

Judge Mike Thomas and his wife Patsy took a special interest in out-of-state students. They guided me by asking the right questions at the right time. I still talk to Mike several times a month.

And of course, faculty at Neeley had a big impact. Sanoa Hensley was an accounting professor whom I actually dreaded. She was a no-nonsense teacher who did not allow me to slide by in her classroom. She made me learn accounting whether I wanted to or not! And David Lobingier had a knack for putting things into a real-world perspective. He gave us license to make decisions and argue about our choices within our "companies."

ADVICE
- Persistence is critical to success.
- Today we emphasize teaching, coaching, and mentoring. But learning from mistakes is important too. If people see you're trying your best, they'll help you.
- Knowing a business requires you to submerge yourself, to learn every aspect of the company.
- People are willing to pay for outstanding performance. Be the best that you can be.
- I'm not the type to hide behind a computer. I believe every business is a "people" business. It's important to know what your employees and your customers need.
- The art and discipline of sending handwritten notes is a skill that should not be underestimated. Write thank-you notes, write notes for no reason, write notes of congratulations, write notes of sympathy, and write notes for fun. Spend 44 cents to stamp a letter and throw it in the mailbox; the impact this has on people is tremendous.

John F. Davis III
Sometimes Failure Is the Best Teacher.

JOHN F. DAVIS III *is chief executive officer of Hotel JV Services LLC, a hospitality technology joint venture that evaluates technology investments in the hospitality sector.*

John has a long history as an innovator in the travel and technology industries. He was previously chief executive officer of BirchStreet Systems, Inc., a procure-to-pay software service, and served as chief executive officer and president of Pegasus Solutions for nineteen years. He led the launch of Pegasus Electronic Distribution "switch" technology, which was created to link the central reservation systems of hotel companies with the major airline global distribution systems. A long-time entrepreneur, John also co-founded the toll-free ordering company 800-FLOWERS for the floral industry.

John has received numerous business honors, including Business Travel News and Travel Industry Hall of Fame; he was named six times to its annual 25 Most Influential Executives. He serves on the board of TRX Inc. and is an honorary consulate for the Principality of Monaco.

A 1974 graduate of the Neeley School, John serves on the board of trustees of TCU and on the Neeley School International Board of Visitors. He has been an executive-in-residence in the Neeley School and was honored with the TCU 2008 Valuable Alumnus Award.

The experience that had the biggest impact on my life, oddly enough, was my first major failure.

My partner and I had started 800-FLOWERS. Pressured by our limited partners, we had to hire a professional CEO, who promptly blew all of the $7 million we had raised in equity. Not only had I put everything I had in the company, I had borrowed $150,000 from my father-in-law — really bad idea! So here I was: broke, no job, and pregnant wife.

We had built a beautiful call center in Las Colinas to handle all the calls for 800-FLOWERS, where a large portion of the blown $7 million had been invested. The center had 600 cubicles, 600 computers, and 600 phones — just not very many calls.

At that point, I came up with the idea of turning it into a telemarketing company. At the time, AT&T was being broken up, and there were a number of new competitors looking for customers. I was able to convince U.S. Telephone (now Sprint) to take 300 positions for outbound telephone sales. From there, I convinced several hotel companies to use our center for reservations.

My relationship with the hoteliers eventually led me to starting Pegasus Solutions. The telemarketing company, ATC, and Pegasus Solutions were all huge successes.

EIF BOARD ROOM
The board room of the Educational Investment Fund was an intense place in 2006, when this photo was taken. It still is.

YOUTH AND COLLEGE

I grew up in Baton Rouge, Louisiana, the oldest of five kids. I am from a middle-class family who really had to scrimp in order to pay my tuition. I am pretty sure my only interest coming out of high school was girls.

I chose TCU primarily due to its size and location. I was looking for a small school as far away from Baton Rouge as possible. I did not know anyone from my hometown who had ever gone to TCU, but after going to a recruitment dinner in New Orleans, I was sold.

My first major at TCU was accounting. After freshman year, I figured out that my personality was not really geared to accounting, so I changed to marketing.

My TCU education really prepared me for the business world. I could read and understand income statements and balance sheets. While this may sound like basics, I am still always amazed at how many "business" people can't figure out if a company is doing well or not by looking at their financials.

I learned much from Dr. Sanoa Hensley She expected us to study every night and fully understand accounting concepts. She instilled study habits that lasted throughout college.

EARLY JOBS AND CAREER

My favorite job in college was selling at a RadioShack. My boss at the store always thought he was a great salesman, so every week we would have a contest to see who could sell the most. It was a very rare week when I lost. Looking back now, I see how he used the competition to motivate me.

My first job after graduation was with the 3M Company on the order desk, taking orders over the telephone. I was quickly promoted to sales, where I learned one of the most valuable lessons in the world — how to sell!

I really had two mentors in my life. Ken Cheairs, my first sales manager at 3M, taught me to talk to everyone, not just the buyer, because you never know who could influence the buying decision. My next mentor was Bob McGrail, vice president of marketing for Days Inn. When I started Pegasus, Bob was the first chairman of the board. He had spent more than thirty years in the hotel business and encouraged me to change the way the industry did business.

I will never forget the meeting where I introduced the concept of a worldwide clearinghouse for hotel commissions paid to travel agents. There were vice presidents in the room from fifteen or sixteen hotel companies telling me it would never work. As we walked out of the meeting, Bob looked at me and said, "You are right. They are wrong. Keep pushing."

Today that business clears $700 million in commissions and nets over $25 million in annual profits.

ADVICE
- The personal attributes that have served me over my business career are perseverance and optimism. No matter how many times I get told no, I get myself right back up and go after it again.
- My mother always said I was like a baby duck hatching every day. No matter what happened yesterday, I forgot about it and moved on.
- Don't hang onto failures or successes too long. Both of these happened yesterday. Focus on the challenge of today.

Ash Huzenlaub
Promoting Entrepreneurship

ASH HUZENLAUB *is vice president of business development across the western United States for TeamHealth, a $1.5 billion NYSE-listed company majority owned by The Blackstone Group. TeamHealth provides emergency physicians, hospitalists, and anesthesiologists to more than 500 hospitals across the country. Before that, through Ashco Group (a firm that delivers project-specific execution assistance to investors), Huzenlaub helped Sweet Leaf Tea Company expand its footprint outside of Texas in order to prove that "sweet tea" could be nationally embraced beyond its southern roots. It became the fastest-growing tea brand in the Whole Foods chain of stores. Prior to this, in 2002, at the age of 26, Ash became one of the youngest CEOs of a public company when private equity investors took over Emergisoft, the electronic medical records company that automates hospital emergency rooms. His four-year turn-around of the company resulted in his becoming a nominee for the Southwest Ernst & Young Entrepreneur of the Year Award.*

Ash graduated from TCU in 1998 with a degree in finance and marketing and has served on the board of advisors for the Neeley Entrepreneurship Center since its founding. He was a two-time recipient of the Chancellor's Leadership Award at TCU and a track and field letterman. Recently he has become an avid skydiver, capitalizing on the extreme sports world present in Southern California where he now lives.

I learned about entrepreneurship early. We lived in Houston, and my father was one of thousands who lost his job in the Texas oil crunch of the early 1980s. It was a tough awakening for him. He was an executive for an oil valve company and was accustomed to traveling the world representing the company and its products. The unemployment rate in Houston and generally across Texas at that time necessitated that my family do whatever it took to keep up with the house payments and take care of my sister and me.

As no jobs were available, Dad and Mom began selling soap, fire extinguishers, and other items door to door. Dad had always allowed me to tag along with him when he was working, so hanging out in an office before the downturn turned to following him door to door and hotel conference room to hotel conference room as he gave sales pitches. More often than not, homeowners would not open the door for him unless I was visible at the curb. Eventually it clicked for him, and he started sending me to the door while he waited at the curb. It became a winning formula. Rather than the homeowner supporting a door-to-door salesman, their purchases became "supporting a dad teaching his kid about business." It worked. This is how kids should be instructed.

For every item sold, I earned $5. The rest went to Mom and Dad and product costs. These were concentrate-based products, so often they sold for $20 or more. Every night we went home and dumped out a Texas Commerce Bank bag that was hidden under a box in my red wagon. We divided the monies up right then and there, and they showed me how they kept their ledger. What a great experience! I was seven years old. If I wanted the new Big Wheel advertised on Saturday morning cartoons, that meant I had to sell eight items. The seed of carrot-driven success is one that is hard to extinguish, and it has stayed with me to this day.

FREE FLOATING
Ash Huzenlaub ('98) advises others to get out of their comfort zones — and he clearly follows his own advice.

After this introduction and witnessing Dad's experience, I believed in working for myself. My Christmas gifts became biographies instead of toys. And on one birthday, Dad raised the garage door with a smile — it was floor to ceiling with pallets of products to sell.

In high school I started a curbside recycling service with my free enterprise teacher called Recycle Now. This service targeted the wealthier neighborhoods that did not want to dirty up their cars transporting recyclables to the city recycling center. We were glorified trash men playing a numbers game. One street had forty homes, and at $3 each, we could make $120 in less than thirty minutes. If you were not using Recycle Now, you did not care about the environment, and in a place like Tyler, you have to fit in. Every first and third Tuesday of the month, Mr. Woodard and I "cleaned house." However, it was my auto detailing business that is the best learning experience I have encountered. I learned about the value of customer service and how that equates to word-of-mouth advertising, the most valuable marketing of all. Do a great job and people talk. Do a bad job and people talk.

When you see your parents lose a job, work hard to put food on the table, clothe you, and break their necks to keep you happy, it makes a big impact. You want to make things better. You want to do everything you can to accomplish a lifestyle where worrying about bills is not the first thing on your list in the morning. Whether you are a pure play entrepreneur or someone working for a large company, experiences like I had growing up teach you to always have a plan B and keep on your toes.

Bottom line, I never considered myself having a career. I am entrepreneurial, and from a career perspective there is nothing more rewarding. But I also find it valuable to work for large companies so that I can expose myself to the inner workings of these businesses. Large companies, especially those owned by private equity firms, need entrepreneurial-minded workers to bring in new schools of thought, to break them out of the status quo. That is why I am doing what I do today.

COLLEGE LIFE
I ran cross-country and the 1600 meters at my high school in Tyler and came to TCU as a walk-on athlete gaining periodic scrap scholarship money for books when it was available. I would sit in TCU's financial aid office in Sadler Hall for hours on end trying to find unclaimed scholarships. They were few and far between, but every once in a while I would come across something

like the TCU Texas License Plate Scholarship, one I received four years in a row. My sister preceded me to TCU, and with Mom serving as a nurse and Dad busting his back at UPS, any scholarships we could find were a gift to them.

TCU was a university 140 miles away from home: close enough to head back to East Texas if we needed, but far enough for the folks not to know too much of what we were up to! For me, TCU had one of the best track programs in the country, and Fort Worth was home to Richard Rainwater, the Bass financier I had read about all through high school. He was like Michael Jordan to me, and I wanted to study everything he was doing.

I became a finance and marketing major and discovered six people who profoundly changed my life:

Charles "Chuck" Williams, now dean of the business school at Butler University, inspired me and genuinely believed in me when I arrived on campus in 1994. When others based their assessment of students squarely on a GPA, Doc looked at the whole picture of a student and invested his time accordingly. Eventually I took three courses from him including his Leadership London study-abroad program. He also served as my faculty sponsor for The Independent Study of Entrepreneurship (ISE), the most rewarding of my hands-on educational experiences at TCU.

ISE was a program Doc and I developed from scratch together that resulted in my traveling more than 6,000 miles across the U.S. and England interviewing entrepreneurs and their financiers one on one. I had the pleasure of spending anywhere from hours to days with entrepreneurs large and small. These included Howard Schultz, founder of Starbucks; Michael Milken, the "junk bond king"; John Mars of the Mars candy empire; representatives of the Virgin Group in London; and many others. Apple provided a laptop (quite bulky compared to today's devices) as long as I kept a daily journal, a journal later titled The World Is My Classroom.

ISE led to Endeavor: Entrepreneurship@TCU, whereby alumni entrepreneurs from TCU wrote letters to the board of trustees lobbying for TCU to launch a full-fledged entrepreneurship program.

Bill Moncrief has to be one of the coolest professors at TCU but not as cool as he used to be. Prior to my getting to TCU, professors were allowed to hold court at The Pub if students were over 21. While we did not have that experience with Dr. Moncrief in the 1994-98 era of Neeley, we did have classes in such places as box suites at Texas Rangers Stadium and at local businesses around TCU. Dr. Moncrief, like Doc Williams, was one who judged students on their work ethic and passion for learning — not your GPA. He would reach out a helping hand to help you achieve your goals. He gave me faith in professors, those I often dismissed unfairly as academics. These were not academics; these were people showing us the path to achieve business success.

TEACHING THE 4 P'S OF MARKETING TO SUPER FROG
Pepsico executives Tom Baltes and Nick Giachino enjoy a meeting with Chancellor Ferrari, Marketing Professor Bill Moncrief, and Super Frog in 2001.

Stan Block is an icon at TCU and in the world of financial education. I could sit in front of this guy for hours and not get bored. I still have tapes of him. Co-founder of the famed Educational Investment Fund, Dr. Block is another of the Neeley greats who goes out of his way to assist an energetic, passionate student. No, I did not make it into EIF. I love him anyway!

Mayor Bob Bolen was not an official professor, but he is the "Statesman of TCU." He took me under his wing and pointed me in the right direction numerous times. There should be a book about him. It should be titled *Mentor*. He learned of my desire to learn from Richard Rainwater before I arrived at TCU. By my sixth week on campus he had me elbow to elbow with this great business leader in downtown Fort Worth.

Professor John Thompson said simply R-E=P (Revenue Minus Expenses Equals Profit). As he would say, "This is not rocket science, folks!"

David Minor was a TCU alum when we met. At Mayor Bolen's request, David started working with me as a mentor straight out of the gate my freshman year. Today, more than fifteen years later, he remains one of my best friends and closest advisors. David, of course, became founding director of the Neeley Entrepreneurship Center and was the first alum to write a letter when the Endeavor project began. There could not have been a more perfect alignment of timing and opportunity — TCU's desire to launch entrepreneurship and David Minor's new availability due to the fact he had just sold his business. And there could have been no better fit — an accomplished alumni entrepreneur who cannot take no for an answer in an academic setting working to exact change. Because of his efforts, TCU now has one of the top undergraduate entrepreneurship programs in America.

ADVICE

- Get out of your comfort zone. Enroll in a study-abroad program as many summers as you can. If you cannot find an open slot at TCU, find one through another university at studyabroad.com. When the official programs are complete, stay on a few weeks more and backpack abroad. You can't change the world if you haven't seen it. Don't wait until your senior year: Start exploring the world, jobs, and life experiences as soon as you finish reading this sentence. When you study abroad, don't just experience the pub-crawls — interview the pub owners, learn their businesses, and open your eyes.
- Entrepreneurship is about sales. It's about finding business needs and creating a way to fulfill those needs. And it's about building strong, trusting lifetime relationships. Roll your sleeves up, explore, and make it fun.

Warren Mackey
Think Big. Talk Small.

WARREN A. MACKEY *is founder, president, and chief investment officer of Arles Management, Inc., which is the investment manager of Arles Partners LP and Homestead Odyssey Partners LP. With more than two decades of experience in the financial services industry, he spent six years as an investment banker in the corporate finance department of Salomon Brothers, where he was actively involved with domestic and international financings, mergers, acquisitions, and divestitures.*

Warren is a former director of Center Financial Corporation, one of the largest Korean-American banks in the U.S., where he served as chairman of the Planning and Asset-Liability Committee. He is currently an organizer, director, and one of the largest shareholders of BankAsiana, a Korean-American bank located in New Jersey.

He is a published writer with articles appearing in numerous newspapers and magazines, including The New York Times *and* The Washington Post. *He graduated with a bachelor of business administration from TCU in 1981 and serves on the International Board of Visitors at the Neeley School.*

In my junior year at TCU, I was fortunate to have the opportunity to meet and then build a relationship with M.J. Neeley, the quintessential entrepreneur. He soon became my mentor, and over the next seventeen years we met many times. Mr. Neeley's greatest gift to those who knew him was his time. He generously gave his time to teach, to encourage, and to motivate. He was a mentor to many.

Mr. Neeley had a pragmatic way of evaluating people: "You judge a tree by the fruit it bears," he said. His words have had a lifelong impact on my career.

COLLEGE

I was an accounting major. My father was an accountant. My next-door neighbor, a close friend, was an accountant. From an early age, I learned that accounting is the language of business.

While completing my studies at TCU, I was on the Educational Investment Fund, which was enormously important. The experience helped clarify that I wanted a career that was broader than just accounting.

For two summers and part time through one school year, I worked in the audit department at Southland Royalty Company, an independent producer of oil and gas in Fort Worth. I spent the vast majority of my time auditing joint ventures of drilling projects.

This was my first office job. All my previous jobs, which I enjoyed and which were well paid, involved manual labor. The work was primarily outdoors. I moved furniture and drove a truck for United Van Lines and worked in local neighborhoods mowing lawns and painting houses.

CAREER

My work at Southland Royalty required me to thoroughly understand the process of drilling an oil and gas well and to work with many different people throughout the company. I also began to develop essential analytical skills. Southland was an ideal work environment. What we did was interesting, and the people were of the highest quality. This unique experience helped create a solid foundation for my career.

I moved to New York City to work in the Investment Banking Group of Salomon Brothers, Inc. There I was actively involved with domestic and international financings, mergers, acquisitions, and divestitures. I gained a broad knowledge of the securities industry and continued to further develop my analytical skills.

The many relationships I formed at Salomon Brothers have been long-lasting; they have developed into some of my most important business relationships today. In fact, a dozen former senior executives from Salomon Brothers provided me with the capital to launch Arles Management.

Clearly, though, the single most important mentor in my life was M.J. Neeley. He inspired me to pursue my career outside the traditional corporate world. He always said, "Think big. Talk small."

ADVICE

■ Find work that you love.

Note: Below is an article written about M.J. Neeley by Warren Mackey in the *Fort Worth Star-Telegram* that captures the value of close mentor relationships.

What Kind Of Fruit Did Mr. Neeley's Life Produce?

Nearly two decades ago, M.J. Neeley told me this parable in the sanctum of his home study:

"A man walks through an orchard in search of a good apple to eat. He sees some inviting apples way up in the branches, but he is too lazy to climb the tree and he is afraid that he might fall and get hurt, so he finds a comfortable spot in the shade to lie down, hoping that an apple will fall into his lap.

Many hours pass before the force of gravity delivers an apple into his waiting hands. However, the apple is rotten and infested with worms. The man enjoyed the day dreaming about eating a delicious apple in the shade of the tree, but he did not enjoy eating the fruit that was delivered to him.

"He eventually gets up and walks over to a peach tree, which is not too big. On a limb that is within his reach are many inviting peaches.

He shakes the limb and a basket full of ripe, delicious peaches falls to the ground. He spends the rest of the afternoon gorging on the fruits of his labor.

"The moral of the story is that when an opportunity comes along, shake the hell out of it!"

In his lifetime, Neeley did something akin to multiplying the loaves and fishes. He died at his home the second week of January.

This quintessential, exceedingly patient entrepreneur — whose keen foresight stretched for decades — had his hand in transportation, banking, insurance, mining, manufacturing, oil and gas, railroading, ranching, real estate, and education.

Neeley was also a generous philanthropist along the road of creating significant wealth. He was a soft-spoken, humble man. "Think

(continues)

big; talk small," my friend and my mentor would instruct me.

During my junior year at the M.J. Neeley School of Business at Texas Christian University, one of my professors suggested that I meet Neeley in person, and the meeting was arranged.

During the subsequent seventeen years, we met frequently, and our special relationship grew. We would get together at his office, at his home, at the Fort Worth Club for lunch, at restaurants. We even attended a TCU football game together.

One Sunday many years ago, we sat in his office talking for eight straight hours.

The subject matter was quite diverse but mostly business-related. We would have protracted discussions on his business ventures, such as Hobbs Trailer Manufacturing, a truck-trailer manufacturer that became the foundation of Neeley's business empire; PVI Industries, a Fort Worth manufacturer of commercial water heaters and boilers; and Texas Crushed Stone and the Georgetown Railroad, a quarry and railroad in Georgetown.

Hobbs and PVI were floundering when Neeley got involved with them. And we talked about businesses he helped give birth to, such as Fort Worth Savings, a savings and loan.

Marion J. Neeley had a knack for spotting value that others had overlooked, and then the patience to wait a lengthy time for his investment to blossom. (As with the "S" in Harry S. Truman, the "J" in Neeley's name was just a letter and not an initial.)

Neeley would repeatedly tell me the importance of keeping tight control on cash — even if the business is succeeding.

We talked about past Fort Worth businessmen such as Charles Tandy and Sid Richardson and present-day ones. We talked about the history of Fort Worth. We talked about TCU, Texas A&M, and the work going on at the Union Gospel Mission.

We talked about women, marriage, raising children, his family, my family, issues related to aging, and the importance of giving. He told me many times that he got much more satisfaction out of giving than he ever did from making money.

In the early 1980s, during one of our visits, Neeley described in great detail the coming collapse in the savings-and-loan industry and the potential resulting opportunities.

Neeley owned several savings and loans. At the time, I was working in the Investment Banking Group at Salomon Bros. in New York City. Although I admittedly was a junior member of a dozen swaggering investment bankers focusing on financial institutions at the time, Neeley was the first to bring the impending savings-and-loan debacle to my attention — and in fine detail.

A glimpse in the rearview mirror today shows that Neeley's analysis was accurate. I have yet to locate his oracle, crystal ball, or tarot cards in his office or home.

Neeley accomplished much without the narrowness of mental concentration on a single purpose or end. His achievements were the result of an intellect that exceeded definition.

I have never met anyone with a comparable mind. Ideas and numbers were in perpetual motion within his cranium. He had an unquenchable thirst to learn — intense curiosity. He was brilliantly creative, a profound thinker, a philosopher.

Above all, Neeley was a teacher, a motivator, an inspiration — a truly great mentor to many. He packaged his thoughts and ideas in a way that was void of sermons and self-importance.

He had the unique ability to make significant achievements through the willing efforts of talented people who went to conquer many unclimbed mountains. Walter Lippmann spoke of men who plant trees that other men would sit under. Neeley was such a man.

M.J. Neeley's greatest gift to our society was his time.

As with others who knew him, there was no better destination for counsel: clarity of thinking, common sense, wisdom, insight, ideas, encouragement, and spirit.

"A man who has taken your time recognizes no debt, yet it is the one he can never repay," wrote Seneca, the Roman statesman and philosopher.

Those who dealt with Neeley over the years need no elaboration of his integrity — his unimpeachable virtue — and the decency of his treatment of all individuals.

In today's world, where it is customary to conduct business with the assistance of a plethora of lawyers, Neeley's handshake was as binding as his signature. The only promise that I am aware that he made and did not deliver on was when he repeatedly told me and many others that he would live to be 100. He missed by less than three years.

Neeley had a pragmatic way of evaluating other people. "You judge a tree by the fruit it bears," he would tell me.

There is no better way to evaluate M.J. Neeley.

Source: *"What kind of fruit did M.J. Neeley's life produce?"* (by Warren Mackey, *Fort Worth Star-Telegram*, March 31, 1996, Section C, page 5). Used with permission.

Jay Meadows
Streamlining the Mortgage Industry

JAY H. MEADOWS *co-founded Rapid Reporting Verification Co. in 1998, and currently as president and CEO, he oversees the company's business, including product development, operations, sales, and support. Rapid Reporting was bought by Equifax in 2009.*

A widely recognized fraud expert, Meadows collaborated with the Internal Revenue Service to spearhead many of the efficiencies that benefit the mortgage industry today. Through his lobbying efforts, Meadows was instrumental in the IRS's decision to provide information in an electronic format and helped transform the IRS process for providing information and shortening income verification tax transcript turn-around times.

Jay graduated from TCU in 1985 with a bachelor of business administration with a major in management.

I married my college sweetheart, a TCU nursing student. We married right after I graduated — she was still in school — and the same week, I started my career in stocks and bonds with Rauscher Pierce Refsnes.

Marriage at such a young age was tough, especially with the added pressure of the brokerage business. We had been married two years, and trying to balance my career and home life was getting difficult.

The arguments were more frequent. My wife said something to me during that time that really stuck in my head. She told me, "When you start leading, I will start following." I never wanted to hear those words again.

COLLEGE TRANSFER

I transferred to TCU from Murray State, a small junior college in Oklahoma. I wanted to play baseball in the Southwest Conference. TCU had a good program, and it allowed me the opportunity to play while getting a great education.

I majored in management. At that time, John Thompson had several marketing classes and also taught a course called Policies, which was basically a strategic management class. We learned how to assess companies and to read annual reports as well as financials. He encouraged me to take who I was and use my strengths to succeed in business.

He is still mentoring me some twenty-five years after I first met him. But I believe the most important thing he taught me was that the person who makes the best grade is not always the most successful in life.

CAREER AND MENTORS

My first real job was working in a small hotel as a bellman; we bellmen took care of most clients' needs. I learned how to deal with people from all walks of life and how to create "raving fans" through over-the-top customer service.

What I learned on that first stockbroker job after graduation, at Rauscher Pierce Refsnes, shaped everything I've done since. I learned about perseverance, finding value, customer service, competition, and staying connected.

I also found that it's essential to be surrounded with great people who add energy to you, versus sucking the life out of you.

I've had many wonderful advisors, including my grandfather, Marvin Brummett, who was senior vice-president and treasurer of Halliburton. He was a top executive full of sage advice — but he would seldom share it.

One time I was facing a huge career decision. He said, "When you kick a jackass, he sits down. When you kick a thoroughbred, he runs. All you need to do is decide which one you are."

My high school baseball coach, Randy Tally, taught me to believe in myself despite what others might say and to persevere. "Pressure," he said, "is self-inflicted."

Retired Army General Vernon Lewis taught me respect and how to lead. I never had a class. I just watched this man of great integrity. Pastor Randy Weeks taught me that it's impossible to fulfill your potential without God. And Tommy Moore, a CEO of many companies, emphasized that you should always be yourself — because in the end, that is who you are.

ADVICE

- Sold out! Whatever your goal, you have to be completely committed and absorbed with it. Focus is not an option; it is what brings opportunity.
- If you were accused of doing something, would there be enough evidence to convict you? There are multitudes of people who talk about what they are doing or where they are going, but is there any evidence of this in their life? As students, it is important to be able to make the transition from the psychological world (thought) into the physiological world (action).

FAVORITE MENTOR
John Thompson ('63) attends the Neeley 75th anniversary celebration kickoff with his wife, Irene, in 2011.

Greg Meyer
Football Referee
Made Career Call.

CALLING IT AS I SEE IT
Greg Meyer ('81) explains a rule to Atlanta Falcons coach.

GREG MEYER *is a National Football League official, where he serves as a side judge. He also evaluates college football officials for the Big 12 Conference.*

Greg graduated from TCU with a bachelor of business administration in 1981. He played baseball for TCU from 1978 through 1981.

He began his business career with Amoco Production in Alvin, Texas. He started officiating football as a hobby and continued that when he moved back to Fort Worth in 1983 to work for Texas American Bank. He travels frequently for six months each year but makes his home in Fort Worth.

The Super Bowl is the pinnacle for players, and it's the same for us officials, too. There's a worldwide audience, people are screaming, cameras are everywhere. I'll never forget the exhilaration I felt as side judge for 2010's Super Bowl XLIV, which paired the New Orleans Saints with the Indianapolis Colts.

That championship game culminated a long season. We officials start with a training camp in July and start refereeing the first of four pre-season games in August. After that, each crew of seven people works a minimum fifteen of the seventeen regular-season games. Then the playoffs start.

At the Super Bowl, I kept thinking, "What a lucky guy I am. Here I am, the only side judge in the world making critical calls throughout the contest. Awesome!"

I've been at this job thirty years now. I started by calling pee-wee football games and then moved to middle school, junior varsity, varsity high school games, then college — and now the pros.

I must know the rules, put myself in the right position to make the calls under significant pressure, and replicate that performance on 150 plays per game.

This is a fantastic profession and a great life.

EDUCATION AND BANKING
As a high school student in Tulsa, I was more interested in sports than in school. I had a chemistry teacher, Charles Brown, who also served as athletic director and head football coach. He treated his students with respect and gave us responsibility too.

Outside of school, I worked for a health food distributor. I packed and unpacked trucks. I learned this lesson from all that sweaty work: Study hard and someday I could work in an air-conditioned office.

For college, I looked at several schools. But my older brother was already at TCU, and Fort Worth is a great place to live. I came to play baseball.

I majored in business and loved it. I also enjoyed other courses like astronomy and geography. I continuously juggled my schedule around baseball. My challenges: Keep my GPA up, learn as much as I could, and find a way to accumulate 124 hours!

After graduation, I started working for Amoco Production. When the oil business declined, I moved back to Fort Worth to work in Texas American Bank's credit training program. Then I became a loan officer.

I left Texas American Bank to join NCNB, which became Bank of America, in the mid-1980s. Over the years, I was a banker for Bank One, J.P. Morgan, Compass, Summit, and Frost.

I moved more and more into officiating, and since 2006 it's been a full-time profession.

THE OFFICIAL'S LIFE

I'm a side judge and work on the same side of the field as the head lineman. I'm in the defensive backfield. I watch wide receivers and punt returners, looking for both defensive and offensive pass interference, defensive holding, and illegal contact. We officials are evaluated for every play. One's aggregate performance determines who'll work the playoff games.

My hardest season was rookie year, transitioning into the pro ranks from college football. I'd gained some experience by refereeing for NFL Europe, which has a spring season. Six teams play ten games each. The league exposes Europeans to American football and also helps the NFL showcase and evaluate potential players.

As a Big 12 evaluator, I watch game videos of officials' calls throughout the season. On the football weekends when I'm not officiating an NFL game, I go to a Big 12 game to evaluate officials there.

I'm often asked what surprises me most about the NFL. Mainly, it's the speed of the game. These players are incredibly strong and fast. My biggest fear is that I'll be making a call and collide with a flying player! Fitness is critical. My neighbor and I run four times a week, and I also lift weights.

My wife and I have a daughter and a son. Our daughter will soon marry another official's son — so I guess officiating runs in the family!

ADVICE

- Whatever you put into something is what you get out of it. The effort tends to benefit you, and you reap the rewards down the road.
- Some people have career paths. In officiating, the funnel gets narrower, and many things have to go your way. Typically it's the guy who works the hardest, treats people well, and displays character who does the best.
- The easy path at times is the one you want to take — but it's not always the right one.
- Learn to appreciate and respect all points of view.

Mike Micallef
Restaurants, Ranches, and Rodeos

MIKE MICALLEF *is president of Reata Restaurant and JMK Holdings. Reata has two Lone Star State locations; the original opened in Alpine in 1995, and its second location is in downtown Fort Worth's Sundance Square.*

Another family-owned business, CF Ranch, has expanded the boundaries of a traditional ranching operation by striving to find and develop innovative profit centers. These emerging opportunities include real estate development, film and television production, and wildlife management.

Mike graduated from TCU with a bachelor of business administration in 1999 with a finance major and also earned a ranch management certificate in 1997.

I always enjoyed hunting, fishing, and being in the outdoors. My original plan for college was to attend the TCU Ranch Management program, which at the time was a certificate program, and subsequently finish with a degree in wildlife management from Texas Tech.

Our family's ranch is in Alpine, Texas, so I started taking basic courses at Sul Ross University to be close to the ranch. While I was there, I also began helping a couple of graduate students in their wildlife management masters' research studies. I quickly realized that these students didn't know much more than I did about wildlife.

I entered the ranch management program at TCU in the fall of 1996 and noticed that the whole focus of the program was on basic business principles such as break even and cash flow analysis. The abundance of field trips was my favorite part of ranch management training.

The hands-on experience gave us the opportunity to meet with ranching professionals and learn more about the business side of these organizations, which helped me realize the importance of cost accounting and commodity markets.

A combination of all these experiences led me to the decision to apply to the business school at TCU. I graduated in 1999 with a BBA, emphasis in finance. Although I chose not to pursue a graduate degree, I believe what makes the graduate school is not just the professors; it's also the students in the class. You should learn as much from your peers as you do from the faculty.

MAJOR INFLUENCES

TCU finance professor, Dr. Joe Lipscomb, was my advisor. He helped me secure a critical internship that resulted in my first job. I still consider him a friend and seek his thoughtful counsel on business and career matters.

While at my first professional job — a hedge fund — I also came to two conclusions. The first: I didn't like measuring success on a daily basis. With a hedge fund, at the end of every day you know exactly how much money you made or lost. Second: I wanted the opportunity to work with my father, Al, who is very entrepreneurial. I believed I could help him, and I knew that eventually I would be responsible for these businesses. We've had our disagreements, but we've learned how to work together and listen to each other's thoughts about an issue before making a decision.

Ultimately I wanted to be part of a company where I could build a foundation and help it grow.

BUSINESS THOUGHTS

Reflecting on education and business knowledge, the hedge fund experience gave me a broad base of knowledge about many different kinds of businesses, which allows me to participate in deeper conversations with a variety of business professionals. That's a major plus when developing new relationships.

Being introspective, I also came to the realization that I'm a numbers guy. I feel comfortable when I can make decisions based on good research and the interpretation of data from a number of sources.

Reflecting on the importance of relationships, it's quite ironic that Reata Restaurant opened in Fort Worth in 1996 because another TCU grad, Bob Semple, president of Bank One in Fort Worth in 1995, ate at our Alpine location. He suggested we re-create the quality and atmosphere in Fort Worth, and that's what we've tried to do.

ADVICE

- It's helpful to learn to relate well with older and more established professionals. Their experience can teach you a lot, for an interest in business transcends generations.
- Learn to ask good questions. Many people will be glad to tell you what they've learned. Asking questions shows them that you care — and you can learn a lot too!
- Work on your public speaking skills, for this will serve you in innumerable ways.

FATHER AND SON TEAM
*Mike Micallef ('99) and his dad
Al enjoy a day on the ranch.*

Keira Breeden Moody
Grounded with a Twist

KEIRA BREEDEN MOODY *is founder and president of Keira Moody, LLC, a contemporary business development firm. She has an undergraduate degree in accounting, having graduated magna cum laude from TCU in 1992. She is a CPA, held a short auditing stint in public accounting, established Crescent Real Estate's then-public investor relations program, and founded one-of-a-kind Eurotazza Coffeehouse in Fort Worth.*

Keira's firm wraps in her experiences of both Wall Street and Main Street, as she approaches business development with a twist — using a highly focused, integrated marketing and communications platform to open up new or underdeveloped business channels.

At Crescent, I was known for having meetings "off campus," preferably at coffee shops, rather than office conference rooms. I am a big believer in getting people away from the familiar, which fosters a much broader spectrum of thinking.

It comes as no surprise then, that in 2003, my affinity for the coffee culture was taken to a new level. While vacationing in Italy for a friend's birthday, I stole away for an hour to enjoy a cappuccino in Florence's Café Gilli, where I jotted down a few notes in the inside cover of the book I was reading. I thought how incredible it would be to bring the European coffee experience to Fort Worth. This led to the founding of Eurotazza or "Cup of Europe." The three years that I operated Eurotazza were invaluable in my developing into a business consultant. I now have stories of operating in the trenches right along with fellow business owners and entrepreneurs.

COFFEE AND INSPIRATION
Keira Breeden Moody ('92) got the idea for Eurotazza on a trip to Italy and now provides consulting clients with fresh perspectives.

GETTING GROUNDED

My father, who is retired from the Air Force and the FAA, says that if I adhere to his three rules, I will be successful in business:

1. Always be early to an appointment.

2. Regularly back up files.

3. Keep your car's gas tank more than one-quarter full. (Of course this one is for his own peace of mind, but it does remind me that I should always be prepared.)

When I'm talking with potential clients, I always lead with the fact that I am a CPA. Before TCU, my interests included music, travel, and testing boundaries. And though I didn't admit it at the time, I loved math. Being a CPA gives me instant credibility because it conveys that, while I present a lot of creative ideas, I come back around to what is driving the numbers.

MORE THAN A BEAN COUNTER

The story I still laugh about to this day is my first meeting with Dr. Robert Vigeland, the accounting chair and my academic advisor. Before the meeting, I was tasked with painting and installing a football spirit sign for my Delta Gamma sorority. With one hand wrapped in duct tape, Three Stooges-like, I jumped in the car and headed for the business school for fear of being late (there's Dad's voice again). When I arrived, Dr. Vigeland stood up from behind his desk and professionally extended his right hand to greet me. All I could do was giggle when I revealed a right hand wrapped in duct tape. He said he knew at that moment that I wasn't your typical accounting major.

Entrepreneurial spirit has always been a driving force within me, even when I didn't know what to call it. I remember, back in seventh grade, conceiving and operating a Saturday "Mother's Day Out" for toddlers in the gym of the middle school to raise money for new playground equipment.

Now it's proven that I can be a source of great value for business owners who have a hard time coming up for clean air in the midst all of the fires they are putting out. We sit down and strategize as business partners do, usually over a cup of coffee.

ADVICE

- Surround yourself with people who are smarter than you, no matter how smart you are.
- Don't be afraid to laugh at yourself. People will know that you are real and honest.
- Remember that anything you do involves an opportunity cost, whether it's money or time. Invest yourself wisely.

David Moran
Innovations Create Successful Marketing Brew.

DAVID MORAN *is a strategic problem-solver and innovation architect with a thirty-year track record of driving growth for Fortune 500 companies. He is the founder and president of Marketing Driven Solutions, LLC, and a director for Green Mountain Coffee Roasters, Inc., recently named by* Fortune *magazine as No. 2 on their list of fastest-growing companies.*

David spent the first eight years of his career advancing rapidly through brand management responsibilities with General Foods and International Playtex, then led three marketing consulting firms: Marketing Corporation of America, The Cambridge Group, and Fusion 5. He's addressed a wide array of challenging growth issues across several industries, Fortune 500 companies, and global brands.

David graduated from TCU with an undergraduate marketing degree in 1975 and earned an MBA in 1977. He held a Charles Tandy Marketing Fellowship and was elected to Beta Gamma Sigma, the national honor society for undergraduate business majors and MBAs.

While in Neeley's MBA program, I fell in love with a Connecticut girl whose career had already started in New York. I knew that after graduate school, I wanted a job in New York too.

I talked to my dad, who suggested I transfer to New York University's MBA program. So I called the dean at TCU.

"You're the first recipient of Charles Tandy's full MBA marketing scholarship," he responded. "How do we tell Charles that you don't want to complete your MBA?"

After mulling this over, we came up with a plan. TCU would work with NYU to let me transfer business credits, which I'd earn in New York as a non-matriculating student. So I got half my credits at NYU and transferred back to TCU for the degree.

The temporary NYU residency worked out, because I signed up for job interviews in New York. They'd see I was taking NYU classes but getting a TCU degree — and that made me stand out from the crowd of other candidates.

When I'd tell various recruiters my school story, they'd say, "You seem like the kind of creative thinker we'd like in marketing."

Upon graduation I started in brand management with General Food's Maxwell House division. And thirty-five years later, coffee is still a big part of my business life.

CONNECTICUT AND NEW YORK

I grew up in Connecticut. As a competitive tennis player, I looked for a college in a warmer climate with good academics.

My first night in a college dorm was ... well, exciting. I was assigned to a room with two large football guys who weren't in the mood to share additional space. In the middle of the night, they set fire to my bed. This made me hot to find a safer room.

Things settled down quickly. I concentrated on tennis, but not so much academics. Then in my junior year, I committed to a business major and discovered marketing courses! My grades shot from a C+ level to all As.

Upon graduation, I received that first Charles Tandy Marketing MBA fellowship. But actually, my first marketing challenge took place every summer from freshman through my MBA years. I was a teaching tennis pro at a private yacht club in Connecticut.

MARKETING OPPORTUNITIES

Initially I had to convince kids that boating shoes didn't work well on a tennis court. The next challenge was to build a competitive tennis program. To do that, I had to find out what family members wanted. After asking lots of questions, I discovered that the wife and mom made most decisions, determining her children's and her own involvement.

So for the kids I developed a fun summer-long program with lots of activities. For the grown-ups, I created teaching clinics and drills, competition with other clubs, and member/guest tournaments.

And I learned a lot about stocking and ordering products by working with major companies in the sporting goods field like Wilson and Spalding.

In recent years, being a director at Green Mountain Coffee Roasters has changed my life. When I joined fifteen years ago, it was a small, privately held regional coffee company with about $50 million in sales. In 2011, it is projected to do $2.1 billion and is publicly traded on NASDAQ.

Green Mountain has created the single-cup-brewing revolution. This system provides consumers consistent quality, great convenience, variety, and value one cup at a time.

ADVICE

- Develop the ability to understand consumers and their personalities.
- Try to build effective collaborative relationships with clients.
- Be honest about your real skills and passions. Try to align them, and you will find a career you will love and at which you will excel.

REVOLUTION IN A CUP
David Moran ('75, '77) and Green Mountain Coffee Roasters pioneered single-cup brewing.

Ricky Paradise
Quit Dreaming. Start Doing!

RICKY PARADISE *is president of Everest Recreation, a producer of commercial site furnishings, and former president of Jayhawk Plastics Outdoor Products, the Olathe, Kansas, manufacturer of outdoor benches and picnic tables that look like natural wood but are made of 100 percent recycled plastic resin. Jayhawk's recycled products — made of milk jugs, pop bottles, plastic bags, and other post-consumer items — save trees and reduce landfill use.*

Ricky is a 1999 summa cum laude graduate from TCU with majors in accounting and finance, with an international emphasis. He serves on TCU's National Alumni Board.

One of my earliest lessons came in first or second grade, when I actually skipped school to go to work with my dad. He and his brother manufactured plastic printing supplies. I'd go into his office and sit with him to hear vendors make presentations or to listen while he worked with customers.

I loved this experience. Even then I knew I'd be an entrepreneur.

I've been told all my life that I can do anything — but never that it would be easy or that there wouldn't be challenges. If someone says that something is impossible — if a vendor tells me he can't meet a deadline or if there's a crisis at work — I quote a great Jim Carrey line from the movie *Dumb and Dumber:* "So you're saying there's a chance."

CHOOSING THE RIGHT SCHOOL

During my high school senior year, I toured a bunch of schools. I remember walking TCU's campus during passing period. I saw about a thousand kids who looked friendly and happy. And something else: Even people who didn't know me said hi. I thought, "What's up with these people, and isn't this great?"

I also picked TCU because I wanted to study business, and I wanted some type of international experience. TCU seemed to emphasize both.

Once at the school, I met several exceptional people. Chancellor Bill Tucker taught me about vision and strategy; he led by example, and his example was inspiring. Dr. Don Mills took an interest in my personal development and helped me grow by providing challenges and opportunities.

Sandra Toumey invested a lot in my leadership development, was a professional and kind mentor, and taught me about being a servant.

Dr. Kay Higgins treated me like an adopted son and made me feel comfortable on campus with the challenges of adjusting to college.

I firmly believe that the magic of TCU is that there are so many professors who will have a profound impact on you. Dr. Robert Vigeland brought the entire accounting curriculum together. Dr. Jane Mackay instructed me about electronic and digital business and spent endless hours as my advisor. Janice Cobb mixed academic accounting with real-world experience. And Dr. Stephen Quinn and Dr. Charles Becker challenged every student and prepared me for graduate school with the hardest tests I had ever taken.

BUSINESS THOUGHTS

I graduated from TCU on a Saturday and started law school the following Monday at the University of Kansas.

After law school my first job was as an associate attorney at a firm in Houston — Ogletree-Deakins — that specialized in labor and employment law. I learned much from that two-year experience, most of which I still use on a daily basis.

The most important thing I discovered: When you get a group of smart people in the same room to solve a problem, you have a very good chance of getting it solved in the best way possible.

Today Jayhawk Plastics provides an environmentally friendly alternative to something people need and use. Benches and picnic tables can be made from metal, concrete, or wood. Our special niche is the environmental implications.

My dad always said, "Work smart." That doesn't remove hard work from the equation. It just means that if you're working really hard, take time to step back and look at the problem from another angle. See if you can find a better way.

At Jayhawk we try to work both smart and hard. And I feel proud we're able to provide good manufacturing jobs to some fine people in a great community.

ADVICE

- Quit dreaming and start doing. The market is set up to reward those who make it happen, not those who dream about it. If you want to be a success in anything, it usually starts with *doing* something.
- Hire people smarter than you are, people who are experts at their specialty.
- Stay optimistic! You must not be limited by challenges, obstacles, or what other people tell you. You must know in your heart that you will be rewarded if you do the right things. In this day and age, I don't think many people really believe that.

Derek Peachey
Taking the Road
Less Traveled

DEREK PEACHEY *is co-founder and managing partner of Floodlight Digital, LLC, a leading provider of mobile strategy and services. Derek began his mobile career after graduating with an MBA from TCU in 2002 when he joined mobile content aggregation pioneer Handango during the emergence of the first wireless downloads. He served in executive-level positions at leading mobile solution providers before breaking out on his own.*

Derek holds a bachelor's degree in geology from Dickinson College in Pennsylvania and currently lives in the San Francisco Bay area with his wife, Stephanie, and newborn son, Lane.

I have never been reluctant to follow the path less traveled when an opportunity emerged.

My father was assistant headmaster at Blair Academy in Blairstown, New Jersey, and I grew up on a boarding school campus, which provided a unique and diverse atmosphere. Following graduation there, I chose Dickinson College and discovered a passion for geology, an unexpected direction. After graduation, I planned to go to law school to focus on environmental law, but after much consideration decided that law school was not the path for me.

When offered a job in the admissions office at Blair Academy, I was happy to return and work with the mentors I had long respected. One of those people was former English teacher and Dean of College Counseling, Jim Moore, who remains a trusted mentor to this day. He sits on what I characterize as my "personal board of directors," and I turn to him regularly for advice. Jim's mentorship influenced my leadership style. He is proactive and honest, often telling me what I need to hear, as opposed to what I think I want to hear.

The experience at Blair opened up the opportunity to be assistant director of admissions at Fort Worth Country Day School, where I also taught geology and math and coached baseball.

While working at Fort Worth Country Day, I learned of the Neeley School of Business through the many TCU alums and supporters who were part of the FWCDS alumni and parent body, among them Mike Reilly and Bill Landreth. After attending a Neeley School open house, meeting the faculty, and learning about their practical approach to business education, I knew TCU was a perfect match for me. I am a big believer that it is the people within the walls of an institution that form its personality.

WOMEN OF BUSINESS: THEN
The members of Phi Chi Theta gather for a photograph in 1972.

WOMEN OF BUSINESS: NOW
The Neeley Women's Business Network members began a new organization in 2010.

MENTORSHIP

Mike Reilly of Metroplex-based Reilly Brothers Property Company dedicated countless hours to helping me with everything from career decisions to day-to-day business strategy. He taught me the responsibility of giving back to the community and, perhaps more importantly, mentoring others. I rarely turn down a request to help another Horned Frog and do what I can to impart the knowledge Mike has passed on. I am not only a better person because of Mike but also a better leader, father, and citizen.

Effective leadership involves the ability to relate to those who report to you while also managing laterally and "up" in working with peers and supervisors. It requires dedicating the time necessary to be an engaged manager who places a premium on listening. I learned as a young manager that the golden rule does not apply to leadership. Rather than treating others as I would want to be treated, I learned that a good leader motivates others by understanding the unique drivers and personalities of the people around you. I learned to listen, to ask for feedback, and to realize that I have a lot of room to grow as a leader.

EARLY YEARS

I spent one summer during my college years working as a geologist in the Mojave Desert, interning for CalEnergy, a geothermal power company with production operations in the Coso Field near China Lake, California. While many friends enjoyed the benefits of a college summer on the beach, I toiled in 110-degree desert heat. I would not have traded the experience for anything, as it introduced me to the corporate world and to the fascinating field of alternative energy production. That summer motivated me to do something different, something unique with my career. In some respects, it may have been a precursor to my decision to pursue an MBA at TCU.

MBA'S ONGOING VALUE

The Neeley School of Business provided me with a balance of practical business skills and the less tangible attributes of leadership and strategic thinking. The environment was more practical than theoretical. The experience gave me the background to constantly draw on what I learned from faculty and classmates.

Rob Rhodes transformed business law into a class so interesting that my classmates and I eagerly anticipated the lectures. And that subject, under other circumstances, could have been relatively dry. Chuck Bamford taught me that strategy is as much or more about execution as it is analysis, now a core tenet of my company's consulting practice. And Bob Greer taught me how to be an effective negotiator with real-world negotiation strategies and practice. I still find myself accessing negotiation strategies, referencing previous case studies, and opening old notebooks to refresh my approach to formulating strategic plans.

I graduated from TCU when Handango began to develop some of the first wireless (at the time "over-the-air") downloads. I joined the Handango team, and at a relatively young age, I found myself negotiating large deals and managing a team of sharp, experienced professionals. I chose the most risky, lowest-paying, and least comfortable opportunity, and it changed the course of my professional life. As one Fort Worth business leader told me, "Drive the Porsche, not the Mercedes. You might end up in the shop, but it will probably be worth the ride." To this point there have been a few pit stops but no regrets.

ADVICE

- Your reputation is your single most important asset. Those who operate with candor and establish themselves as straight shooters will ultimately find success and sleep well at night.
- Building and maintaining a strong network is achieved by offering help to others and by maintaining regular contact with individuals in your network regardless of their current importance to your business.
- People should find an opportunity that gives them experience early in their careers, while avoiding the draw to the highest salary. If compensation is a motivator, the right experience early in one's career will yield a far greater impact on salary later.
- Give something back to your community. Mentor others whenever you get the chance. Give back to TCU. Strike the right balance between career success and life success. You will be richer for it.

Michael Stanley
Listen Carefully, Work Hard, and Manage the Details.

MICHAEL STANLEY is *president and CEO of the CIS Group of Companies (www.cisgroup.net), a mid-market, industry-leading field underwriting services company headquartered in Fort Worth, with satellite offices in Chicago, Atlanta, and Los Angeles.*

CIS has managed the completion of more than 17 million underwriting transactions since 1996. This unique company and its subsidiaries don't sell insurance or banking products; instead, they're a logistics and supply-chain management and staffing company. In large-risk management or loss-containment projects, these outsourcing firms are hired by insurance companies or banks to supplement internal staff.

Michael completed his Executive MBA from TCU in 2008.

Two major events in 1995 changed my life.

I worked for a large company that's now a competitor. That year, while still a newlywed, I was away on business travel more than 270 nights. I'd just gotten back from another trip, and my wife said, "You look really different. It would be nice to see you now and then!" Obviously I needed to be home more, so the math on that part of the decision was simple.

Concurrently, the major client I worked with decided to pursue an outsourced underwriting solution for a portion of their business. They approached me and asked, "Have you ever thought about doing this type of work for yourself?"

Thus, by nothing more than good fortune, I was offered the chance to serve the firm that today remains the largest single client in our portfolio. I was able to stay home a lot more, move back to Texas, and build a company.

EARLY DAYS

I grew up in Kermit, Texas, between the Midland-Odessa area and El Paso. I chose the University of Houston for college because several family members lived near there. I majored in economics and math.

After a series of blunders and personal mistakes, my first meaningful job after graduation was with the U.S. Army. The most important lessons I learned were that bullets are real and that war is not a game played on some video station. And I most grateful to Pastor Mac, Larry Burkett, and many others. I could talk a long time about what they did for me, but they all know what I would say.

In the Army, I evolved from an immature, selfish boy into a full-blown adult. I learned that I must carry my own weight, carry the weight of others when required, and lean on others for help when needed.

I chose a business career because I was young, married, and didn't have any money! I couldn't do anything about being young. I was incredibly lucky to marry my wife, Summer — and I knew that I'd best take action concerning earning money.

When the sponsoring company made me the offer described earlier (truly good fortune), we took a loan against everything we owned and launched Risk Management Services with six employees and twenty-five contractors. We moved back to Texas.

With some hard work, continued good luck, many blessings, and really good people, we've grown into the largest provider of field underwriting services to the insurance and mortgage banking sector in the United States.

BUILDING THE COMPANY

I was a later-in-life graduate of the Neeley School Executive MBA program. I'd already started the CIS Group. My experience was not so much preparation for career as it was a confirmation of best practices and recalibration around new ideas.

I chose TCU because of the excellent reputation within the local and national community and because it was reasonable from a geographic perspective.

Several professors made huge impressions on me: Nancy Nix taught me that every business is a supply chain. That may have been the single most important take-away from my classroom experience. Chuck Bamford is simply brilliant in his assessment and transmission of corporate strategy. Chris Barry taught me that one can't place too much emphasis on not violating the net sustainable growth equation. In-Mu Haw confirmed my suspicion that when you have the choice between being right and being kind — and the world is no worse for making either choice — then kindness is the best option.

ADVICE

- There is simply no substitute for working hard. You must be willing to outwork your competition, no matter what the cost. The notion that "working smart, not hard" is the best work philosophy is nonsense.
- Jobs are more than just hands-on — you must get your fingers dirty too. You must know your job from the below the ground up!
- Listen carefully to people twice your age.
- Show up for work on time.
- Once out of school, hit the ground with feet moving and mouth shut.
- A big key to success is learning how to manage details.
- Never, ever spend more money than you make. Period.

Marketing and Strategy

"Keep your eyes open and don't assume you know what you want today. I don't want to miss the opening of a door because it's not on my planning list."

LORNA C. DONATONE

"Don't 'radar lock' on anything in life. Keep your interests wide and varied and never stop learning and growing."

MICHAEL HEARD

"The most important skill one can have: the ability to excite an audience to take risks in order to achieve extraordinary results."

BRYAN KOOP

Businesses succeed by creating and sustaining better value for their customers than the competition does. Gaining this competitive advantage involves identifying distinct market opportunities, developing clear strategy, and responding to the rapidly changing business environment. The executives in this section have demonstrated keen business intelligence in implementing highly effective strategies, motivating consumers, and leading in difficult economic times.

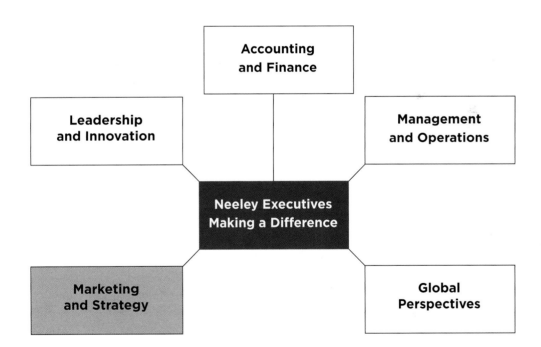

SPENCER HAYS
SELLING PEOPLE
ON SUCCESS

SPENCER HAYS *came to TCU on a basketball scholarship and decided to major in business. He graduated in 1959 with a B.S. in commerce. While looking for a part-time job, he discovered a lifetime profession in personal selling. He began his career with The Southwestern Company as a student dealer in 1956 and progressed through increasingly important sales management positions. He now serves as executive chairman of The Southwestern Company.*

Just over a decade after graduating from college, Spencer founded Tom James Company, the world's largest manufacturer and retailer of custom clothing. Tom James has become an international trademark for custom men's clothing, with offices in thirty-nine states, England, Scotland, France, Germany, Holland, Chile, Australia, and beyond. Spencer is a business owner, entrepreneur, leader, recruiter, trainer, and hard worker. He was named to the Direct Selling Association's Hall of Fame in 1993.

Over the last half-century, he's built businesses in several fields, including financial planning, publishing, clothing, insurance, and real estate. Says his longtime friend, former TCU Chancellor William E. Tucker: "What Spencer sells is not a product — but people on themselves."

Note: Spencer's remarkable story is told here by his friend of fifty-five years and business associate, Jim McEachern, longtime senior executive officer of the Tom James Company. He provided these remarks shortly before his passing on July 12, 2011. At Jim's memorial service, Spencer Hays noted that "Jim served as an example to me and literally thousands of others for how we should live our lives. He was the most unselfish person and by his actions and deeds exemplified the life we should all lead."

In January 2001, at our semi-annual meeting, Spencer told us that when he was very young, his father left his mother, his sisters, his brother, and Spencer. He grew up in Ardmore, Oklahoma, and Gainesville, Texas. Much of that time he lived with his grandmother, who was a seamstress and who taught him the value of good work habits and maintaining a positive mental attitude.

His grandmother also gave him his first selling job. He learned the value of dramatizing the products when she put pretty bows around the necks of kittens and puppies for Spencer to sell. Spencer's grandmother taught him: "There is a destiny that makes us brothers. None goes his way alone. All that we send into the lives of others comes back into our own."

Spencer learned the lesson well. He's been motivated, and is still motivated, to put as much into the lives of others as he can, and that accounts for much of his extraordinary success.

It's been said that "You can have anything in life you want if you help enough other people get what they want." Spencer has demonstrated that very well.

COLLEGE YEARS AND EARLY LIFE

Spencer finished his freshman year at Texas Christian University in May 1956. He and Marlene were married in June, and Spencer spent that summer selling books for Southwestern Company. He continued to sell during the summers of 1957, 1958, and 1959, and in each of those later three summers had a team of students selling with him. Most of those students were recruited from TCU and other nearby colleges.

"I first had the opportunity to meet Spencer Hays in 2008 and the basis for his success was quite clear. This incredibly successful executive was one of the most authentic and genuine persons I had ever met. Anyone who receives his business card immediately knows that he is with a person who is spot on about his calling. The title on his business card is simply "Salesman." Indeed, his most famous philosophy has permeated his business ventures and his life, "You don't build a successful company; you build successful people and they build the company."

HOMER EREKSON
DEAN, NEELEY SCHOOL

After the summer of 1959, Spencer became a Southwestern Company sales manager. Over the next five years, he built a very large organization of student sellers and brought in some full-time managers to work with him.

In 1964, Spencer managed a political campaign for a man who was running for a seat in the U.S. House of Representatives. The man worked for Genesco, which owned both English American Tailoring Company and Individualized Shirts. By this time, Spencer had seen students he'd managed complete college and go on to other careers. He also had seen some of them get away from the success principles they had learned while selling books.

Spencer wanted to start a business that would provide a great career opportunity and also continue to promote the principles of success that he so strongly believed in. He saw English American and Individualized Shirts as sources for products that could be sold to provide that career opportunity.

HOW TOM JAMES COMPANY BEGAN

Spencer presented the idea of starting a division of Southwestern Company to sell clothing, but the Southwestern Company president didn't buy the idea. So Spencer asked for permission to open the business on his own. Permission was granted, and Spencer set into motion a plan to open the first location of Tom James Company in Nashville, Tennessee, in 1966. Tom Ed James, Mack Isbill, and I were the first three employees.

When Spencer decided to start the Tom James Company, his motive was to provide opportunity for earning unlimited income and building net worth. At the outset, we didn't have a stock-purchase plan, profit-sharing plan, or 401k plan. But even from the beginning, Spencer intended to set up a plan for us to purchase stock so we could share in the equity growth as we helped build the company.

Looking back, I can say that the stock purchase opportunity has been very lucrative for everyone who has taken advantage of it. Many are becoming millionaires or multimillionaires through their Tom James Company stock, profit-sharing plan, and 401k plan.

In my experience, I've never known anyone who set up his businesses to share prosperity with others the way that Spencer Hays has done. Those who helped build Tom James — and other companies Spencer has owned — have a great opportunity to earn a very good income and build a big net worth.

One thing for which I greatly admire Spencer is that he's risen from a very humble beginning in life to great successes because of good work habits, a positive mental attitude, and the development of skills. And Spencer has applied himself to providing opportunities for thousands of others.

ADVICE
- Stay hopeful about the next prospect and differentiate yourself from the competition.
- Pay attention to appearance. If you dress well, you feel better about yourself.
- Keep sales calls short and make lots of them. Embrace the law of averages.
- Remember the advice of Spencer's grandmother: "None goes his way alone. All that we send into the lives of others comes back into our own."

John Cockrell, Sr.
Sell the Idea First.

JOHN COCKRELL, SR. *grew up in Fort Worth, played football for Paschal, then declined out-of-town scholarship offers so he could attend TCU. He graduated from TCU with a bachelor of business administration in management in 1969. He has served on the Neeley Alumni Executive Board.*

John's father, Cleat, founded Cockrell Printing and Office Supplies in Fort Worth in 1964. Cleat and John developed this large family-owned printing company that continues to flourish in a crowded, competitive field. John assumed leadership of the company as president in 1985.

Cockrell Printing, now a third-generation company since TCU grad son John joined the business a few years ago, has become a leader in digital printing and marketing programs. John, Jr. founded enovation group in 2003, focusing on advancing print through digital solutions. In 2009, Cockrell Printing and enovation group combined to form Cockrell Enovation, a company focused on creating opportunity and growth through print and technology.

My dad Cleat — my role model and mentor — was a printing company veteran who always wanted to build his own firm. So when I was a high school junior in 1964, he left his partnership in another company to start Cockrell Printing.

We began with a small press and also sold office supplies. I came to work after school, helped in any way I could, then delivered the jobs. Even then I knew you had to sell something before anything else happens.

COLLEGE LIFE

I had a cousin already at TCU. Before I started freshman year in the fall of 1965, she suggested I take English composition in summer school. My teacher was Kirby Post, a graduate student and an outstanding instructor.

He taught me ways to express myself in writing and composition that I still use today. For instance, he'd give an assignment like "Describe a train to me." He'd teach us how to explain things, build transitional sentences, and make the writing flow.

ARMY TRAINING

I took ROTC training in college and reported for active duty not long after graduation.

In Vietnam, Major James Stocker taught me a lot. He was a West Point graduate who wore wire-rimmed glasses and smoked cigars. Major Stocker reminded us to make the best of any bad situation and to always do the assigned job well. He was a master at unifying people for a common cause and turning a negative into a positive.

For a while, I worked as a photo officer for the first cavalry division weekly paper. I learned about photo composition, along with the highs and lows of newspaper deadlines. And I experienced the creativity of crafting and publishing a newspaper.

TODAY'S BUSINESS

The printing business has changed dramatically in the last four decades. In 1998 there were 56,000 printers nationwide — today there are only 37,000. Today's printer must not only apply ink to paper but give customers ideas for the items they print, working with them on how to merge print with other technologies.

Digital technology offers us the flexibility to create personalized but mass-produced items. We can even change and personalize text in some presentation manuals.

When you call on clients, give them a new idea! Today's company must be a valuable consultant. It must specifically show clients how to save money, add customers, create new ideas, or find new uses for current products. We show clients how to increase response with direct mail and demonstrate ways to combine photo ideas with text.

And with print-on-demand technology, we can help clients reduce inventory costs by producing only the quantities immediately needed. We combine print and technology for marketing and product promotion.

ADVICE

- Read biographies about successful people, people you hope to emulate.
- Get a broad undergraduate experience. There's more than just classroom attendance. Consider organizations and clubs that broaden your horizons.
- Take history, speech, and writing courses. They give you perspective about the past and offer ideas to present your skills to future employers.
- As a manager, create a good working environment, treat people fairly, and articulate common goals for success.

BUILDING CONNECTIONS
Mr. Mayor, Bob Bolen, confers with John Cockrell, Sr. ('69) at the 2006 Tandy Executive Speaker Series.

Donald Cram, Jr.
Give Service
Wherever You Can.

DONALD CRAM, JR. *received 2010's Valuable Alumnus Award from TCU, which notes, "He has long been counted among TCU's most involved alumni. He has served on the National Alumni Board, was president of the Fort Worth Chapter Board and chaired the Class of 1961 reunion, Frog Club Board, Committee of 100, Committee on the Future of TCU, and is a patron of the Clark Society." He graduated with a finance degree from TCU in 1961.*

His volunteerism extends in many directions, including work as a board member of the Texas Boys' Choir and the Texas Academy of Fine Arts.

The large mortgage company he built is now part of Saxon Capital, Inc., a subsidiary of Morgan Stanley Mortgage Capital Holdings LLC. Currently he owns The Marc Hogan Group, a private investment firm, and Hear Hear, LLC, a wine distribution company.

Way back in the early 1960s, Dad provided a home loan for an elderly couple. This was the first house they had ever owned. They were so proud. They came in every month by bus to make a payment. They always asked for my father and gave him the money personally. He always spent time talking with them.

If he wasn't there, they'd ask to see Mr. Mortgage, because the company name was Cram Mortgage Service. I'd go out to talk to them, so they assumed Mortgage was my name. Mom tried to correct them, but they didn't catch on.

PROMISING YOUNG MEN
Donald Cram, Jr. ('61), left, was president of Lambda Chi in 1960. He is shown here with two fraternity brothers.

One day, something happened to their Social Security check, so they didn't have enough to live on. They first went to a small finance company but got turned down. So my dad loaned them money to make the payment. They paid him back $10 per month, and of course he never charged them interest. He did that for them several times.

"This business is much more than loans," he insisted. "It's about helping people become homeowners."

EARLY YEARS

When I was in the second grade, my parents moved to Fort Worth to start a mortgage company for a group of investors. Beginning at age 12, I worked every summer at various title companies and eventually at my father's company. I worked in every department. I made collection calls and worked in bookkeeping.

My career path was somewhat pre-ordained. I had been unsure what I wanted to do, and when my father decided to start a new company and said he wanted me to join him, I couldn't have been happier.

I started college as an arts and science major at St. Louis University. While I was in St. Louis, my father decided to leave his position and form his own company. This prompted my move home and my switch to a business major. If I could start college again, I'd major in accounting. It's the foundation for all business.

My father's move happened sooner than he anticipated, and we actually formed Cram Mortgage Service, Inc., during my senior year, with my father as president, me as vice president, and my mother as secretary-treasurer. I learned that being a vice president doesn't mean you know anything.

I believe it's important to know not just what happened, but why it happened. I love history today because of Dr. Eugene McCluney, a remarkable professor. He wouldn't just say, "This event happened in 1920." He'd give the entire background of the period, including fashions and political intrigue.

MORE ABOUT THE MORTGAGE BUSINESS AND LIFE

Dad had a way of teaching and assigning responsibility that made my learning curve virtually seamless. I could find myself in charge of some aspect of our business almost before I realized it.

Full-service mortgage work is detailed. The clientele is mostly customers of realtors and builders. The mortgage company originates the loans, securitizes them, groups them, and creates a mortgage-backed security. But we'd retain the loans, servicing them and collecting payments. I also liked working with the realtors and builders who already understood the mortgage business, as well as the individual homeowners, for whom we provided a valuable service.

Today my son-in-law and I run a wholesale distribution business. While many consider the manufacturing and retailing fields, there's not as much attention paid to this critical business category. A wholesaler must be an expert in a chosen product line. When the wholesaler markets to retailers, he or she also talks to a product expert. So it's a very high level of communication — professionals talking to professionals.

ADVICE

- Business ethics is not an oxymoron. Success comes without corporate or personal greed, and you can sleep better at night.

Lorna Donatone
Keep Looking for Growth Opportunities.

LORNA C. DONATONE *is chief operating officer and Education Market President of Sodexo, Inc. Headquartered in Gaithersburg, Maryland, Sodexo operates in the U.S., Canada, and Mexico, with $7.7 billion (USD) in annual revenue and 120,000 employees. Donatone oversees Sodexo's operations at college and university campuses, public school districts, and private schools in the United States where Sodexo provides facilities management services, food services, and nutrition.*

Lorna received her MBA from TCU in 1982. She serves on the boards of directors of the National Restaurant Association, the Women's Foodservice Forum, and Entertainment Cruises and is a member of the board of trustees of the Culinary Institute of America.

We never know when a door will open and what unexpected opportunities we might find behind that door. Not long ago, I was president of Spirit Cruises, a company providing dining and sightseeing cruises in several major cities. As part of a diversity strategy, we started a women's network group, and I was asked to lead it. I didn't really want that volunteer assignment because I thought I might get branded as a single-issue executive.

I went to my boss, the company's CEO, and expressed my concerns. He looked at me quizzically, then said, "If not you, then who?"

I took the assignment. Because of that, I've become much better known throughout the entire corporation. Instead of branding me, it extended my expertise and introduced me to new executives at other companies.

I work often with women leaders. Finance can sometimes be a barrier to them, because in school many girls self-select out of math.

EARLY DECISIONS

I've always liked working with numbers — and not just the numbers, but the results of those numbers. In undergraduate school at Tulane, I majored in management. Besides, I was terrible at liberal arts! My German professor advised me to go to business school. Actually, what she said was, "I advise you not to come back to liberal arts."

I decided to get my MBA because I felt it would have the most value after I graduated. That was a good choice. I began to look for a great graduate program. TCU's Neeley School kept coming up in my search. I wanted to stay in a warm climate. That was important to me at 22. I liked the South.

When I visited TCU, I felt comfortable with its size and was especially impressed with the admissions team.

CAREER ADVANCEMENT

My MBA concentration was accounting, because I liked the "right and wrong" of that profession. The background gave me credibility. I was prepared to read financial statements and to sit at meetings with charts, graphs, and numbers without being intimidated.

On my first job at Touche Ross — now Deloitte and Touche — I learned to work a ten-key calculator and the expectations of the workplace. I also learned the importance of colleagues and work teams.

When I worked for Comsearch — which provided engineering to fixed, mobile, and broadband wireless applications — the CEO taught me about the value of human resources. I learned to manage not only from the head, but also from the heart.

At the time of my first president's role, which was at Spirit Cruises, I joined the Women's Foodservice Forum (WFF). I met Bill Anton, who was chairman of Anton Airfood; he and I were partnered in a mentoring program through the WFF. His guidance was critical to my career advancement then and continues to this day. He pointed me in the right directions. It is so important to have a mentor.

Over time, a business background is extremely helpful if you can bring people skills to it. Many have academic smarts but no ability to adjust style for situation. If you're in the service industry, you must have people skills and the ability to communicate. I hire for attitude. We can train the rest.

ADVICE
- Keep your eyes open and don't assume you know what you want today. Be open to new opportunities and projects. Personally, I don't want to miss the opening of a door because it's not on my planning list!
- Financial acumen can help propel people in a business career.
- Be amazing in whatever you do. That will help you find your next great job.
- Get a network. Start building your contacts now, whether you currently need them or not. Students, don't wait until you enter the work environment. Get business cards from people; ask them if you can contact them.

CAMARADERIE
Lourdes Hassler, Beth Humphrey, and Irene Young (Executive MBA alumni '06) share a lighthearted moment.

Byron Dunn
Sales Career Started
with a Newspaper Ad.

W. BYRON DUNN *has been a principal of the wholesale marketer of steel tubular products, Tubular Synergy Group L.P., since 2008. Before that, he was president and chief executive officer of Lone Star Steel Company, a subsidiary of Lone Star Technologies, Inc. He was a member of the company for thirty-three years.*

Byron graduated from TCU with a bachelor of business administration and management major in 1975. He is a member of the advisory board for TCU's Energy Institute.

My sales career began in a strange way. When I was only 16, I answered a "salespeople wanted" ad in a Dallas newspaper. I wrote a resumé and went to the motel advertised. In the lobby I found several guys with huge cardboard boxes of panty hose, which they'd sold over the phone.

They didn't look at my resumé. They told me I was hired and gave me a list of names and addresses. They said they'd pay me 50 cents per delivery, but I had to collect the money for each sale they had made (over the phone) or I didn't get anything for my efforts.

What an experience! I'd get to the houses and hear every complaint imaginable about the order being the wrong color, wrong size, or wrong quantity. I'd go back out to my panty hose-filled Mustang and try to piece together an acceptable order to satisfy the customer so I could earn my delivery fee. I became one of their best closers.

I remember my dad asked me what my new job was, and I described it to him — but I don't think he told many people, fearing that I was being trained as a scam artist, which in reflection may have been the case. What legitimate business is run from a hotel room?

The silver lining was that after this indoctrination, I had virtually no fear of meeting new people. I leveraged that experience while in high school. I started a window-washing and home domestic services business and built it going door to door asking housewives to hire me to help them keep their windows clean.

When I sold that business three years later, I had several guys working for me. And even today, I run into people who remember when I washed their windows.

In college I worked in Clyde Campbell's men's clothing store, right by the campus. I learned the value of pleasing the customer and about getting referrals.

All my early jobs involved selling, and those lessons have served me well.

COLLEGE AND GRAD SCHOOL
What's my most memorable moment? When I received the letter from TCU admissions telling me I'd been accepted! My mother attended TCU, and my sister did too, but I had no idea what I wanted to do or what I might enjoy studying. Since I'd started a company in high school, I thought maybe a business degree would hold my interest. TCU was a good fit for me.

Because I am a poster child for dyslexia, reading was difficult — so much so that I even considered not going to college because my high school business was doing fine. But my parents insisted, and I sold my company to some of the students who worked for me. That helped pay a portion of my tuition.

The BBA gave me the tools I needed. I learned about margin management and value creation. And I met wonderful, genuinely caring administration, faculty, and other students who helped me through the process. I chose the best professors and benefited from the smaller class sizes at the time, which created the optimal environment for me to learn in my own unique way.

I later attended SMU to get my MBA. Because of my reading difficulties, my wife read each case study to me. I listened, and that's how I continued to learn.

CAREER

After graduating from TCU, I went to work for Lone Star Steel as a sales trainee. I retired thirty-three years later after the sale of our company to U.S. Steel, having served as president and CEO the last twelve years of my career at Lone Star.

The guy who hired me at Lone Star, Robbie Robertson, was a wonderful example to me — a great guy, gentleman, leader, and friend. He saw more in me than I saw in myself.

After the sale of Lone Star, we started a company selling casings and tubulars to oil and gas clients in Texas. We have built the client acceptance base worldwide; today Tubular Synergy Group L.P. ships to and from about forty-eight countries.

I have learned hard work pays off and that your employees must be both willing and able in order for the company to be successful.

ADVICE
- If you do not trust people, they do not trust you. I place a very high priority on taking care of my employees. They know that, and they all seem to work harder.
- Think globally. The world is smaller than you think, and the business opportunities in this world are greater than you could ever imagine.
- You should help people of various abilities achieve common goals. If you have confidence in others, they'll carry you across the goal line. Surround yourself with people whom you know have greater skills than you do. It will challenge your leadership skills and make you collectively more successful than you would be on your own. That is why we named our company Tubular *Synergy* Group.

Jim Estill
It Takes More
than a Green Thumb.

JIM ESTILL *is chairman of the board and chief executive officer of Calloway's Nursery Inc. Along with John Cosby and John Peters, Mr. Estill co-founded Calloway's Nursery Inc. in 1986. Calloway's is the largest lawn and garden retailer in Texas, operating seventeen stores in the Dallas-Fort Worth area and three Cornelius Nurseries stores in Houston. He is a Texas Master Certified Nursery Professional.*

Jim received two degrees from TCU — the bachelor of business administration degree in management and finance in 1969 and an MBA with a finance concentration in 1977 — following in the footsteps of his mother and father who graduated from TCU in 1941 and 1940, respectively. He is a member of the Neeley School International Board of Visitors and former president of the Neeley School Executive Alumni Board.

One might argue that I have always been looking for greener pastures. I grew up in Independence, Kansas, serving as president of the Kansas Association for Youth and the regional representative for the Kansas Methodist Youth Fellowship. I also achieved the Life designation as a Boy Scout/Explorer Scout and traveled to England, France, and Switzerland on an exchange program.

ACADEMICS
But I found a home at TCU and, just as my parents had done, considered TCU a foundation for my success in life. Dr. Stanley Block introduced me to business through a course in statistics that captured my interest. And it's a good thing, as I had had four majors prior to taking that course. His teaching method and the very logical means of evaluating outcomes really resonated with me, so I chose business and never looked back.

CAREER PATH
After graduating, I started at Pier 1, a rapidly growing organization made up of quality individuals who challenged me. As a manager trainee, I helped open the first Pier 1 store in Detroit in 1969, one of the biggest grand opening weekends for Pier 1 ever. I learned a lot about customer service, managing the store team, and the importance of presentation. Pier 1's approach was so distinctive, and customers loved both the product and the experience. I also learned that when the customer cannot compare a product easily at another store, the retail price is aligned with the value in the customer's mind.

We try to bring that same sense to Calloway's. Our customers seek us out because of our ability to provide them with an unequaled shopping experience. Gardening is a creative process, adding value to a home and providing pleasant diversion and environmental benefit.

GUIDING LIGHT

Luther A. Henderson, president, chairman, and CEO of Pier 1, had a brilliant financial mind and was very approachable. After being promoted to become the second individual in a two-person real estate department at Pier 1 in Fort Worth in 1970, I was in close contact with Mr. Henderson on many projects. I felt fortunate to gain his trust and support, and he gave me many opportunities that kept me growing.

From my early career experiences, I learned the value of people working together. I have been blessed with members of my management team who get it done against all odds. I have achieved nothing of significance with my performance alone.

ADVICE

■ Never take anyone for granted. That person just may have the solution that makes the difference between success and failure.

HONORABLE GROUP
The members of Neeley Fellows first class in 2006, pictured here with Associate Dean Christine Riordan (front row, right), prepare for the future. Neeley Fellows challenges top Neeley students to stretch themselves with advanced coursework and opportunities to meet with executives both inside and outside the classroom.

Katie Farmer
Learn to Articulate
your Thoughts.

KATIE FARMER *is vice president of domestic intermodal marketing at BNSF Railway Company. In this capacity, she is responsible for BNSF's sales and marketing activities for the domestic intermodal business unit, including truckload, LTL, parcel, and temperature-controlled freight. Prior to this appointment she was vice president of sales, industrial products, where she was responsible for leading the carload sales effort across the U.S. and Canada.*

Katie began her career in the railroad industry with Burlington Northern Inc., a BNSF predecessor, in 1992 as a management trainee in Fort Worth. During her career, she has held a variety of roles with progressive leadership responsibility in customer service, marketing, sales, and equipment management.

Katie earned two degrees from TCU, a bachelor's degree in marketing in 1992 and an MBA in 1996.

My sixth-grade English teacher, Mrs. Gordon, made a lasting impression on me. She was a fiery, red-headed woman who was just brutal on us! I remember diagramming sentences and writing millions of papers. But what I remember most about Mrs. Gordon is her belief that the most important thing in the world was the ability to skillfully articulate your thoughts and ideas. We heard this from her time and time again. She made me miserable for a year of my life but gave me a gift to last a lifetime!

COLLEGE DECISIONS
I graduated from high school in Deerfield, a suburb north of Chicago. My father was on the board of church extension at the time, and he wanted me to visit a Disciples of Christ school.

We came to campus for a visit, and I fell in love with Fort Worth and TCU. I attended a large high school, and TCU felt like a great fit. It didn't hurt that it was 60 degrees in February in Texas, while we had several inches of snow on the ground back home in Chicago!

The job I enjoyed most in college was my internship with Burlington Northern (one of the predecessor companies to BNSF Railway). Through this internship I learned to appreciate the value of diversity of background and thought. I experienced the tremendous loyalty and pride that employees at the railroad had for our company and its rich history. It was also my first exposure to emotional intelligence.

My undergraduate degree was in marketing, and I went back to school at night to get my MBA. I chose TCU for several reasons. It's a challenging program, and I liked the idea of going to graduate school with working professionals. The program afforded me access to a great network in Dallas-Fort Worth, which added a unique dimension to the curriculum.

CAREER
After graduation, I was accepted into the corporate management training program at Burlington Northern. I learned many things from that experience. During that rotation, I learned how a major transportation company functions, how great leaders find ways to create compelling visions, and how hard change can be for people and companies. John Hovis was my first boss, and he put me in developmental roles where I could learn the business and lead people early in my career. John Lanigan, Carl Ice, Steve Bobb, Dave Garin, George Duggan, and Steve Branscum are all great leaders who believed in me along the way and gave me the flexibility to balance

family with the responsibilities of being a senior-level contributor. Matt Rose created a culture focused on the leadership model, took calculated risks, and gave me developmental opportunities. For that I will always be grateful to him.

I can't say that there was one specific experience that changed me from a business standpoint. Instead, there have been a series of significant experiences and people helping to shape the kind of leader I have become. My first role models were my parents, and I have a true appreciation now for how hard they both worked to balance their careers and the needs of three children. They gave everything to provide us opportunities to be successful. This sacrifice, along with the strong Christian values they instilled in us, has made the most significant impact on my leadership style and approach.

ADVICE
When I speak to the TCU BNSF Next Generation Leadership students, I always give them my David Letterman Top Ten List of things I wish I'd known as a student:

10. Work hard, and the opportunities will follow. Worry less about the money, and more about the experience.
9. Take jobs where you get to lead people, either formally or informally.
8. Find two mentors: one who's just like you and one who's not.
7. Listen, learn, and know your stuff.
6. Treat people with respect. You may be working for them someday.
5. Sometimes it's better to be right than liked. Sometimes it's not.
4. Enjoy what you do; companies will never be able to pay you enough if you don't.
3. Have a destination in mind. The route you take may change, but you need to know where you want to end up.
2. You shouldn't fit the model. Challenge it and make it better.

And the number-one thing I wish I'd known as a student ...
1. Great leaders hold themselves accountable not only for the results they achieve, but how they achieve them. The BNSF Leadership Model lays out behaviors that are critical to that success:
   - Create a compelling vision.
   - Model the way.
   - Lead more, manage less.
   - Communicate, communicate, communicate.
   - Make development a priority.

FOCUS ON SOFT SKILLS
M.J. Neeley cuts the ribbon to mark the opening of the Center for Productive Communication in 1989, the first national business school communication center.

Michael Heard
A Frightening Lesson from Eighth Grade

Michael Heard riding high.

MICHAEL HEARD *is vice president of feature production at Twentieth Century Fox Studios. He graduated from TCU in 1992 with a bachelor of business administration and major in accounting and was part of the track team at TCU. His first professional position was as a staff auditor for Ernst & Young.*

Mike joined Fox, Inc., as a senior financial analyst in 1997 before entering the production field in 1999. He has worked on a variety of productions including Fantastic Four, X-Men: The Last Stand, The Darkest Hour, Glee: The 3D Concert Movie, *and* In Time.

I was shocked and sad.

I got a D in math my eighth-grade year. That one event struck a chord of fear in me. It was this fear of failure that motivated me in ways that continue today.

When I got to high school, I had Ms. Hoose for English my freshman year. She was truly the first teacher who took an interest in me as a student. Instead of seeing me as a C student, she saw a student with untapped potential.

Her guidance led me to obtaining straight As as a sophomore.

ACCOUNTING MAJOR

I was born in Torrance, California. I first heard about TCU through my minister, who had attended Brite Divinity School.

When combined with its nationally recognized track program — and family roots that trace back to the 1840s in Texas — the choice was easy.

My BBA in accounting prepared me extremely well. In fact, when compared to accounting graduates I worked with from "powerhouse" schools like USC or Texas, I felt I was educationally on par, or better prepared, than they were.

Dr. Robert Vigeland, chair of the accounting department, was truly extraordinary. He made a dry subject like accounting exciting and interesting.

While in school, I was an accounting tutor for the athletic program. In tutoring more than thirty different athletes, I discovered a true passion for teaching and mentoring others.

CAREER PATH

After graduation, I worked at Ernst & Young in Los Angeles in valuation analysis and audit. I learned that accounting was not necessarily a career fit that made sense for me.

I well remember my first day. A presentation for new employees was scheduled for 8 a.m. in the company's conference room. I showed up a little after 7:30, and the trainer in charge of orientation told me to look around while I waited. I walked the corridors, noting executives in the largest offices.

When I got back to the conference room, I asked, "Who are those distinguished-looking older guys in their seventies and eighties?"

The trainer replied, "Those are some of the partners — and they're in their fifties and sixties."

That's when I decided that accounting pressures might age me quickly, and I altered my career goals.

In this business, one particular person who's impressed me is Ralph Winter, producer of *X-Men*. In Ralph, I found a mentor who was an inspiration both professionally and spiritually. Because of him, I finally had a tangible example of someone who showed me it was possible to be a Christian and work at a top level in the film industry.

ADVICE

- Cultivate a relentless drive not only to succeed but to achieve that success at the highest level possible.
- Don't "radar lock" on anything in life. Keep your interests wide and varied, and never stop learning and growing.
- Take chances on yourself! You may think you want to be something when you grow up, but don't stay locked into something that doesn't fulfill you.

Christine Kalish
Defining Answers Helps
Define Career.

CHRISTINE KALISH *is an executive consultant with Beacon Partners, which provides management consulting services to the health care industry.*

Before that, she served as vice president and chief transformation officer for the University of North Texas Health Science Center, vice president and chief of staff in the office of the president of the Center, and administrative director of the Department of Internal Medicine at the Center.

Chris earned an MBA degree from TCU in 2003 and serves as president of the TCU Neeley School Alumni Executive Board of Directors.

I never really had an "Aha!" experience. My professional life has truly been a progression.

My work background was in retail: first grocery, then banking. Then I sort of fell into health care. My friend worked at her physician brother's office. She was moving out of state, and he needed some help. It was a good fit, and I stayed with him for ten years. I ran his office. His idea of a "retirement plan" for me was to pay my way through school!

I finished my health services administration degree that way. I did my undergraduate work in finance at TCU, first because UT Southwestern Medical School's Allied Health Science Program offered only one health care finance class and — more importantly — because I had chosen TCU for graduate school.

Honestly, my only "major" moment came recently, when I realized that I would not spend the rest of my career doing the day-to-day operational tasks. That bores the heck out of me. That's why I'm consulting now. I always have to be on my game and be able to get to the root of the issues pretty darn fast. As we advance in our companies, we become more oriented toward strategy and project management. The current environment requires that we think at different levels than we did in the past.

SELECTING A CAREER

I wasn't always attracted to business. After graduation from high school in Carrollton, I started North Texas State University as a design major. I thought I was going to be a great fashion designer, so I saw myself as an artist. But I learned that designing costumes and clothes was fun only when I wasn't dependent on my income from it.

I worked all the way through school. There were maybe six months, while I was finishing my undergraduate degree, when I didn't work. I couldn't stand it. I've always found I accomplish more when I have more to do.

For me, improving health care has become an important career focus. Our health care system has to change. We are the only country where people declare bankruptcy due to medical bills. It's not right. Maybe I can be a tiny piece of fixing it.

VALUE OF MBA

I finished my undergraduate degree in 1999 and my MBA in 2003. I learned that my graduate degree helped me move to the next level in job opportunities. Don't misunderstand: I worked like crazy to get there and paid my dues. It just helped give me that boost.

Realistically, the MBA didn't make me a better whatever. It's not magic. In fact, I walked out of school pretty sure of myself. It took me awhile to re-learn that it's about the people you support, the front-liners who do the jobs every day. We need to be the folks who clear the way for them to do what they need to do. It's more of an inverted pyramid.

Also, my MBA training says that I know I don't always have the answers, but I can go through the process of defining the question. That's the most important part of the process anyway.

I learned these valuable lessons especially from two incredibly humble and effective professors at TCU. I had Rob Rhodes for three classes in a row, so he had three opportunities to make an impact or make me crazy. Honestly, he is one of the most gifted teachers I have ever had; he is a true academic and passionate about his profession and students.

Larry Peters is one of the most networked people I know. He understands strategy, the psychology of companies, and why people interact the way they do. When I was going through some tough times in my career recently, he reminded me that we all need to be open to change. It made me think really hard about who I am and what I do. He just has that effect on people.

ADVICE

- Be fearless. Don't be afraid to try and fail. It's in failing that we push our limits and learn our lessons so we can improve for the next time.
- Be passionate. Try lots of things so you can find what you love in life and in work.
- Be true to yourself. Tell the truth always, especially to yourself and to those who matter in your life.

David D. Kinder
Mastering Business Details
Is Critical.

DAVID D. KINDER *is vice president of corporate development, treasurer, and head of investor relations for Kinder Morgan, one of the largest pipeline transportation and energy storage companies in North America.*

David's responsibilities include leading Kinder Morgan's acquisition and divestiture program. As treasurer, he is involved in managing the company's financing and investing activities.

David is a 1996 cum laude graduate of TCU with a bachelor of administration in finance. He joined Kinder Morgan as manager of corporate development in 1999 and was named vice president of corporate development in 2002, treasurer in 2005, and head of investor relations in 2009.

Getting lots of responsibility at a young age matures you in a hurry.

I remember my first job as a waiter when I was only 15. I quickly learned a lot about customer service and how hard it is to run a retail business. And after that job, I definitely started tipping a lot better!

I had been at Kinder Morgan only six months when we started going through a large-scale merger. I was only 25 at the time and was given lots of responsibility to divest certain assets following the merger. I made mistakes in that process but learned more in one year following that acquisition than I would have in probably twenty years at any large-scale company.

COLLEGE

I was from a small town, so for college I preferred to go to a smaller school instead of a larger state university. I liked TCU because of the class sizes, and I would have the opportunity to get to know the teachers instead of being instructed by a teaching assistant.

I decided to major in finance and minor in history. This gave me the foundation to look for a variety of jobs in the business arena.

I was especially impressed with Dr. Stan Block, who was extremely bright. He could remember every sentence out of the textbook — but then again, he wrote it! He was very open to meeting with students to assist them in areas they didn't understand. He pushed me to apply to the Educational Investment Fund, and his class and the Fund were most influential to my college experience.

CAREER

After graduation, I started working as an analyst at Enron Corporation. It was a very fast-paced environment. For the first four months, I just tried to keep my head above water because of the huge amount of new information that was coming at me.

I learned quickly that I was more comfortable in a company where you owned hard assets and focused on the cash flow that could be produced from those assets over the long term vs. the next couple of years.

Kinder Morgan owns or operates about 37,000 miles of pipelines and 180 terminals in North America. We're the largest independent transporter of refined petroleum products and one of the largest natural gas transporters and storage operators. We are also the largest independent terminal operator, the largest transporter and marketer of CO_2, and the largest handler of petroleum coke.

We have minimal exposure to commodity price volatility because we typically don't own the energy products that we transport, store, or handle. As a result, our businesses are relatively stable, and our fee-based assets have consistently generated superb cash flow in all types of market conditions. Where we do own the commodity, such as in our CO_2 business, we hedge to lessen the impact of commodity price swings.

ADVICE

- Work ethic is very important. I want someone who will work hard in his or her job. I've worked with many people who are extremely smart and have graduated from some of finest institutions in the country. However, if they have a poor work ethic, they are not able to cut it.
- You must understand the details of a business. If you ever work for a company or invest in one where the CEO or president says he doesn't have the time or isn't focused "on the numbers," then I think it would be wise to move on.

SNOW DAY
Fort Worth doesn't often get a major snowfall, but the Tandy Hall lawn provides a rare opportunity in 2011.

Roger King
Commit Yourself to Going the Extra Mile.

J. ROGER KING *has served as a director of BJ's Restaurants Inc. since April 11, 2002. These restaurants began in 1978 and now have multiple locations in the United States.*

Roger spent thirty years in the human resources field for PepsiCo, Inc. During that tenure, he served as senior vice president of human resources at PepsiCo, Inc., vice president of labor relations at Frito-Lay, and vice president of human resources at Pizza Hut.

Roger received his bachelor of commerce with majors in marketing and management from TCU in 1963. He serves on the board of trustees of Texas Christian University. In addition, he has served as chairman of the Employee Relations Committee of The Business Roundtable and vice chairman of the Labor Policy Association in Washington, D.C. (Source: Forbes.com)

I had a Sunday school teacher in high school, John Summers, who made a lasting impression on me. He was very smart and a successful businessman.

I'll never forget the day he said this: "When you are accepted in college, you have the capability of making As in every class, or the school would not have accepted your application."

He continued, "It is your choice whether you make Cs or As, and it all depends on how hard you are willing to work and to apply yourself."

This man was so accurate, a great mentor and friend. I wanted to grow up to be just like him. I later asked his counsel again when I considered graduate school. "If you take the hours you will put forth in graduate school," he said, "and apply them to your job, you will be just as successful."

I did exactly that, and it worked for me. However, my feeling today is you need the graduate school learning experience!

SCHOOL CHOICES

I first went to Georgia Tech to be a chemical engineer. In the late 1950s, many young people felt that the most successful career path was to be in a professional job, such as being a doctor, lawyer, or engineer. After a short time at that school, I discovered that my personality and aptitude did not match engineering. So I took a battery of aptitude tests that sent me toward the business world.

At the same time I came down with an illness that required a special diet, which I could only get at home. So I came back to Fort Worth and enrolled at TCU. I majored in marketing and management. Back then, the degree was called a bachelor of commerce. It provided me a good fundamental understanding of various facets of business.

BUSINESS TRAINING

My last three college years I worked part time (about twenty-five hours a week) at J. C. Penney's. The biggest learning came from observing some of the young managers there.

I discovered that just doing a job was not enough if you wanted to progress in a company. You must do your job plus more than is expected of you. I also learned how important the customer is to the success of a business. And I learned the art of managing others. This was the single most important job I ever had in developing my career.

After graduation I immediately went to work for Penney's in Dallas as manager of the men's and boys' shoe department. Because I'd worked part time for the previous three years, I skipped the two-year training period that most college grads went through at that time.

I had several promotions within a short period at Penney's. The reason was: I just flat out-worked my peers! I went the extra mile in everything I did at Penney's. Later, when I worked for PepsiCo — where I worked for thirty years — I applied the same principle.

I was inspired by many mentors who contributed to my success. John Ewing, vice president of human resources for PepsiCo, set the gold standard for quality of work. He expected the best and never accepted anything less. He was tough to work for, but he took me a notch higher in my own performance expectations.

PepsiCo CEO Wayne Calloway taught me to be a good listener and to treat everyone in the organization with respect and dignity. "Be a servant to those who work for you," he said, "so they can do their jobs better."

ADVICE
- I've been told by several of my bosses through the years that what they respected the most was my integrity. That went beyond telling the truth, but more to telling it like it is — whether it was good news or bad news.
- Your future begins today. How well you do depends on your commitment to being as good as you can be, and that begins with a commitment to learning.

SETTING PRIORITIES
Norman Bulaich ('70) focuses on accounting back in 1967.

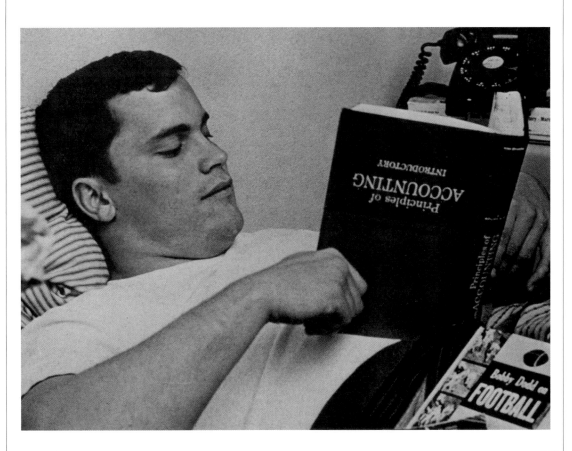

Bryan Koop
Learning to Lead During Tough Economic Times

BRYAN J. KOOP *serves as senior vice president and regional manager of the Boston office of Boston Properties. The company is a self-managed real estate investment trust. It is one of the largest owners, managers, and developers of first-class office properties in the United States, with a significant presence in four core markets: Boston, New York City, Washington, D.C., and San Francisco.*

Bryan is responsible for overseeing the operation of a 13 million-square-foot regional portfolio in the Boston area, which includes the Prudential Center, John Hancock Tower, and Cambridge Center. He is also responsible for all new development, which totals over 3 million square feet over the past ten years, including Boston's first green skyscraper, Atlantic Wharf. He has been selected by Boston's Mayor Thomas Menino to serve on the City of Boston's Green Ribbon Commission advising the mayor on sustainability policy.

Bryan received two degrees from TCU, a bachelor of business administration with a major in management in 1980 and an MBA in 1983.

I can't say that one specific business experience influenced my career. Actually, it was a series of events based on the "Great Texas Real Estate Crash" of the 1980s.

That's when I started my career — and when I think about how that period influenced me, it turns out to be a blessing. It provided innumerable lessons for a life in real estate and business. Every day I witnessed examples of what not to do! And I learned that the ability to underwrite risk, avoid overconfidence, and focus on what's important were key lessons that have served me well.

FROM CHICAGO TO FORT WORTH

I grew up in Chicago and heard about TCU through their recruiting efforts in the Chicago area. I received the BBA and MBA from the Neeley School.

At TCU, Drs. Joseph Lipscomb and Stan Block made lasting impressions on me.

Dr. Lipscomb had an enthusiasm for real estate and finance that was contagious. He was an early adapter in teaching through real-life experiences he encountered in the marketplace.

Dr. Block taught me to challenge financial analyst reports and think independently.

TCU's MBA program was clearly building momentum, and I had a strong interest in the Educational Investment Fund. I was chosen to serve it as portfolio manager. The Fund was way ahead of its time and provided the best possible real-world business experience and a quantum leap into my business career.

My favorite job in college was an internship with the Trammell Crow Company.

THE REAL ESTATE BUSINESS

After graduation I joined the Trammel Crow Company in Houston as a leasing agent. In that job, I learned to sell and market real estate. I gained an understanding of all aspects of deal making, which is an essential skill set in commercial real estate.

While market conditions were awful, Trammel Crow gave me tremendous autonomy and responsibility. I was fortunate enough to complete several hundred transactions in the first five years of my career. The early deal-making experience in the worst possible market conditions has proven valuable to this day. Starting a career in a poor market can be incredibly valuable, as you see every possible challenge in a short period of time.

A positive attitude is the one personal attribute that has carried me through my career. The real estate industry tends to be very cyclical, where poor market conditions can last for years. When challenges or crises hit, no one wants to work with a whiner, and no one will passionately follow a leader who is not optimistic and positive. A positive attitude is an essential personal attribute to becoming an effective leader in the real estate industry.

Chris Roth, a partner at Trammell Crow Company in Houston, was my first supervisor and best possible mentor. Chris was an incredible deal maker and salesperson. The negotiation and sales skills Chris taught me have proven invaluable throughout my career.

ADVICE

- Two things will improve a person's life: the people you meet and the books you read. First, find and invest in mentors. They will provide training and opportunity. Second, continue to read and become a life-long learner. Surprisingly, many people don't invest in relationships and shut down learning after the first three years of their career.
- Building adaptive capacity is essential in building a sustainable career. Continuous learning is the most important ingredient in building adaptive capacity.

Gary Naifeh
Learn How to Motivate an Audience.

GARY NAIFEH *is a principal with Brand Savvy, Inc. The company guides organizations through the strategic and tactical phases of effective brand development and evolution. This includes appraising a product's current brand equity and developing tools both to position brands in the marketplace and to distinguish them from their competitors.*

Gary has worked with a diverse group of Fortune 1000, health care, and start-up companies. He has held vice president of marketing positions at Coors Brewing Company, PepsiCo's Pizza Hut International, and Boston Market. He's also served as vice president of operations for PepsiCo's Taco Bell restaurant division.

He received an MBA from the Neeley School in 1974 and was recently a vice president of TCU's National Alumni Board.

Late in 1973, I made a decision that when I got my MBA in May 1974, I wanted to get into the beer business. I felt that in this industry, big money could be put behind what I thought were my big ideas. I chose Schlitz Brewing Company as my target, because it was number-two at the time. I felt my contributions would be better noticed there than at Budweiser, which was number-one.

My work on the TCU Educational Investment Fund taught me how to prepare for my Schlitz interview. My preparation meant exhaustive research into every facet of their business. In February 1974 I interviewed at Schlitz headquarters. The various interviewers were fascinated that I knew so much about the company. I got hired on the spot for $12,000 a year. So in the middle of the early 1970s recession, I had a job before I graduated. I thought I was rich!

This launched my career in the beer industry. I later became vice president of brand management at Coors Brewing Company.

STARTING EARLY
When I was nine years old, I began helping my mother and uncles in their grocery store every Saturday morning. I learned firsthand about merchandising, pricing, promotion, and advertising. I also learned about human nature, because a grocery store has a very diverse clientele. My mother paid me 25 cents an hour, and at the end of the day I got a six-ounce soft drink and a Hostess cupcake (which added up to another 25 cents).

When I took my first college marketing course and the professor began discussing the four Ps — product, price, place, and promotion — I realized I'd been practicing them since I was a child.

Starting in my early teens, I worked in my father's business and realized that I wanted to pursue a business career. When I graduated from Stephen F. Austin University — it was Austin State College then — I applied to TCU's MBA program. It was close to my home in Longview, the smaller classes were attractive, and the campus appealed to me.

In the MBA program I learned the benefit of being a strong communicator. There's incredible power and personal satisfaction knowing how to take command of a room of strangers and focusing their attention.

CAREER

Robert A. Rechholtz, now retired, was one of R.J. Reynolds Tobacco Company's youngest vice presidents. Bob became a vice president of marketing at Schlitz, and we spent many late nights together thinking about how to salvage the company.

He later became executive vice president of sales and marketing at Coors, where he recruited me from Schlitz. When I joined them in 1982, Coors was in only eleven states and bleeding money. Bob's challenge to me was, "Do what you have to do, and I'll watch your back."

I did — at times to Bob's chagrin. He'd give me a good scolding and then forget about it, which I found motivating.

Working with lots of talented, committed people, Coors began its journey to become a national brand in 1983. Today it's a leading international brand.

The lesson is that when you have someone believe in you, and you believe in the product, great things are possible.

ADVICE

■ The most important skill one can have is the ability to excite an audience to take risks in order to achieve extraordinary results.

■ Right-brain MBAs who focus on marketing must remember that — to have their ideas reach fruition — they must sell those ideas to CEOs and CFOs, who are typically left-brain and struggle with abstract thought.

■ My advice to these right-brainers is to think like a marketer, but talk like a CFO. By making your narrative start with a financial focus, your big marketing idea will quickly gain their support.

BUSINESS WEEK
Mayor R.M. Stovall and Dean Joe Steele join students Charles McGuire ('72) and Doug Tyler ('71) in the mayor's proclamation for TCU's 1971 Business Week.

Don Thomas
Act Responsibly and Value Other People's Time.

DON THOMAS *has been a principal with Reata Real Estate Services in San Antonio since its beginning in 2001. With more than twenty years of commercial real estate experience, Don has leased and/or sold over 5,000,000 square feet of retail space.*

He is currently involved in the redevelopment of the historic Houston Street and Rivercenter Mall in downtown San Antonio, as well as the management and/or leasing of approximately 7,000,000 square feet of retail and office space in San Antonio and South Texas.

Don graduated from TCU in 1987 with a bachelor of business administration and major in marketing. He was student body president at TCU and now is a member of the Neeley Alumni Executive Board.

A close friend during high school made a major error in judgment our senior year that affected his life for many years and caused me to re-evaluate mine. I quickly realized how life can change in a moment. I decided that day to pay better attention to the people I surrounded myself with and the decisions I made. I became a better, more focused individual from that time forward.

My high school job was running an ice rink for the Atlanta figure-skating club during weekday mornings before school. I drove the Zamboni, a machine that resurfaces the ice at rinks, and opened the rink at 5 a.m. most days. This taught me a lot of responsibility. Participants spent a lot of time and money on the sport, including, in some cases, parents driving two and a half hours to bring their children to the rink, so my job was very important. (I also met a lot of really cute girls.)

My first college job was working in two men's clothing stores (Harold's and Mark Shale). I learned how to fit the right clothing with the personality and needs of the customer. I also learned to cross-sell. Someone coming in to purchase only a suit would usually end up with a pair of shoes, belt, socks, dress shirt, and a few ties as well.

I was good at maximizing a sale, following up with customers, and building loyalty with them. I learned to schedule appointments with clients. I didn't just wait for a customer to walk into the store.

EARLY YEARS
I was born in Texas, and my family was middle-class, maybe upper-middle-class. We moved to Marietta, Georgia, when my father transferred with his job. In high school I played five sports and lettered in three.

I chose TCU because it was so familiar. My sister was a sophomore and my uncle a senior when I started. I had another uncle who had graduated from TCU during my high school junior year, and they all loved it. I liked the size and student-teacher ratio in classrooms. It was a private and Christian-based school. I felt I could flourish academically and socially and not be just a number.

My favorite college job was serving as student body president. I worked with other students, faculty, alumni, and the board of trustees on matters that improved and enhanced the education and lives of those who were a part of TCU.

My degree is a BBA with emphasis in marketing. I took a variety of business courses and other electives that provided me a well-balanced education related to the specialty I pursued, commercial real estate.

BUILDING A CAREER

My first job after college graduation was as a leasing agent for a commercial real estate company. We specialized in shopping center leasing and tenant representation. I'm still doing it and learning all the time.

In my business, it's most important to attract the best possible retailers, restaurants, and service users to provide very specific goods and services to the demographic profile of the customers shopping the specific center. Attracting the best mix involves understanding these types of businesses and matching them up with the right centers and other complementary businesses. When this is successfully achieved, tenant sales are usually higher. This ultimately leads to higher rents for the center, creating more value for tenants in shopping centers and owners of centers.

Mike Jaffe and David Nicolson at Trammell Crow Company taught me the skills to research and market shopping centers and the art of lease negotiation.

Bob Barnes, my boss at Trammell Crow and now business partner at Reata, taught me to approach business with a long-term mentality, treating people respectfully and valuing their time.

My parents taught me about honesty, integrity, and strong work ethics. They are wonderful examples, and I owe them the most for the success I have experienced.

ADVICE

- Once you identify the industry or field you want to work in, research the best company or individuals in that industry or field and pursue a job with them at any reasonable means or expense (including an internship, if necessary).
- Identify the one person who is most successful at the job you desire, an individual who possesses similar ethics and ideals as your own. Attach yourself to that person and learn all you can. This will pay off in the long run.
- Do your research well and make yourself available.
- Figure out what you are passionate about and make a career of it. If you do what you love, success will come in many ways. Life is short, so enjoy it!

Ronnie Wallace
Placement Office Experience
Leads to Perfect Place.

RONNIE H. WALLACE *is a rancher and former executive vice president of Ben E. Keith Company and president of Ben E. Keith Foods, one of this country's largest food and beverage distributors.*

He has served as chairman of International Food Service Distributors and president of the board of the Nation's Produce Marketing Association. Formerly, he served on the boards of Chase Bank of Texas, Health Care of Texas, and Fired Up, Inc. (owner of Johnny Carino's Italian Restaurants.) He is chairman of Nolan Ryan's Guaranteed Tender Meats.

Ronnie graduated from TCU in 1970 with a bachelor of business administration and degree in general business.

It's spring, 1970. I'm about to graduate with a business management degree and ready to begin my job search. So I go to the TCU job placement service and start flipping through "job opportunities" index cards. One catches my attention.

At first glance, it looks like the Binyon-O'Keefe Company, a Fort Worth moving and storage firm. I recognize the name, because one of my friend's dads worked there. So I take the card out and start to write down details. But the job opportunity's not at Binyon-O'Keefe. It's at Ben E. Keith.

I schedule the interview and talk to several people. Howard Hallam — now president of the company — asks me what I want to do. I say, "Sir, I want to wake up each morning and know that the harder I work that day, the more I will be paid." He told me later that he hired me because I said that.

I got the job and was sent to Big Springs to learn to sell produce. Later, I was transferred to Abilene and became manager there when I was 25, the youngest branch manager in their history.

So that day in the placement office changed my life and started me on a great career in the food business.

FORT WORTH FOUNDATIONS

I was born and raised in Fort Worth. I went to TCU football games even when I was a young kid with my dad, Minor Wallace. Dad was my best friend and taught me how to work. He owned Henslee Auto Parts on Camp Bowie, where Texas Grill is now.

I loved TCU as a child and never stopped. I played baseball and football at Arlington Heights High School and nearly played football at TCU.

I started college in 1964, spent two years in the Marines, and completed my degree in 1970. Business law case studies and the course's essay tests taught me how to dissect and articulate issues in writing.

One of my favorite college jobs was selling programs at the Fort Worth hockey team games at Will Rogers Coliseum. I worked for Rip Johnson, concessionaire of Will Rogers complex. That was my first sales experience, and I liked it.

OTHER GREAT TEACHERS

In my last semester, I signed up for a night class called salesmanship. I'd never considered being classified a salesman, but I found that's exactly what I wanted to be. I was a low-A, high-B student, but this teacher later told me that I made higher grades in that class than anyone else — the first time that ever happened to me. I've thought about him many times — and his inspirational influence on my career — but I cannot remember his name!

At Ben E. Keith, former executive James Rogers was a wonderful mentor. Then I was an assistant to Johnny Beauchamp, the former president, the most optimistic and best salesman in the organization. He believed in me, taught me how to interview and hire people, and later picked me out to be his successor.

- Everyone is a salesperson. It doesn't make any difference what you do — you must sell yourself and your ideas and get along every day.
- Those who work hard generally move ahead.
- Never quit trying to learn more, in any way you possibly can, about the project you're working on.
- Remember to listen and not to always talk.
- The person who succeeds isn't necessarily the polished performer but the one with honest appeal and the desire to help the client.

MIDNIGHT OIL
Just because the day has ended doesn't mean Neeley students quit studying. This photo was taken in 1979.

Chip Webster
Strive for Increasing Responsibility.

FRANK T. WEBSTER *(known as Chip) is president and chief operating officer of Adams Resources & Energy, Inc., the Houston-based company engaged in crude oil marketing, natural gas marketing, oil and gas exploration, refined products marketing, and interstate truck transportation of petrochemicals. He's responsible for $2.0 billion in revenues, 700 employees, board relations, strategic planning, and day-to-day operations.*

Although he's spent most of his career as a banker, he first started work in the oil industry more than forty years ago — not in an office, but in the field.

Chip received his undergraduate degree from TCU with a management major in 1970 and continued on to earn his MBA from TCU in 1972 with concentrations in finance and economics. He serves as a member of the Neeley School International Board of Visitors and the TCU Houston Breakfast Network Committee. He is active in many community and civic activities and is president of The Petroleum Club of Houston.

It's ironic that I've found a second career in this industry. It's a flashback to my early life. Dad and Mom built their oil business a little bit at a time. They lived in a trailer and went from one job site to another. When they made some money on a well, they invested it in the next one.

Eventually, Webster Drilling Company operated four inland barge rigs. Sadly, before I finished my Neeley MBA, my father developed health problems, sold his business, and passed away. My mom had died a few years before.

Dad always felt grateful to the industry. He told me, "The oil business took me off hamburger and put me onto steak."

A REALLY TOUGH JOB
In high school and college, I worked summers for my dad's contract drilling company on inland barge drilling rigs. Several people work on a rig, and job descriptions are distinct. There are swampers, roustabouts, and floor hands who work to move up to become crew supervisors, called drillers. Eventually a floor hand or roughneck could rise to become the rig supervisor or toolpusher after years of being a driller.

There's a definite hierarchy. I learned from my dad and others that the only way to move up is to work harder. Dad would say, "If you're a ditch digger, work to be the ditch digger's boss. Always strive for increasing responsibility."

Dad wanted me to get a business school degree. I think he worked me really hard in the summers to encourage me to go back to school!

COLLEGE FOCUS

I received a management BBA from Neeley and went directly into the MBA program. Dr. Allen Self selected me as his graduate assistant, and he became a great mentor. He also hired me to assist in some of his external consulting engagements.

Upon graduation I had two offers: one from a Fort Worth bank and one from First City National Bank of Houston for their management training program. I loved Fort Worth but decided to return to Houston, where I had roots. And besides that, First City offered $50 more per month.

BANKING EXPERIENCE

I joined the management training program at First City and spent twenty years there. I eventually become executive vice president and head of Energy and Corporate Banking.

When I joined First City, our training program was an eighteen-month, comprehensive rotational program including one where trainees made marketing calls on non-customers. Meeting business owners and taking plant tours convinced me that I wanted to go into the commercial lending department.

After training, the executive vice president and banking division manager, Grover Ellis, called me in to welcome me. He had known my father when he was a bank customer. Mr. Ellis gave me two books, *The Art of Negotiation* and *Elements of Style*. The latter is still readily at hand and used often in my written communications.

He told me to read those and to re-read them in future years. This polished Harvard man mentored me. He was always quick to pen a note of congratulations to me when I brought in new business or received a civic award.

TURNING POINTS

In 1992 changes in banking made me decide to become an independent financial advisor. I paid $10 for an assumed name certificate and hung out a shingle for Webster & Company. I sought energy consulting, financial advisory, and related engagements. Attorney friends provided referrals for sell-side engagements and expert witness work. Friends at Arthur Andersen referred fiduciary roles as a receiver and trustee.

After five years, I was hired by Arthur Andersen to set up an energy merger and acquisition practice in 1998 to focus on sell-side engagements in the relatively new corporate finance department.

Then in 2001 my superior at Andersen and old First City colleague, Robert Ladd, asked me to join him in establishing Duke Capital Partners, a new business unit of Duke Energy. So we resigned from Andersen and established a private equity and mezzanine debt shop focused on independent oil and gas producer clients.

MBA ASSOCIATION
Members of the MBA Association gather for a meeting in 1983.

In 2004 I received a call from a former bank customer, Bud Adams, who asked me to join Adams Resources & Energy, Inc. as president and chief operating officer. Back in the tough energy markets of the 1980s we at First City Bank had worked with Adams, and he recalled our loyalty and support during trying times.

While we are an oil and gas producer, we are primarily a "midstream" company with 700 employees. With more than 350 tractor trailer trucks transporting product around the country, safety is integral to our business and our success. Safety is part of our culture, and I think it will become a major part of many businesses in the next few years.

ADVICE
- Strive for increasing responsibility in every job.
- If you want to learn debating skills, argue your case before a loan committee.
- Honesty and integrity are a person's most important qualities.
- A great quote from the oil business: "Never take 8/8's of a well." Always have partners. Diversify your risks.
- Be comfortable with every person you hire. You must depend on them.
- Volunteer for worthy causes. Whether serving on the board of a children's hospital or heading up the bank's United Way campaign, I seemed to run into the same group of leaders in Houston. Busy people are the people who accomplish things for their company and community.
- Your mentor can be a parent, teacher, or supervisor. A mentor who believes in you can build your confidence, knowledge, and career.
- Try to help others achieve their goals. Share beneficial books with them. We are all students and teachers in the world's learning community.

Management and Operations

> *"Be a great listener to employees up and down the organization chart, to customers, to competition — and then act!"*
>
> JOHN V. ROACH

> *"A business degree is the first step to any occupation. It's the key to open whatever professional doors you choose."*
>
> JENNIFER DUNCAN EDGEWORTH

> *"In school, sample a variety of classes in all academic disciplines. College is not just for grades. It's for searching for ideas and careers you might enjoy."*
>
> CHRIS KLEINERT

Few business leaders would claim to have been self-made, arguing that they achieved success or recognition solely by their own efforts. In this section we find highly accomplished executives who have grounded their success by listening to the advice of trusted mentors and asking questions to constantly keep their companies and organizations on track. Moreover, they have found that business training and expertise can be useful in many different industries and across many different occupations, in both the for-profit and not-for-profit industries.

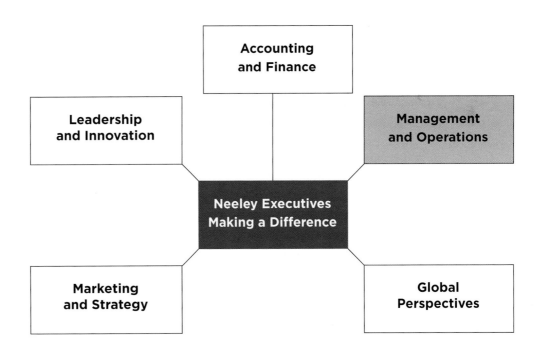

FEATURED ALUMNUS

JOHN ROACH
THE MOST EXCITING JOB INTERVIEW STORY YOU'LL EVER READ

JOHN V. ROACH *is considered one of this country's top technology executives. He served as chairman of the board of two of Fort Worth's largest companies: Tandy Corporation and Justin Industries.*

He's received an astounding thirty-four local and national awards, including Financial World *magazine's Executive of the Year (1981),* Forbes *magazine Business Speaker of the Year (1988),* Financial World's *CFO of the Decade in Specialty Retailing (1989), the Electronics Industries Association Medal of Honor (1993), Texas Business Hall of Fame (1994), Golden Deeds Award as Fort Worth's Outstanding Citizen (2000), and the Tops in Marketing Award from Sales and Marketing Executives International (1990).*

John received his undergraduate degree from TCU in 1961 with a double major in physics and mathematics and then earned his MBA from TCU in 1965. Over the last several years, he's served as TCU trustee, chairman of the trustees, and chairman emeritus. He also serves on the Neeley School International Board of Visitors.

TCU has recognized him with the Distinguished Alumnus Award (1984) and the Royal Purple Award (1997) and has named the university's Honors College and the Neeley School Dean's Chair for him.

It was 1967, and I'd been interviewed twice about managing Tandy Corporation's computer department. The CFO, Charlie Tindall, said, "Charles [Tandy] would like to interview you too. He'll meet you at 6 p.m. at his apartment."

I told my wife I'd be gone a couple of hours. I had no idea I was about to witness a major catastrophe.

I got to Charles' place; we talked for a while, then sat down for dinner about 9 p.m. The phone rang. Charles answered it, then said, "I'll be right there." We jumped into his Cadillac and took a wild ride toward University Drive, site of the enormous Tandy Craft & Hobby Mart. The building was engulfed in flames. Charles meandered through the park, making his way through police and fire blockades, to reach the site.

The building housed thirty-five craft and hobby shops. The first person we met was a media guy, who asked Charles if the property had insurance. So he, Charlie Tindall, and I raced back to Tandy Headquarters to check that out. I got home at 1 a.m., very tired — and still unhired! I immediately took my wife back to the site to show her the remains of this cataclysmic event.

But I did get the job and began a great ride with some terrific people who helped shape technological history.

EARLY EDUCATION

I grew up in a modest eastside Fort Worth neighborhood and graduated from Carter Riverside High School in 1957. My academic interests were physics and math.

The only colleges I considered were Arlington State (now UTA) and TCU. I chose TCU because my cousin had played football there. I double-majored in physics and math. This developed my ability to analyze problems, and that's been beneficial over the years.

I also unloaded boxcars and roughnecked on a drilling rig in college. These were the highest paying jobs I could get — and they taught me that I didn't want to spend my future in manual labor!

FROM CALIFORNIA TO TEXAS

After graduation, I worked two years, mostly in engineering, for California's Pacific Missile Range. I'd married a Fort Worth girl, and after awhile we wanted to come back to Texas.

Dr. Jim Moudy, one of my favorite TCU professors, had become dean of TCU's graduate school. I wanted to get an MBA, so he suggested I try for a Computer Center Fellowship. This helped pay my way through graduate school and laid the foundation for my career.

I got a computer-related job at General Dynamics, but after graduation I took another job, with a small finance company. I managed a department of about ten employees. Before too long, however, I began to worry about the company's future.

That's when I heard about the Tandy opportunity. My future was about to change in a big way.

EARLY TANDY YEARS

What led to my eventful job interview was Tandy Corporation's need to automate many departments for the first time. You may remember that Tandy — especially RadioShack — requested every customer's address at the point of sale. Those addresses formed the basis of a huge mailing list. Customers received catalogues based on how recently or frequently they'd visited a store and how much they spent.

At that time there were about 300 RadioShack stores. They kept addresses on a magnetic tape-based system, and they employed thirty keypunch operators. It was also my duty to streamline the P & L statements, which Charles referred to as his "bible."

By 1975 Tandy Corporation comprised about thirty companies. Fortunately, we spun them off into three large publicly traded firms: Tandy Corporation, which included electronics and RadioShack; Tandycrafts, which included Tandy Leather; and Tandy Brands, which included belts, billfolds, and multiple leather products.

After several promotions, I was named vice president of manufacturing, and I put together a small group to develop the first microcomputer system in 1977 to be sold nationally at retail. (Later, of course, these would be known as personal computers.) The huge success of the TRS-80 microcomputer — plus my breadth of understanding the company — propelled me to the corporate level upon the untimely death of Charles Tandy in 1978.

REMEMBERING CHARLES TANDY

You gain from lots of people, but Charles Tandy was a larger than life leader and teacher. He's the most unforgettable character I've ever met — and I've met many nationally known executives. Charles had an uncanny ability to get extraordinary results out of ordinary people. He managed by the numbers and demanded performance. He was motivational, but he motivated with compassion. He might give someone a lesser position but would not fire them.

Among all of Charles' attributes, he was a teacher. He would take an unusual amount of time to be sure you understood a concept and understood what he expected.

SUCCESS AND INNOVATION

Fortunately, I was the management guy behind microcomputers as computers took off. The time was right for innovation. I gathered several designers and engineers to develop our system.

Since no one knew what a microcomputer was, we made a "barnstorming" computer tour. Our plan: Advertise our arrival in a city, rent a ballroom, and set up about twenty-five computers so people could touch and experiment with them. I'll never forget Washington, D.C. We booked a conference room at the Hay-Adams Hotel. So many people showed up that we didn't know what to do! However, we were sure of one thing: We were on to something big — and it turned out we were right.

Over the years, we were Microsoft's first credible customer. We brought the first cordless telephone and digital receiver to market. We brought Nokia to the U.S. We bundled start-up AOL software with a computer. We developed the first notebook computer, the predecessor of the Palm Pilot, and more.

ADVICE

- Be a great listener. Listen to employees up and down the organization chart, to customers, to competition — and then act!
- You want to be considered for every opportunity that occurs. The way you assure that: Perform your current job the best it has ever been done. Actions speak louder than words. You will not be chosen every time, but you want to be considered.
- A good leader must be a good teacher. The leader should understand the business well enough to teach it.
- Sometimes a leader, especially a good businessperson, can lead best by setting a good example.

GLOBAL PERSPECTIVE
Charles Tandy was always looking for ways to capitalize on market opportunities.

Brenda Cline
The Call that Changed Her Life

BRENDA A. CLINE *is executive vice president, chief financial officer, treasurer, and secretary for the Kimbell Art Foundation in Fort Worth. She graduated from TCU with a bachelor of business administration and major in accounting in 1982. She is a member of the advisory board for the Department of Accounting in the Neeley School.*

She also serves as a trustee for Texas Christian University and the American Beacon Funds. She is a certified public accountant and was with Ernst & Young for more than ten years, becoming senior audit manager.

I vividly recall the afternoon I received the phone call from an executive recruiter describing a financial position at a private foundation. Just the day before, I'd resigned from Ernst & Young after more than ten years' employment to accept the CFO position at a small, privately held company. As much as I thought that CFO position was perfect for me, the private foundation position seemed even more "perfect." I told the recruiter about my dilemma, but also acknowledged that I would be interested if a decision could be reached quickly, since I was to start the CFO position in a month.

Within two weeks I was offered the financial position at the private foundation. I had to make one of the hardest decisions of my life: Should I resign from a position I had not even started and break the commitment I had made to that company? The mere thought went against everything my parents had taught me about integrity, character, and loyalty.

Wisely and persuasively, the recruiter helped me see the long-term, rare opportunity I had with the private foundation. With great anxiety, I resigned for the second time in less than a month and accepted the new offer. I have now been with the Kimbell Art Foundation for more than eighteen years as its executive vice president, chief financial officer, treasurer, and secretary.

Yes, that phone call changed my life.

SCHOOL AND TRAINING

I grew up in Wichita, Kansas, graduating at the top of my class at Wichita High School West. In addition to being a strong academic student with broad interests, I was (and still am) a cellist. I participated in the Wichita Youth Symphony, Kansas All-State Orchestra, and other performing ensembles.

I chose TCU for a number of reasons: its openness to allowing me to explore various fields of study as a freshman, its location within a day's drive of my hometown, and its significant scholarship support.

For three summers in college, I was the administrative assistant for the high school summer driver education program. I learned to work independently; interact confidently with teachers, administrators, and students; and be highly organized and dependable.

At TCU, Dr. Gere Dominiak taught me — and everyone else in intermediate accounting and auditing — to think and apply principles, not just know them. I had the privilege of teaching her intermediate accounting lab my senior year. I learned as much as the students taking the class did, just by preparing for the lab, reading her notes to me, and discussing her teaching philosophy with her. That experience taught me to explain complex accounting issues and theory in a straightforward, understandable manner, and that's proven to be a lifetime skill. Indeed I believe that accounting is the foundation for all business. Fundamentally, businesses make a profit (or at least break even), and the numbers tell a story if you understand them. Learning how to read the story and interpret it is paramount to the success of any business.

MAJOR MENTORS

Mr. Turner Almond, an audit partner at Ernst & Young, was encouraging and supportive even when I made mistakes. I remember once being very disappointed in myself. I missed something that he caught in his review. Turner viewed that as a learning experience and told me, "When you've been doing this job as long as I have, and you still miss something like that, only then can you be mad at yourself." He taught me to lead by example and how to reward and develop my staff.

Since I left public accounting, Mr. Ben Fortson, Vice President of the Kimbell Art Foundation, has been my mentor. From my first days at the Foundation, he has included me in the decision-making and has patiently taught me about the oil and gas business. He has supported my exploration and education in the investment management field and regularly listens to and discusses with me new investment ideas and opportunities. He is my champion and supports me in any endeavor.

ADVICE

- Perseverance is critically important. I mean that in the broadest sense — determination, persistence, commitment, hard work, a "whatever-it-takes" attitude, thoroughness, etc. Over time, with perseverance, those individual accomplishments multiply and lead to a successful career.
- Become a good communicator, both in writing and orally. Good communicators understand their audience. Write and speak clearly and concisely. Learn to explain complex theory in a straightforward, understandable manner.

THE LANGUAGE OF BUSINESS
Professor of Accounting, Mary Stanford, shares insights about accounting and business strategy with two Master of Accountancy students, Scott Boyd ('04, '05) and Ashley Davis ('05, '06).

David Coburn
"Dr. Detail" Advises Multiple Industries.

DAVID L. COBURN *is a senior executive for Accenture, formerly Arthur Andersen and Andersen Consulting. He manages and delivers projects to companies around the world to assist them with technology infrastructure operations and application development maintenance.*

He has advised clients in the insurance, chemical, industrial equipment, financial service, utility, and hotel industries and has also assisted federal, state, and local governments.

David earned an undergraduate degree in accounting from TCU in 1981.

I'll never forget my first accounting class in Rogers Hall. The professor walked in and looked around.

"There are too many people in this classroom," the professor commented. "But that's OK — because two weeks from now, half of you will be gone." I stayed, and I'm glad I did. My accounting degree taught me metrics, trending, and the numbers side of client businesses. It taught me that if you can't measure a problem, you can't develop a solution.

I'm very thorough, and that's why some of my co-workers call me Dr. Detail.

As a consultant, I've also had some flexibility to take care of family matters. For instance, I was able to relocate to Florida, so I wouldn't need to travel so much when our son was in middle school. This was an important time in his life, and I got to be there for him.

Professionally, I've been able to learn lots from some big assignments. My biggest challenge was providing support services for a company with worldwide operations. We navigated multiple cultures and client expectations halfway around the world. During this two-year period, I gained expertise that could help many other clients too.

Somebody once told me, "Stay as close to the revenue-generating side of the business as possible." That's been good advice. And I've also been shaped by those who've worked on my teams, including those I've had the opportunity to mentor.

HIGH SCHOOL YEARS

I grew up in Maryland and moved to Fort Worth when I was 15. My stepfather was a minister at University Christian Church, just across the street from TCU. My mom worked at TCU in the music department. So my connection to TCU was established. I was destined to be a Horned Frog! I was interested in a business degree, and TCU had a solid business school.

I worked at the Region XI Education Service Center as a programmer during high school and part-time during college. I began this as part of a vocational education program at Southwest High School. I had a few other jobs, but this was my favorite because it taught me about workplace relationships and working independently. I kept the job through college; it's where I got interested in the technology side of business.

Accounting taught me structure and discipline. And my involvement in the Delta Sigma Pi fraternity taught me about leadership.

ACCENTURE CONSULTANT

When I graduated, there were eight large national accounting firms. I received four or five offers, including one from Arthur Andersen in the consulting division. I've been here about three decades, and the consulting field has grown tremendously. When I started, there were only 5,000 Andersen consultants in the entire world. Today we have more than 200,000.

The consultant must be a quick learner, because every company is different. A consultant must discover what's going on to make the customer successful. When times are tough, "hug" a client. In other words, the closer you are in your organization to the delivery of services/goods to the end customer, the more relevant you are, and the less likely you become a target for down-sizing, right-sizing, layoffs, or whatever you want to call it. This is true not just when times are tough, but all the time. It's always a good thing to be close to the customer.

I guess I'm an anomaly for having stayed in one place for so long. I've had six or seven careers inside this company, really enjoy my opportunities here, and learn something new every day.

ADVICE
- Facts are powerful. Emotional decisions are risky.
- Manage your career. Nobody else will do it for you. Don't be bashful about your accomplishments; but at the same time, don't be cocky.
- Take the time to mentor and coach others. There's tremendous satisfaction in seeing others succeed.
- Listen, listen, listen. Then act. Listen some more, then adjust your actions. Repeat.
- Don't let yourself be a victim. In other words, be proactive, show up. When you see the "writing on the wall" where an issue or problem is coming your way, take steps to get out in front of it. Don't let yourself be a victim of circumstances when you have the ability to influence the outcome.

GO FROGS
Christopher Del Conte, Director of Intercollegiate Athletics (far left), joins Jackie Coburn ('80), David Coburn ('81), Cathy Daniels ('85), and Charles Daniels ('84) for a tail-gating party before a TCU football game in 2011.

Jennifer Duncan Edgeworth
The Persuader

JENNIFER DUNCAN EDGEWORTH *is a partner at the Hermes Sargent Bates law firm in Dallas, where the Junior Chamber of Commerce recently named her one of "Five Outstanding Young Dallasites of 2010."*

"Jennifer is the type of lawyer many aspire to be — she is cognizant of her role in the community as a professional, and she seizes the opportunities she is given to help others," said Hermes Sargent Bates partner Kimberly Wilson.

Jennifer's practice is primarily devoted to environmental litigation, product liability, construction, and commercial litigation.

She graduated from TCU cum laude in 1996 with a management major and earned an MBA and law degree from Baylor. She is a member of the Neeley School Alumni Executive Board.

My work today is a natural progression from high school. That's when I joined the debate team and competed in a Lincoln-Douglas format. Each team was required to defend a value position. In preparation, I studied some profound documents, like John Locke's Second Treatise. Locke talks about how this country's founders created the government by stressing that each individual is free and equal and owns the results of his or her own labor.

As I adapted to each debate, I realized the value of learning to be persuasive whether you agreed with a position or not. Your job was to convince debate judges that your position was best. I got hooked then on speech and debate, and when I began college I knew I would ultimately attend law school.

CAREER PREPARATION
My first paid job was as a cashier at Target before college. I found that minimum wage working behind a cash register wasn't my ultimate goal — there's value in getting a higher education.

I did not expect to choose TCU. I went with my parents to a Monday at TCU because my grandparents lived in Fort Worth and recommended I visit the school. I made the decision to attend while listening to the presentation on the third floor of the business school. I was so impressed. This business school is cutting-edge, I thought, and these professors want to be part of my learning experience.

MENTORS
I chose a management major because I'm fascinated by factors that make an organization successful and productive. And the process of managing people requires the ability to persuade.

Dr. Jane Mackay led the Management Advisory Council of management students. I was impressed with her success in the business world as a female. She's a successful woman and role model, which to me was very empowering.

Dr. Kay Higgins was adviser for orientation student assistants. She gave me the opportunity to be creative and work with students coming to TCU, allowed me to lead and develop my leadership style, and gave me unfaltering support not only during, but after college. We're good friends today.

Dr. James Atwood taught my freshman year survey of religion course, and I also took an elective course from him as a senior. He helped me understand other religions and cultures.

I went to Baylor for a joint MBA-JD degree and completed it in three years. I wanted both degrees with the goal of one day having the option to join a company as a corporate attorney.

ADVICE

- In law, I've learned that everyone has the right to be represented.
- Details are very important in any career.
- Public speaking experience benefits most everyone. Look for opportunities to learn more about it and speak more often.
- A business degree is the first step to any occupation. It's the key to open whatever professional doors you choose.
- At the end of the day, your integrity is far more important than your paycheck. Treat others as you would want to be treated and maintain humility with every success.

SHOOTING STRAIGHT
Caitlyn Morrisey, current Neeley junior, is an accounting major but also was an All-American athlete in the Air Rifle competition.

Charles Florsheim
Business Training Is
Helpful to any Profession.

Charles Florsheim ('71) was recognized as Who's Who in Business in 1970.

CHARLES FLORSHEIM *graduated from Texas Christian University magna cum laude in 1971 with a bachelor of business administration in accounting. He attended law school at Southern Methodist University, receiving his JD in 1974. Following four years of service in the Army Judge Advocate General's Corps — which included a thirteen-month assignment in Korea — he returned to Fort Worth, where he has been in private practice since 1978.*

He is a partner at Cantey Hanger law firm in Fort Worth. His practice includes a variety of areas, with a primary focus on business organizations, franchising, real estate, securities, and mergers and acquisitions.

My life really began at TCU. I met Sam Wood the first day of school. We started in honors accounting class together and have remained close friends. He changed my life by introducing me to Ann Collins.

When Sam got engaged, he asked me to be a groomsman. At the wedding, he set me up on a blind date with Ann, who was in the house party. Since 1971, Ann — also a TCU graduate — has been my wife, best friend, closest advisor, best critic, and love of my life. Without her I would not have accomplished the things I've done.

After graduation, I immediately went on active duty in the Army while attending law school, and after law school I served four years on active duty. In the Army, I learned how wonderful it was to be able to practice law without worrying about how much time I spent on a project and whether I got paid for it. It was a truly rewarding experience, both in the context of serving my country and practicing law within the military.

FOCUS ON ACCOUNTING

I was born in Longview, Texas, but raised in Dallas. I chose TCU for several reasons. It had a reputation as a school that offered more personal interaction with faculty. I wanted to major in accounting as a prelude to law school, and the reputation of the business school and the honors accounting program was also most appealing.

My favorite college job was teaching freshman accounting labs. It was rewarding to be able, for the first time, to really use knowledge gained in my first couple of college years. The accounting training has always given me a leg up in my law practice. I primarily have a general business practice, with a focus on franchising and mergers and acquisitions.

Because I'd gone to SMU law school, I had a great advantage over other non-business majors who attended law school, and the same applied in the practice of law.

LASTING IMPRESSIONS

One of my major scholastic influences was my high school French teacher. As a freshman, I was just rocking along in school, with mediocre grades. That French teacher recognized my potential and once gave me a test grade one letter higher than I deserved. She told me that she gave me that grade because that was what I could make — and should make. She challenged me to prove her right. After that I never made less than an A in high school, graduating with honors. I always remembered that lesson and how she gave me confidence. I've strived to live up to the potential she saw in me.

Victoria MacLean, my TCU English teacher, was not only a wonderful instructor but a friend who guided me in college, helped me develop valuable communication skills, and recommended me for various honors, including Who's Who at TCU. She took a strong personal interest in students and loved education.

In my personal experience, a business education was very beneficial. Our son Charlie was a TCU finance major, and our daughter Claire was a TCU philosophy major with a double minor in business and Spanish. Both also graduated from SMU law school, and I think business training helped both of them.

Just recently, our family set up an endowed scholarship for the Neeley School, based both on academic achievement and financial need.

ADVICE

- Develop communications skills. In all aspects of legal and business professions, communicating and expressing your ideas clearly and concisely are important aspects of success.
- The key to every profession is ethics. Always carry out your business activities in an ethical fashion, but remember that others may not have the same standards.
- Never lower your standards because those on the other side of a transaction act in unethical ways. Keep your guard up but never lose sight that ethical behavior will win the day.

Jeffrey Guy
Financial Expertise Can Also Be a Work of Art

This photo of Jeff Guy ('72, '74) was taken when he was a student in 1972.

JEFFREY R. GUY *is chief financial officer and director of finance and administration for the Dallas Museum of Art. The Museum — established in 1903 — welcomes more than 600,000 visitors each year and features more than 24,000 works of art from around the world, from ancient to modern times.*

Jeffrey graduated from TCU with a bachelor of business administration and management major in 1972 and earned his TCU MBA in 1974. He is a member of the Neeley School International Board of Visitors.

The atmosphere in the somber room was like a funeral service.

In March 1988 I worked for FirstRepublic when it failed. At the time it was the most costly bank failure in history. We went to the building where The First National Bank of Fort Worth charter, dated 1875, was stored in a vault. While FDIC officials waited, we retrieved it. At this point, I realized things were going to change dramatically and that I needed to adjust, remain flexible, and take advantage of opportunities that arose out of the chaos.

The banking industry taught me a lot. I've traveled quite a bit and have become very attached to this region. Sometimes people ask, "How'd you get to Texas?"

I reply, "Do you know what a snow blower is? I drove south with one on top of my car. When somebody eventually asked, 'What's that?' I knew I'd found a warm place to stay."

FROM OHIO TO TEXAS

I grew up in Shaker Heights, Ohio, where I received a college prep education and participated in various sports, including swimming, soccer, and cross-country. I was also actively involved in band and orchestra, playing trumpet and French horn. And I played in various garage bands throughout high school.

I got accepted at Ohio State and Denison universities in Ohio, but on the recommendation of a swimming team friend already attending TCU, I applied, visited, and accepted a swimming scholarship. The university felt right. It wasn't too big or too small, and the location put just the appropriate distance between an 18-year-old and his parents.

I majored in business with emphasis in management and minored in history. I purposely kept course selection broad and had intended early to secure an MBA with a focus in finance.

During college summer breaks, I worked as a part-time bank teller. I'd travel to various branches throughout Cleveland, relieving full-time tellers who went on vacation. I liked the challenge of helping people, could count money really fast, and enjoyed providing good customer service. I also learned that even the nicest of people can act weird when it comes to their money!

I started working toward my MBA at Neeley, focusing on finance, immediately after getting my BBA. I got a part-time job at a local bank as an afternoon drive-through teller; my salary helped pay for my tuition.

FROM BANKING TO MUSEUMS

My first job after MBA graduation was as a management trainee at the local Fort Worth bank where I'd worked as a part-time drive-in teller. I learned all aspects of the banking business, from finance to operations to lending.

I discovered that I was good at quietly leading people through change and improving processes and procedures. I worked with my long-time Bank of America boss, Billy Murray, from 1988 to 2001. He taught me how to successfully navigate and achieve positive results in a large, growing, constantly changing company. He also taught me the importance of trust, respect, and ethical conduct in the business environment and placed me in challenging positions that allowed for my personal growth.

In my last seven years at Bank of America, I traveled a lot, serving as senior vice president and managing director of global corporate investment banking. I officed in Fort Worth on West 7th Street.

One day a friend nominated me for the job of chief financial and operations officer at Amon Carter Museum. I joined them in 2001.

I came to the Dallas Museum in 2007. I get to contribute to this community and use my skill sets to make this incredible museum even better.

ADVICE

- Demonstrate passion to do the right thing
- Listen to those around you, learn from all experiences, and use them to apply creative and innovative thinking to all that you do.
- My father always encouraged me with gentle support and counsel, and he exhibited a sense of humor and grace in all situations. I find that by using the same approach, I usually receive positive responses and results.

Thomas Hund
On the Right Track

THOMAS N. HUND *assumed his current position of executive vice president and chief financial officer of Burlington Northern Santa Fe Corporation in Fort Worth in 2000. He began his career in the railroad industry with Santa Fe Pacific in 1983 in the accounting department.*

Tom received his undergraduate degree in business from Loyola University of Chicago and his MBA from the University of Chicago. His background includes experience with KPMG as an audit manager.

He is a member of the Financial Executive Institute and the American Institute of Certified Public Accountants and serves as chair of TCU's Neeley School International Board of Visitors.

My wife and I grew up in Chicago. I received business degrees in accounting and finance from Loyola and the University of Chicago. I worked for the public accounting firm KPMG in the Chicago office for seven years. Next, I joined the corporate offices of Santa Fe, also in Chicago, and worked there for six years.

In 1989, our lives changed. I was transferred to Topeka, Kansas, a smaller town away from family, friends, and the city we knew. I moved from a non-union environment — working with small staff groups — to a department of 1,000 people, 80 percent of whom were union-represented.

This changed our family in several positive ways. Our children were young: eight and four. Because we were separated from our extended family, we formed new networks of friends. We met our neighbors, enjoyed the surroundings, and appreciated the town's atmosphere and easy commute.

Professionally, I discovered the many strengths of the railroad business. I learned about union issues like collective bargaining and the great work ethic of union members. I also learned much about leadership, setting clear objectives, leading by example, and inspiring others to excel.
TRAINS AND FREIGHT

MINDING THE RAILS
These Neeley graduates — Mitch Curry ('07), Brian Goodfriend ('02), Stephanie Remigio ('10), Sara Warren ('10), Kelly Parcher ('11), Jace Thompson ('08), and Chris Reed ('11), left to right — are now key employees at BNSF Railway.

My current job is twofold: First, I'm the CFO of Burlington Northern Santa Fe, LLC, the parent company, which means being the central banker and administrator of financial functions. Our only subsidiary is the railroad, a transcontinental freight company that operates in twenty-eight states.

As CFO, I am involved with many operational issues. I work on people-related issues like compensation, benefits, pension plans, personnel development, training, and evaluation. I also spend time with experts in marketing, operations, technology, and law. We work cross-functionally on such questions as "Where should we locate our next train yard to expand capacity?"

This company has a terrific culture — it's more than 150 years old. We perform a vital service: We transport coal for energy, agricultural products, industrial products for building, food, clothing, and other commodities.

When we make decisions, we take a long-term focus. We make large investments in railroad yards, locomotives, track, and railcars that will provide years of service.

A GREAT OPPORTUNITY

I love my job and the people I work with. Today's railroad industry is state of the art. We're highly computerized and very efficient. Our job is to convince the public that — in addition to being less expensive to ship by rail — it is also quite reliable. From the people standpoint, we're putting a lot of emphasis on development of skills. For instance, if an individual has been in a job for three or four years, we rotate that person to a different job to broaden those skills.

Also, we're a green industry. For instance, a train can move a ton of freight about 500 miles on a single gallon of fuel.

I see myself carrying the company baton for one leg of a long race. My generation wants to hand an even greater company to the next one.

ADVICE

- If you chase artificial success (promotions, salary, etc.), you will experience only short-term satisfaction. Look for a job you enjoy.
- Try to understand not just your job, but the business your company is in. Then ask yourself: How does what I do fit into the picture?
- Expand your reach. Think of your job as a sheet of paper. Do everything on your sheet of paper, then look for jobs that may fall outside the paper. Think about other ways you can help the company.

Thomas Klein
150-Year-Old Company
Expands Product Line
and Reach.

THOMAS R. KLEIN *is president and secretary/treasurer of Klein Tools, a family-owned hand tool company founded in 1857 and based in Lincolnshire, Illinois. Klein Tools is now in its fifth generation of management and is in the process of opening a new operations facility in Mansfield, Texas.*

The company's product line has broadened to include virtually every major type of hand tool used in construction, electronics, mining, and general industry, in addition to the electrical and telecommunications fields. Internationally, Klein's products are available around the world through a well-established network of agents and distributors who stock the products required for their particular markets.

Tom received his undergraduate degree from TCU in 1984, majoring in finance and accounting.

I've had some cool summers and some hot ones too. I spent my coolest summers out in the country visiting my mom's dad. His house had a stream running right through the property. Grandpaw kept me busy outdoors helping him with various projects. He'd lived through the Depression and knew the value of hard work coupled with a good education. Throughout those summers, he mixed math skills and reading into our projects. We worked, learned, and had a great time.

I spent my hottest summer at Klein Tools, serving in the heat-treat department. I gulped water all the time and drank a half-gallon of milk at lunch. But by the end of each workday, I'd lost ten pounds.

In both situations, I realized I could learn something from each of my labors and that every job has value.

Our company sells into the electrical distribution, industrial wholesale, and consumer markets. In each, we've had to find a way to differentiate ourselves from the competition. Being able to explain that differentiation is critical.

TRAINING AND EDUCATION

I grew up in a family that has owned and managed its hand tool manufacturing business since 1857. At age 14, I began working summers there. I started in the warehouse and toiled in various other departments, including the tool room, engineering, and finance.

When it came time for college, I looked at several schools, including Michigan and Michigan State. But my sister Susan, a few years older, had been recruited by TCU, and she was a strong TCU advocate!

As a freshman I entered the Neeley School and majored in accounting and finance. This combination gave me a solid understanding of business principles. Utilizing a business major, you can ultimately do anything. A business education also prepares you to conduct your own personal business. Finance courses were my favorites, because they taught me how to understand business financial proposals, explaining such things as internal rate of return, payback analysis, and margin analysis. Many who study other non-business disciplines do not learn this.

Dr. Sanoa J. Hensley was my advisor and taught several accounting classes. She was a direct-to-the-point instructor. She taught principles and emphasized them with real-world examples. I will always value the many things I learned from her.

GRADUATE SCHOOL AND CAREER

My first job after graduation was in finance. While my later summer jobs at the company involved cost accounting issues, this job concerned finance-related matters such as insurance, profit sharing, debt finance, and financial reporting.

For graduate school, I chose Lake Forest Graduate School of Management, which was near our business. They wanted four years' work experience before admittance and full employment while in attendance, so I worked full time and took night classes. The school was very group-oriented; students remained with the same small groups throughout each class in the program. We learned from one another's strengths and weaknesses and benefitted from small-group dynamics.

I've been president of Klein Tools since August 2006 and enjoy working within the family company. Several family members work here, including my two sons, Tom Jr. and David.

My wife Sara is a graduate of TCU, and my middle son David and his fiancée Lindsay Brackett graduated in 2011, while my daughter Leah is a Neeley Fellow at TCU right now.

ADVICE

- Learn to work with your peers and be tolerant of others.
- Don't be afraid to hire the brightest talent available. Too many times, I've seen managers select inferior talent because they fear for their own jobs.
- Best advice I ever got: Our company's family attorney emphasized the importance of hiring the right person for the job, with a focus on strong managerial traits.

A HANDLE ON HISTORY
The Klein family has a long history with TCU and the Neeley School. Pictured here are Sara Stuelke-Klein ('84) and Thomas R. Klein ('84), front row, and Lindsay Brackett-Klein ('11), David J. Klein ('11), and Leah K. Klein ('14), back row, left to right.

Chris Kleinert
Right Answers Result from Asking Good Questions.

CHRIS KLEINERT *is president and CEO of Hunt Consolidated Investments, a subsidiary of Hunt Consolidated, Inc. He oversees the operations of Hunt Realty Investments, Hunt Investment Group, and newly created Hunt Energy Solutions. Hunt Consolidated's other business interests include oil and gas exploration and production, petroleum refining, electric power generation and transmission, ranching, and agriculture.*

His affiliation with Hunt Consolidated began in 1996 as investment manager for Hunt Financial Corporation. Prior to joining Hunt, he was employed by Texas Commerce Bank (now JPMorgan Chase) and General Mills.

Chris received his MBA from TCU in 1982. He and his wife, Ashlee, have endowed an MBA scholarship at TCU and have been strong supporters of the Collegiate Entrepreneurs Organization in the Neeley Entrepreneurship Center.

My first boss at Texas Commerce Bank, Bob Stack, ran the regional corporate group. He was a former rear admiral in the U.S. Navy, and he was very disciplined. He took young guys like me right to the front line. He went with us on client calls.

Bob was an old-school banker. He believed we must be methodical in how we approach a prospect and find out the ways we could best serve each company. He said the key to gathering that information was asking the right questions.

The best part was that he was willing to let us make mistakes to learn. He wanted each of us to be better.

ROLE MODEL

I grew up watching my father start as an entry-level salesperson and work his way up to being president of a large company. He had a great work ethic and was a terrific role model.

I went to undergraduate school at Southern Methodist and got a marketing degree. Then I went to work for General Mills as Oklahoma territory sales manager. After two years, I went to TCU to get an MBA.

I was very green when stepping onto the TCU campus. I'd been fortunate to get a great job with a Fortune 500 company out of college, but I felt unprepared when faced with situations that involved any degree of financial complexity. I was eager to learn various aspects of finance and accounting that I took for granted while an undergraduate. When interviewing for a position after the MBA program, I got a very positive reaction to my coursework at TCU and how prepared I would be for a commercial banking position.

I realized then that I really could transition to a new career path given a much broader and firmer foundation.

SHARING EXPERTISE WITH OTHERS

I benefitted during my time at TCU from many classes and interactions with much of the faculty, but I was especially impacted by Dr. Chris Barry and Dr. Stan Block. They were both great, challenging students while encouraging them at the same time. They, along with the other professors at Neeley, created an environment that developed confidence in each student's ability to succeed out in the real world. Upon graduation, I felt that I was really prepared and equipped to accomplish something for my employers.

It's rewarding now to help other professionals share their expertise. In 2008 my wife, Ashlee, and I formed a nonprofit organization called Executives in Action, which engages transitioning senior executives in short-term consulting projects for nonprofit groups. Thus far, we've launched more than 200 pro bono consulting projects at more than 120 nonprofits.

ADVICE

- In school, sample a variety of classes in all academic disciplines. Then, if you see a club or special interest group that interests you, join it! College is not just for grades. It's for searching for ideas and careers you might enjoy.
- Be reliable! Honor your word, work hard, be proactive, be the person that everyone else knows will get something done — and done well.
- Remain open-minded. Try new things. Challenge yourself to learn and be adaptable. The world is changing. What works today may not work tomorrow, and it's important to learn the skills to identify where change will occur and to react accordingly.
- I don't see many people today staying at the same job. Don't go to a company thinking that you must be there your entire career, but look for opportunities to learn.
- Don't take the job that pays the most unless it's the job you like the most.

Benjamin D. Loughry
The Lunch That
Changed My Life

BEN D. LOUGHRY *is managing partner, founding stockholder, and on the board of directors of Integra Realty Resources in Dallas/Fort Worth. He has been an independent fee appraiser since 1981.*

From 1977 to 1982 Ben served as vice president of Ashland Development, Inc., which included townhouses, office buildings, and land. Before that, he was president of a Fort Worth-based real estate company.

An active member of the Fort Worth community, Ben served as president of the Fort Worth Association of Realtors and is on the board of directors of the Fort Worth Chamber of Commerce. In addition, he is serving as chairman of the Greater Fort Worth Real Estate Council.

Ben received his bachelor of business administration with a major in marketing from TCU in 1970. He has served on the Chancellor's Advisory Council at TCU.

I'm one of several people whose life was changed by the Neeley School. But even more than that, my life was changed by its namesake.

Dad worked for Mr. Neeley at Hobbs Trailer Company in the late 1940s, right after World War II. He was a top salesperson and was fortunate to know Mr. Neeley personally. When I was in junior high school, Dad, Mr. Neeley, and I met for lunch downtown. I really did not know much about him at the time except that my father always spoke highly of him.

During that lunch, Mr. Neeley asked me what I wanted to do with my life. My visions of playing baseball were foremost. Then he asked me several questions regarding activities, faith, friends, family, and the future. I was very impressed to be asked these things.

We left the lunch with handshakes all around. I especially remember Mr. Neeley's firm handshake. He made a huge impression on me that day, and later he'd make a major impression on my future.

HIGH SCHOOL AND COLLEGE

When I was in high school, Dad asked if I intended to go to college. He encouraged me to continue my education and wondered if I had thought about TCU. Neither of my parents had attended a university, so I was a little surprised at the mention of TCU because of the cost. After several family meetings, we decided that, if I got accepted, I would attend TCU. Dad was adamant, which was not his character.

I was not a great student but had a knack for taking entrance exams. My application was submitted to TCU, and I received a provisional acceptance. This meant I was required to maintain a certain GPA. I received a phone call from Mr. Neeley congratulating me on my acceptance. He asked what major I had picked and if I had any thoughts about the business school.

The rest is history. I graduated in 1970 from the Neeley School, and today I enjoy a prosperous business.

TWO GENERATIONS OF ALUMS

But there is more to the story. Dad sat me down many years after graduation and explained how this had all come together.

Mr. Neeley had told him to get me to TCU! In no uncertain terms, the die was cast when I was in junior high school, at a lunch in downtown Fort Worth. Mr. Neeley told my dad he would watch over me and help me in business as a friend to my father. I have wondered many times why opportunities came my way.

There's a part of this story I wish I could change. I never knew how much Mr. Neeley affected my life until after he had died.

Today my family and I are very blessed. My son, daughter, wife, and I are proud TCU alumni — all due to a great man. I asked my dad why he did not tell me about all this sooner. He said, "Mr. Neeley wanted it that way."

ADVICE

■ You never know when your life can change or what person can help you find success.

A PIECE OF HISTORY
This image is of an original stock certificate for Hobbs Manufacturing Company, issued to M.J. Neeley in 1946.

Pylar Pinkston
Listening to the
Call of the Wild

PYLAR PINKSTON *is first vice president and investment management consultant at Morgan Stanley Smith Barney in Dallas. She joined the firm in 1994. Before that, she was vice president of wealth management at Banc One Securities.*

Pylar is founder and director of Furry Friendzy Animal Rescue and Wildlife Rehabilitation. It's a 100 percent volunteer mission located in Kaufman, Texas, that adopts, nurtures, and provides foster care to both domestic and wild animals. The web site is www.FurryFriendzy.org.

Pylar graduated cum laude from TCU in 1986 with a bachelor of business administration and major in finance and real estate.

Work can help you get an education, and learning those new skills helps you find even more meaningful work. Both also provide new opportunities to help others.

For me, work began at an ice cream store in a Tyler mall. I was under age, but because it was privately owned I was able to get hired at 15. When I turned 16, I worked part time my last three high school years at J.C. Penney.

I worked in the accounting department of a nursing home all four years at TCU, reconciling bank statements and helping with payroll and billing. This helped build my business skills and also fed a hunger I have for helping others, especially those who can't help themselves. I also have a natural passion for the elderly, thanks to my great aunt who helped raise me. She taught me to love and respect others, for God made us all and has a purpose for each of us.

As graduation neared, TCU's Career Planning and Placement taught us how to seek employment, conducted practice interviews, and encouraged us to look through career guides.

EAST TEXAS CHILDHOOD

I grew up in Tyler and always knew I wanted something different in my life, as I would be the first in my family to go to college.

I was very active in the Disciples of Christ church, and due to my leadership role in the Christian Youth Fellowship throughout high school, I learned about TCU and ultimately applied. TCU was the only place I applied, and thankfully they accepted me; otherwise I would have only been able to attend the local junior college. Scholarships, financial aid, and working all four years through TCU allowed me the opportunity to get my college education.

Originally I felt out of place. It seemed the other freshmen had declared a major. I initially took a variety of classes to see where my interests and strengths were. One of those areas was radio-TV-film, yet my East Texas accent didn't lend itself well to broadcasting. So I took a speech and diction class to help develop a more neutral dialect, a requirement for an on-air news career.

That wasn't my calling. The class helped, but as the saying goes, "You can take the girl out of the country, but not the country out of the girl."

But once I settled in as a business major, I was selected to participate in the Educational Investment Fund. It was truly one of the most beneficial classes, and it paved the way for my business career.

BANKING AND INVESTMENTS

I received my BBA in finance. After interviewing with banks both locally and on the East Coast; in Washington, D.C.; and in New York, I began my career with the former MBank. It had the same feel that TCU had given me — one of family.

I worked there a total of nine years and went through the bank failures, government ownership, and ultimate revitalization of the banking industry. I learned that I am in charge of only one thing: my attitude. As Chuck Swindoll says, "Life is 10 percent of what happens to you and 90 percent of how you react to it."

I've been in my present position sixteen years and love the challenges and growth each day brings. Wonderful supervisors and mentors allowed me to learn by making mistakes. They taught me to be a giver, not a taker. Those who touch our lives so often, like teachers and mentors, are often the ones who go unnoticed. Yet they make a lasting imprint on who we become. I've tried to pass these blessings forward.

ON A RESCUE MISSION

I work in Dallas, but when I go home to Kaufman, about an hour away, I devote each evening to caring for animals in need. I founded Furry Friendzy Animal Rescue and Wildlife Rehab in 2004, and we became a nonprofit 501c3 in 2006. Our mission is to act as a shepherd for animals in need of help — to care for and find loving homes for unwanted, abandoned, neglected, and abused animals. Volunteers make up 100 percent of our staff; we have no paid employees. Every single donation is put to use for the direct benefit of the animals. It seems to me that God has a purpose in creating all things, and there are many lessons the animals can teach us if we are just willing to listen, observe, and learn.

We take in animals of all kinds and provide rehabilitation, medical attention, socialization, and a chance to find a loving and caring owner for the domestic animals, while the wildlife is released back into nature on private property.

ADVICE
- Walk in faith and trust.
- Believe in yourself.
- Do what you love.
- Never give up — continue to reach for your dreams.

MAKING A DIFFERENCE
Pylar Pinkston ('86), in foreground, and some Furry Friendzy volunteers have a great day in the sunshine with their four-legged buddies.

Roger Ramsey
Deal with Honor, Act with Courage, and Refuse to Fail.

Roger Ramsey ('60) was recognized as Who's Who in Business, 1959.

ROGER RAMSEY *is chief executive officer and managing partner of Ramjet Capital in Houston. He was a 1960 graduate of the Neeley School with a bachelor of science in commerce and major in accounting. He has held senior executive positions and was founder and chief executive officer of Allied Waste Industries and co-founder and chief financial officer of Browning-Ferris Industries, both NYSE companies. In the private company arena, he was founder and chairman of both VeriCenter and MedServe, Inc., both of which he built and sold to public companies.*

Roger has used his experience and knowledge of accounting and finance as a director of several public and private companies. He is a member of the board of trustees of TCU. He has been a member of the Neeley School International Board of Visitors and has been instrumental in helping to build the Houston Business Network.

My first job came when I was 14. I told my dad that some of my friends had gotten jobs after school and on weekends at gas stations or grocery stores, and they had plenty of spending money. I thought I should drop out of school or at least drop school activities and get a job at a gas station. He told me he would give me a job so I could see how I liked it.

Dad apprenticed me to Jake, his long-time porter and jack-of-all-trades. Jake was pleased as punch; this was his first job in "management," and I was his staff. Jake started every day at 7 a.m., so I was going to have to get up earlier than usual.

Our first task was to build an auto-wash rack behind my father's dealership. To accomplish this, we needed sand and gravel from the San Jacinto River. Jake drove us to the river in the shop truck and picked out a nice clean deposit of white river sand. He handed me a shovel, curled up under a tree, and told me to wake him when the truck bed was full of sand.

After I woke him up, he drove us back to the dealership, where I unloaded the sand. When that was completed, Jake took me down to the railroad siding where a boxcar waited. The building supply guy in town had ordered a carload of cement, and my dad bought some of it at a good price because we were going to unload it and save the owner the expense.

The cement sacks weighed almost a hundred pounds each, and it was about 120 degrees inside that boxcar. After awhile, Jake took pity on me and stood just outside the door to take the sacks from me and toss them in the back of the truck.

After the wash rack was completed, our next big task was to re-tar the roof over the repair shop area. Somehow Jake got the melting pot up onto the roof without my help. I had to climb up a two-story ladder carrying a 90-pound block of tar. It was late June or early July, and I was dragging.

Jake took pity on me and cut the blocks in half with an ax so they were easier to handle — but only after he showed me that he could run up that ladder carrying a full block of tar on each shoulder. I couldn't pass that test. After a few ten-hour days in the hot July sun, melting tar, slopping it on the roof with mops (if you got the tar on your skin, it immediately raised a blister and if you didn't get it off soon enough, it burned a hole), and shoveling gravel on top to hold everything together, we finally finished the roof.

That afternoon, my dad said it was time to see how the business worked and that tomorrow I would work with him in his air-conditioned office.

The next morning we got up at a leisurely hour, had breakfast, drove downtown to the post office to get the mail, and went to the drugstore for coffee. My dad met a man who was looking for a new pickup, so we all went to the dealership. The prospect looked over the truck, decided it was just what he needed, and they negotiated a price. The customer wrote out a check for the down payment and signed a note for the balance while someone put paper tags on the truck. The happy customer drove away.

My dad turned to me and said, "For the last month you have been getting up early, shoveling sand and gravel, emptying a hot-as-an-oven boxcar, digging post holes and building forms for concrete, melting tar and spreading gravel for the roof, and burning your body with splatters. For that work I paid you $150.

"This morning we got up late, met a few people downtown, came out here to my air-conditioned office, and sold a man a truck. I made $1,500, and it is just now 10 a.m. I'll let you decide whether you're going to spend the rest of your life working with your back or your brain."

I've never forgotten that lesson, and I've always been happy I stayed in school and learned to work with my brain.

SCHOOL AND TRAINING

I was raised just outside Houston in the farming community of Crosby. My father was the Chevrolet dealer in town, and he imbued (or cursed) me with the entrepreneurial spirit.

I came to TCU in 1956 because I thought I was a football player and Abe Martin gave me a partial scholarship. It took only a year for me to realize that I wasn't big enough, fast enough, strong enough, or good enough to play football for TCU. It was a small, friendly school and felt comfortable to a small-town boy from southeast Texas.

My major was accounting, the language of business. I chose it because it was easy for me, and I felt that if you understood accounting, you could understand business.

Dr. John Wortham was my economics professor, and we connected on a special level. He challenged me and made me think and perform at my top level. I learned to be prepared, and when I'm prepared I usually win. I don't always get a good result when I'm unprepared. I almost majored in economics, but I just wasn't sure how an economist made a living.

I took a position with the international accounting firm of Arthur Andersen & Co. My seven years there taught me how to exist and excel in a very competitive employee environment and honed my finance and accounting skills so that I could quickly learn to be CFO of a public company.

EXPERIENCE COUNTS

In the early days of Browning Ferris Industries (the late 1960s and very early '70s), we were busily consolidating the waste industry. The conglomeration trend of the early '60s had only recently come to a disappointing end. The general view at the time was that when a company acquired other companies or assets that increased their size in revenue or assets by 10 percent or more, the acquiring company had to stop and file a new registration statement with the SEC, laying out the transaction and providing audited, consolidated financial statements of the combined companies.

BFI was a small company at the time, and 10 percent of revenues was a small number. The accepted process meant that we couldn't continue our game plan of acquisitions of solid-waste companies at a rapid pace. We had a large pipeline of acquisitions that needed to be closed, and we were in danger of losing some of them if we had to halt for several months to wait for the SEC to approve our filings. That was unacceptable, and we needed some way to continue our rapid growth.

We talked to several investment bankers and law firms in Houston and New York, trying to identify the best securities lawyer in the country to help create a way to continue our acquisition program. Their unanimous selection was a man named Manny Cohen, who had been an appointee to the original SEC in the 1930s and had risen to chairman for a number of years. Manny had just retired to become a partner with Dewey Balantine, et al, a large D.C. law firm. Manny's clients were the giants of American industry — companies like General Motors and General Electric — and no one thought he could possibly have time for a little upstart garbage company from Houston.

My partners and I thought we really needed Manny and that we should take our best shot at him regardless of what all the smart Wall Street guys said. We managed to get a thirty-minute appointment with him, and we flew to Washington, where we pitched him as hard as we could (and one of my partners was very charismatic), but he said he just didn't have time for us.

Manny was having a hard time shooing us out of his office until his secretary finally came in to remind him he had a plane to catch and needed to leave for the airport. As they were herding us to the door, one of my partners piped up and asked where he was going. Manny replied that he was giving a speech the next day in San Francisco. We exclaimed about the amazing coincidence — just where we were headed!

We had our corporate jet at National Airport (now Reagan International), so why didn't he ride with us? Our jet just happened to be the fastest corporate aircraft of the era. Manny thought that might be fun, so he decided to ride with us. By the time we landed at Las Vegas to refuel and restock our liquor cabinet, he had agreed to represent us in securities matters.

Within two weeks, Manny had written a two-page memorandum to the staff of the SEC (who had all been working for him until a few months before) that essentially said he understood the law said "ABC," but it really meant "XYZ," and that hereafter BFI would halt their acquisitions when they exceeded 10 percent of revenues. We would then file a "sticker" of one to a few pages, which would contain a description of the changes since the last full SEC filing, including audited financial statements of the combined companies (pro forma), and that sticker would be filed with the SEC and attached to a copy of BFI's latest filing.

BFI's stickered filing would be provided to the selling shareholders of the target and made available to the investment community in their normal method of accessing financial info from the SEC. In the next thirteen months, BFI completed the acquisition of 220 companies instead of the eight or ten we might have managed under the old rules. I believe this was the first time a prospectus was "stickered" with updated information and was the beginning of the shelf registration statements that are in common use today.

This experience obviously taught me about the value of refusing to fail, acting with courage, and the power of a group of good minds focused on a common objective.

ADVICE
- Creativity is relating seemingly unrelated things.
- Focus on recognizing talented people and get them engaged. Then focus, focus, focus. Shut out distractions.
- Stay out in the middle of traffic so something good has a chance to run over you.
- The game is not over until you leave the field and go to the locker room.

MIXING MUSIC AND BUSINESS
Tim Halperin ('10), American Idol finalist and Neeley Marketing grad, and Maddison Grigsby ('10), high school Spanish teacher for Teach for America and Neeley Finance grad, perform a duet at the 2010 Honors College Convocation.

John Robinson
No Matter What You Do in Life, Accounting Will Be Part of it.

JOHN H. ROBINSON *is executive vice president of the Amon G. Carter Foundation. He joined the organization as controller in 1980 and is now in charge of all grant-making activity. The Foundation awards grants in excess of $20 million yearly. Among its many gifts have been capital contributions to support TCU's Moudy Building, the School of Education, the Amon G. Carter Residence Hall, and the Amon G. Carter Stadium renovation project.*

John is a trustee of the Amon G. Carter Star-Telegram Employees Fund, president of the Boy Scout Foundation, and past board chair of Carter BloodCare. He has served on the boards of the Fort Worth Chamber, Tarrant County United Way, Exchange Club, and Rotary Club.

John graduated magna cum laude from TCU in 1977 with a bachelor of business administration in accounting. He has also served on the AddRan College Board of Visitors and The Campaign for TCU. He received TCU's Royal Purple Award in 2010.

There comes a time when everyone has to think for themselves and not just repeat what someone else has done. One of my duties as an intern at Ernst & Ernst was to proofread audit reports. Late one afternoon, I was comparing the handwritten copy of the footnotes to the typed version. Although all the words were there and spelled correctly, what it said just did not make sense to me.

The only person I could find still in the office was the partner in charge of the job. When I showed him the section I questioned, he read it, frowned, and agreed it did not make sense to him either. He then told me to go rewrite it and bring it back to him.

This was the first time I remember questioning what someone else had done, being challenged to think differently, and creating something better.

MAKING A COLLEGE CHOICE
I am a lifelong Fort Worth resident. During my high school junior year, TCU sent a letter to the top twenty or twenty-five students in each area public school with an invitation to apply for a two-week introduction to the TCU business school. I was selected for this immersion opportunity, and after that experience and hearing what TCU had to offer, I never even applied to another school.

One of the messages from that summer experience was no matter what you do in life, accounting will be part of it. TCU promised that if I came to TCU, majored in accounting, and made good grades — a really important qualifier — they would guarantee I would be offered a job by one of the Big Eight accounting firms. Then, after graduation, one career option would be public accounting. But more than likely, I would meet a client in a business I did not even know existed. I would like them, they would like me, and that is where I would go.

In my case, that is exactly what happened. I went from public accounting to working for the Amon G. Carter Foundation, where I have been for the past thirty years.

CAREER DEVELOPMENT

During my freshman and sophomore years at TCU, I worked every afternoon as a teller at a local bank. The summer before my junior year, I started working for the accounting firm of Ernst & Ernst as an intern.

My favorite job during college was teaching a freshman accounting lab during the fall of my senior year. Having to stand up and explain what I knew to others really helped solidify what I had learned.

Ernst & Ernst offered me a job during my junior year and encouraged me to graduate a semester early so that I could be there full time for tax season. I quickly learned that there needed to be a correlation between the work I was producing and the amount that could be billed for the time it was taking me.

David Bell ran the tax practice in the Fort Worth office of Ernst & Ernst and was responsible for my first job evaluations. I had no frame of reference of how well — or poorly — I had done during my first tax season compared to anyone else. But one of the things he wrote in that review was that I was going to be a "shining star." This praise was not coming from my parents, but from someone I thought was smarter than anyone I had ever met.

As long we worked together, David continued to give me challenging projects and opportunities to be creative. My potential and the expectations I had for myself were forever changed.

ADVICE

- When I was in school, I wondered why anyone would consider hiring me if I did not get everything 100 percent right. As ridiculous as that sounds, I still believe attention to detail is critical.
- Regardless of what others are doing or not doing, approach every task by anticipating what others might need to know or understand and be prepared to respond.
- Guard your reputation and integrity. Even people you may not know are watching and evaluating your actions.
- It is not about what others do, it is all about the decisions you make. People remember both good and bad.
- Learn to communicate clearly in both speaking and writing. Spelling and grammar are critical; do not rely solely on computer programs to check your work.

P.D. Shabay
The Suit with
Two Pairs of Pants

P.D. SHABAY *graduated from high school in Graham, Texas, as a four-sport letterman. As a gifted all-state quarterback, he received multiple scholarship offers but felt most comfortable at TCU, where he loved the Dallas/Fort Worth region plus the opportunity to work for a large company.*

He spent forty years with Textron's Bell Helicopter, retiring in 2007 as executive vice president. An expert in human resources and labor relations, Shabay created a program at TCU called C-Level Confidential, where twelve MBA students spend three hours with corporate executives at dinner and an intensive question/answer session.

He graduated from the Neeley School with a degree in management in 1968 and serves on the Neeley School International Board of Visitors. He also serves on the board of the Fort Worth Air and Space Museum, which will be housed in Alliance Airport.

My dad owned a men's and boys' clothing store in Graham. One day while I was there, a lady came in to buy her husband a suit. Dad asked her to bring him in for a fitting. "That's not possible," she said, "because he died. This will be his burial clothing."

Dad worked with the measurements she provided and quickly altered a suit. When she picked it up, he'd added a second pair of pants with it. "What do I do with that other pair of pants?" she asked.

"Every suit sold right now gets a second pair of pants," he replied. "We've offered that to everyone, and a promise is a promise."

THE EXTRA MILE

That story reminds me what honorable people my mom and dad were. They taught us the value of hard work, sacrifice for the family, and absolute integrity.

When I came to college, I decided I wanted to major in business, with the goal of working for a big company.

Dr. Murray Rohman made a profound impact on me when I took his labor law and labor relations courses. He was a no-nonsense guy teaching a no-nonsense course, and it later became the foundation for my business life.

Each summer I worked in the paint department at Bell Helicopter. During my third summer there, somebody asked me about my college major. When I answered personnel management, they moved me into that department.

LIFE-CHANGING EVENT

After graduation, I began work as a management development training instructor at Bell, but I got little satisfaction or motivation. My students were supervisors and managers who came from various Bell Helicopter disciplines.

I learned how radically different an engineer dealt with a problem compared to someone from marketing, or a line supervisor versus an accountant supervisor. I also learned that I would struggle in a job that was difficult to measure.

LAUNCHING A PASS
P.D. Shabay ('68) was a star
quarterback for TCU in the 1960s.

NO FEAR OF HEIGHTS
P.D. Shabay ('68) focused on helping Bell Helicopter fly high.

Then the manager of labor relations, Al Sauerwein, reached out and said, "I believe in you, kid. Do you want to work for me in labor relations?" To this day, I do not know why he chose me, but it changed the entire course of my life. Al was raised above a bar in Buffalo, New York. He had a BA from Syracuse University, an MBA from TCU, and a doctorate of law from SMU. He prepared me to take on any battle.

The first two years I worked for him, I literally followed him into negotiations with the UAW reps. I listened to what he said and how he said it, and then followed up with questions as to why. He made me supervisor of the department at 30 years old and gave me the best advice ever given to a labor relations professional: "Don't ever lie to the union. It will come back at you a million times." I never did, and it was a source of my strength through countless situations.

PHILOSOPHY OF NEGOTIATION
In a negotiation, it's critical that each side believe what the other is saying — total honesty should prevail. It's also important to realize that both management and the union are on the same team. Neither side wins if the company doesn't sell a product. If the company is successful long-term, that will help the union too.

It is beneficial to discuss everything each side wants and to get everything out on the table. Only then can we can begin to structure a successful package both sides can present to their constituents.

Sometimes I asked both management and union teams to sit down together before negotiations started. Then I asked everybody to put themselves in the other team's place for a while. That completely alters the perspective and builds empathy at the same time.

ADVICE
- Be totally honest at all times. A lie can come back to haunt you.
- People in different specialties approach problems in different ways.
- Finding common goals is critical. It's the initial part of settling a disagreement.
- People who can find acceptable middle ground in a negotiation are the ones who make things happen.
- All of us need incentives and challenges. People want to rise, to be the best. Discover how you can help others get there.

Richard W. Wiseman
65 Yards Away from a Scholarship

RICHARD W. WISEMAN *is a partner with the Fort Worth firm Brown, Dean, Wiseman, Proctor, Hart & Howell, L.L.P. He focuses his practice on litigation in the areas of business, condemnation, construction, contracts, landlord/tenant, public housing, and real estate development. He is a fellow of the Texas Bar Foundation and a charter fellow of the Tarrant County Bar Foundation.*

Richard has been recognized as one of the Best Lawyers in America and is listed in Texas Super Lawyers in Texas Monthly magazine, as a Top Attorney in Tarrant County by Fort Worth, Texas magazine, and as an Attorney of Excellence by the Fort Worth Business Press.

He graduated from TCU in 1973 with a bachelor of business administration and a major in management and then attended law school at the University of Texas at Austin. He has served on the Chancellor's Advisory Council.

I intercepted the pass and stood sixty-five yards away from a football scholarship.

It was the third freshman football game of a five-game season that pitted the TCU Wogs against the Baylor Cubs and my first start as a defensive safety. I'd worked my way up from fourth to first team, and I desperately needed a good game.

That fourth-quarter interception gave me the opportunity. I ran it back for a touchdown and helped us win the game by only two points.

Although I didn't get the scholarship until after Christmas break, I knew that night I'd won it. I'd spent my life's savings to pay for the first semester and had only $40 in the bank. If I hadn't gotten that scholarship, I would have had to drop out of school. And who knows where I'd be or what I'd be doing today?

COLLEGE EXPERIENCES

At L.D. Bell High School in Hurst, Texas, I played football, ran track, was involved in a number of school activities including theater, and graduated in the top 5 percent of my class.

I also started my own concrete construction contracting company in order to earn enough money to pay the first semester of tuition for a chance to earn a football scholarship as a walk-on.

I actually wanted to play football at SMU because an older classmate of mine was captain of that team. But after reading a *Fort Worth Star-Telegram* article about TCU head coach Fred Taylor, who walked on as a TCU freshman football player by asking the head coach for a scholarship, I decided to choose TCU. I believed Coach Taylor could identify with me. He encouraged me to pay my first semester for a chance to get a scholarship the second semester.

My major was management, with a minor in marketing. One of my professors provided me addresses of area mobile home park developers in the DFW area that led to my advertising to those developers for a summer project. I was able to land a huge concrete construction contract with Trammell Crow & Co. for construction of 85,000 square feet of driveway/sidewalk concrete work and two miles of curb and gutter. I hired eight other football players, trained them, and we completed the project before the start of fall football practice.

SOLIDIFYING A CAREER

I had only one job in high school, every summer from ninth grade on, and that was with Shirley Concrete Construction Company. But at a salary of $2.50 per hour, I could never earn enough to pay for even one semester of college at TCU. That pushed me to start my own business the day I graduated from high school. I learned that quality work attracts new customers by word-of-mouth.

I continued my concrete construction business in the summers at TCU, using teammates as workers. Not only did they learn the trade, but it made for great camaraderie. We constructed all the concrete for a huge mobile home park in the summer between my junior and senior years. Not only did we take great pride in completing the project, but it was extremely profitable and earned me approximately $30,000 in today's dollars for two and a half months of work. It paid for my law degree from the University of Texas law school.

Later, in the legal field, Richard Miles was my mentor. He was like a father to me as well, giving practical advice. Mr. Miles told me six weeks into my associate law practice, "If you promptly return your phone calls and work hard, the biggest problem you will have is that there's not enough time to handle all the business."

He was dead-on right. With little to no marketing and only word-of-mouth from satisfied clients, the biggest problem I have today is not enough time to handle all the business coming in the door.

ADVICE

- Hard work and preparation in the practice of law are no different than any other business area or, for that matter, than in life in general. Ninety-nine percent of the time, you'll come out on top.
- Take all the advantages that a great university like TCU has to offer — not just academically, but socially and civically as well.
- Get to know your professors! They are a great resource of knowledge and experience, not to mention a possible invaluable reference because of the Neeley School's reputation nationally and internationally.

SCHOLARSHIPS MAKE
A DIFFERENCE
Ron Parker ('76), Chair of TCU Scholarship Campaign, receives a Neeley Heritage Scholarship check for $150,000 from Brad Wallace ('95), chair, Neeley 75th anniversary kickoff celebration.

Rick L. Wittenbraker
Team Members Work
Toward Common Goal.

Rick Wittenbraker ('70), no. 22, playing defense for TCU.

RICK L. WITTENBRAKER *is senior vice president, general counsel, and chief compliance officer for Waste Management, Inc. The company provides comprehensive waste management services to municipal, industrial, commercial, and residential customers throughout North America.*

Before that, Rick was a partner in the Houston law office of Bracewell & Patterson, L.L.P. He headed the firm's business practice group, which included mergers, acquisitions, and various other business structures.

Rick graduated from TCU in 1970 with a bachelor of business administration and a marketing emphasis. He was a basketball letterman at TCU and is a member of the TCU Board of Trustees.

Teamwork is vital, off and on the basketball court.

In the summers during college, I worked construction jobs in Dallas. I set electric power poles for a utility, did electrical work in apartment construction, and was a laborer for a hotel construction project. As far as I know, everything I worked on is still standing.

In construction, you learn the same sorts of things you learn when you're on a sports team. The members come from a wide variety of backgrounds, maybe very different from your own, and they may have future plans that are also very different from yours. To be successful, you have to put aside those differences and concentrate on doing the best job you can.

I was always proud that I put myself through college on an athletic scholarship. And I played on a team with James Cash, Bill Swanson, Jeff Harp, Mike Sechrist, Tom Swift, Carey Sloan, and others who were just as serious about school as they were about basketball. We all knew that what we learned in school would carry us a lot longer and farther than sports. All of those teammates remain big sports fans, but our business and professional careers are more important.

YOUTH AND COLLEGE

I was born in Indiana and lived there through my junior year in high school. I went to a big suburban Indianapolis high school and had time only for school and sports.

Dad's company relocated to Dallas, so we moved there for my senior year. We bought a house in Richardson so that my brother Tom and I could attend school there. Then someone told my dad that interscholastic league rules made transfer students ineligible for sports for one year.

Tom and I had never come home after school at 3:30 before. Mom told Dad that she wanted us home at 6, and she wanted us tired after sports practice. So Dad's assignment was to find us some place where the school was good and the coaches would make us tired. We ended up at St. Mark's School in Dallas. The school was very good, and so was our basketball team. All five of our starters went on to play basketball or baseball in college, and I received an athletic scholarship at TCU to play basketball.

I chose TCU over three other schools that recruited me because I liked the people. I wanted to major in business, and the Neeley School had what I wanted.

I was dating Connie, and she said she would go to TCU instead of Texas Tech if I went there. That worked out pretty well, and this year we will celebrate our fortieth wedding anniversary.

LAW SCHOOL AND CAREER

Right after graduating from TCU, I went to law school at the University of Texas at Austin. I studied business law subjects to the extent I could get the courses to make a concentration. Most law schools — and Texas was no exception — focused most of their attention on teaching people how to be trial lawyers, so you had to work at it to put together enough business law courses. You have to learn a lot of business law in your first job.

Following law school, I started at Bracewell & Patterson in Houston. Two things give you an advantage when you start in a business law practice: a basic understanding of business concepts and financial statements and a willingness to put in the extra time to learn your trade on the job. TCU's Neeley School gave me an excellent understanding of business and finance, and I was willing to put in the extra time learning to serve real business clients.

New lawyers often struggle in two areas. First, they do not know how to write in clear, simple sentences. Second, they do not understand business or know how to read financial statements. TCU gave me a great background in both these areas.

Mom and Dad had the biggest influences on me and on my career. They tried to give me some very basic principles of family, hard work, and honesty, and then they let me make my own choices. I always knew they were there for support if needed, but they expected my two brothers and me to take care of ourselves.

Mom and Dad were very independent people, and they raised three very self-reliant sons.

ADVICE

- Take all the accounting you can stand, even if you're not going to be an accounting major. It will always be relevant, and you will use your accounting knowledge every day in almost any career.
- Be prepared to work extra hard early in your career so you have options later.
- Life and career are more than an IQ test. The tortoise often beats the hare in the intermediate and in the long term.
- Recognize that every person in your company or other organization can make an important contribution. Every person deserves your respect, no matter what position he or she holds. You never know when you will need help, and often the help you need will come from people below you in the organizational chart.

Global Perspectives

"Your value to the world isn't what you make; it's what you give."

DAVID BREEDLOVE

"I encourage every young person interested in business to subscribe to the Wall Street Journal. *Ten minutes every morning opens up a world of possibilities."*

SETH HALL

"Life is an adventure. Be open to what the world offers."

SALVADOR RODRIGUEZ

The challenges of globalization have transformed the environment facing business leaders in all industries. Technology has erased geographic borders, and the globalization of markets has led businesses to form strategic worldwide alliances. The Neeley alumni in this section have recognized the challenges and opportunities presented by the global economy and have adapted strategy, resources, and organizations in creative ways for business success, and they've found ways to give back to society.

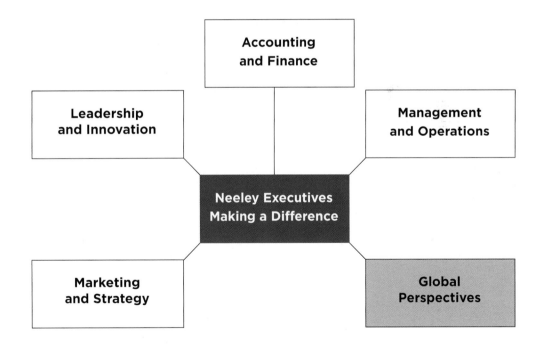

GORDON ENGLAND
THE SOFT STUFF
IS THE HARD STUFF.

GORDON R. ENGLAND *is the president of E6 Partners, LLC, which builds international business opportunities and government relationships, with special emphasis in the defense and security sectors. Mr. England has served as the twenty-ninth Deputy Secretary of Defense, the seventy-second and seventy-third Secretary of the Navy, and the first Deputy Secretary of Homeland Security, all in the administration of President George W. Bush.*

Prior to joining the federal government, Mr. England served as president of General Dynamics Fort Worth Aircraft Company (later Lockheed), president of the General Dynamics Land Systems Company, and corporate executive vice president of General Dynamics Information Systems and Technology Sector, Ground Combat Systems Sector, and the International Sector. His business career spanned more than forty years as an engineer and senior executive, beginning with Honeywell and working on NASA's Project Gemini space program.

Mr. England graduated from the University of Maryland in 1961 with a bachelor's degree in electrical engineering and then earned an MBA from TCU in 1975. He has served in a variety of civic, charitable, and government organizations, including city councilman; vice chair, national board, Goodwill, International; the USO's board of governors; and the Neeley School International Board of Visitors.

In 2011 he was the recipient of the inaugural Bob Bolen Civic Leadership Award presented by the Neeley School to honor a civic or corporate leader of national stature for his or her contributions to the building and stewardship of our communities and nation.

Every time I walked into the Oval Office, I thought about events that brought me there. I thought about my random luck being born to hardworking parents who instilled in me a strong work ethic. I remembered how my dad, a bookkeeper, went back to school in his forties to get a general equivalency diploma. Later he graduated from the Baltimore College of Accounting and eventually became president of the Maryland Accounting Association.

I thought about my electrical engineer training and the opportunity to participate in America's early space flights. I remembered the sacrifices my wife and children had made so I could return to school for an MBA in my mid-thirties.

I thought about great bosses and co-workers like Larry Sill in the Gemini program, Juan Sandoval, Bob Lee, Bill Dietz, Ted Webb, Herb Rogers, and Dick Adams — wonderful colleagues! I thought about my bosses at the time, President George W. Bush and Secretary of Defense Donald Rumsfeld and Bob Gates, who expressed confidence in me.

This is a land where a person can study, work, and prepare for the right moment to make the most of the skills acquired. That's what I've always tried to do.

CHILDHOOD

I grew up in a Baltimore row house, a series of identical homes that share a common side wall. Mom and Dad were great people, and they worked constantly. Because of economic circumstances, both had to drop out of school after eighth grade to help support their families. Dad had become an orphan early. His mom was dying and asked a neighbor to take him in. That family's last name was England. Dad used the last name England all his life but didn't get it changed legally until near-retirement.

I started working young and had a number of unusual jobs. I began as a baseball park peanut-counter. My job was to put ten peanuts in each bag, then fold and seal them for vendors. The boss often came by and randomly pulled a few bags to count. If I had put eleven peanuts in a bag, I got in trouble, but I was OK. I learned economics early in my life!

For high school, I wanted to attend nearby Mount St. Joseph Catholic School, but yearly tuition was a huge $325. My parents couldn't afford it, so I needed a job to help pay. I found after-school work as a movie theater usher, making 47 cents an hour. After I'd been there a while, the manager called me in.

"Gordon," he said, "You're doing a great job. We're giving you a raise." I got a huge increase — to 49 cents. But he lauded my efforts and showed it financially, so I appreciated that.

COLLEGE AND EARLY CAREER

I went to the University of Maryland and majored in electrical engineering. I also liked literature classes. I remember being the only guy in one English literature class! As graduation neared, I began a job hunt. One day my wife Dotty and I went shopping and passed a men's clothing store. There was a beautiful suit in the window with a sign that said, "Suits for successful executives who want to make $10,000 a year." Wow, we thought, if we ever get there, we'll be rich!

My first salary was $5,800 per year, working for General Electric in Syracuse, New York. But it snowed 112 inches that winter, so I eagerly took another job in Florida, with Honeywell. I worked for NASA's Project Gemini launch program. As that program ended, many engineers went to the Centaur program. I got the opportunity to come to Fort Worth to work at General Dynamics.

CAREER ADVANCEMENTS

As I moved into supervisory positions at General Dynamics, I realized I needed more business skills, like management and accounting, so I enrolled in TCU's Neeley MBA program, taking one night course per semester. I also took several undergraduate business courses as prerequisites.

After about six years, I decided I'd finish the last twelve hours in one semester and work full time too. We had three children at home, but we decided I should try it. So I practically lived at work or school, studying in TCU's library until it closed each night. Upon graduation, I'd acquired new skills I could immediately apply and use for the rest of my career.

After that, I worked as director of avionics and then moved to Detroit as vice president of General Dynamic's ground combat (Land Systems) division. In the early 1990s, I was brought back to Fort Worth as president of General Dynamics.

GOVERNMENT SERVICE

During President Bill Clinton's administration, Secretary of Defense Les Aspin called to ask me to consider government service, but I didn't feel the time was right. A few years later, in George W. Bush's administration, I got another opportunity.

I worked for the Defense Department, which has a budget similar to the world's seventeenth-largest country. The entire government is astoundingly complex. When I worked for Mr. Rumsfeld, we separated Defense responsibilities into three categories. Each of us had primary tasks, and we shared responsibilities for the third category. For the most part, he became Mr. Outside, dealing with interagency, international, and public situations. I was Mr. Inside, dealing with budgets and internal operations. Secretary Gates and I used the same formula.

When I reflect back about this service, several thoughts occur to me:

I spent eight years in various jobs and found experience a great asset. The average appointee stays only between nineteen and twenty-two months.

In government, there's not much appreciation for money, because it just comes in. It's not viewed as an asset, but a tool.

People are sent to Washington either to make new laws or to spend money. So every year you get new rules, whether you want them or not.

Voting is a great privilege. If you don't like who's making the rules, you can vote them out. That's a safety valve unique to democracies.

We must provide businesses the environment to improve and provide individuals the incentive to move up by working harder and learning more.

ADVICE

- The soft stuff — working with people and relationships — is the hard stuff. Interpersonal skills are critically important. Many people with good technical skills can improve their careers by mastering the soft skills.
- Nearly everyone can teach you something.
- The most valuable gift you can give is your time. It's finite. When you give it away, you can't get it back. And it's a gift when people give you their time.
- In a large organization, centralization rarely succeeds. It's more beneficial to develop a decentralized system, with a uniform set of metrics to use for management and measuring the work of all groups.
- In a big manufacturing plant, it's not just the product but the infrastructure. Value everybody's talent and find ways to nurture it.
- Every business benefits itself by creating an environment where people can excel.
- Never stop learning.

Laurent Attias
A Job Is What You Make It.

LAURENT ATTIAS *is president of Alcon-Europe, Middle East, and Africa. Founded in 1947, Alcon is one of the world's largest eye-care companies. With operations in seventy-five countries, the team is constituted of nearly 15,000 dedicated employees. Alcon sells a range of pharmaceutical, surgical, and consumer eye-care products used to treat diseases, disorders, and other conditions of the eye.*

Laurent has held many different professional positions with Alcon, including marketing research, international marketing, pharmaceutical sales, and sales and marketing of surgical devices and laser vision correction.

He graduated from TCU first in 1991 with a bachelor of business administration and major in marketing, then with an MBA in 1994.

One of the first things I learned is that a job is what you make it. My first job at Alcon was as a marketing research analyst. This was a good starting point for learning the pharmaceutical market Alcon competes in.

By definition or job description, that job was only about generating secondary research, or published data reports. Within my two years in this responsibility, I changed the job scope by focusing more on primary research. Thus I could provide guidance helpful to the marketing department for strategic and tactical decisions.

By making this shift, my role and perception changed from a "report-writing" person to a strategic and tactical partner to the marketing product managers' team.

CHOOSING AN AMERICAN BUSINESS SCHOOL

At TCU, I received a BBA in business with emphasis in marketing and the MBA in finance. Being originally from France, I always wanted to study business in the U.S. I admired the hands-on practical approach of teaching business in the United States versus the theoretical approach in France and Europe at the time. TCU accommodated flexibility that I needed to allow me to pursue the MBA. I applied for the program very late in the summer due to some unexpected issues with France's requirements for military service, requiring me to return to France.

For both the undergraduate and MBA programs, the size of TCU and the Neeley School in comparison to programs at larger schools ensured a more immersed experience and close attention from and access to faculty.

Dr. Shannon Shipp's marketing strategy class spurred my initial interest in marketing at a strategic level. The class was taught through real-life case studies and emphasized understanding the big picture and crystallizing the key variables of an issue.

During my MBA studies, I really enjoyed working as a graduate assistant in the Center for Professional Communication in the Neeley School. This allowed me to become very comfortable in formal presentation settings. I became conversant with different multimedia options, like video conferencing. And I got to teach others.

CAREER AT ALCON

There is no doubt that the emphasis on those presentation skills was a great benefit to my career and to actually getting my job! During my MBA internship at Alcon, I offered my skills of designing presentations to directors and vice presidents. This resulted in my being noticed and receiving a job offer.

Bill Barton, Alcon senior vice president of international markets, mentored me in marketing strategy and tactical execution. With his coaching, I learned not to just compete and gain share in a given market, but instead to drive the market and be the game-changer. He taught me to create the opportunities and capitalize on them.

Kevin Buehler, president and chief executive officer of Alcon at the time, taught me how to transfer best-in-class marketing skills to effective skills in the management of entire operations or businesses. He taught me to constantly measure progress, reassess, and adapt.

I learned how to drive a business as a whole, balancing the resources at hand, marketing being only one of them, and how to become an agent of change at an organizational level.

ADVICE

- Focus on execution. Drive decisions into actions.
- Make your passion contagious through strong communication skills.
- Consider any job you are in as your time to acquire certain skills. As soon as you have proven to others in your organization that you have acquired these skills, you must seek the next set of skills to acquire.
- You have to manage your career. Don't wait for others to manage it for you. Be cognizant and realistic of where you are in skill development.
- Consider your career as a set of "boxes" you must check in order to keep elevating. How quickly you check the box and get to the next skill development will depend on your level of personal drive.

Michael Baer
Find a Business That Fits Your Personality.

IT'S A MATCH
Michael Baer ('85) and Susan Oliver Baer ('87) met at TCU in 1983 and married in 1988.

MICHAEL BAER *has more than twenty years of experience in investment banking, trading, and private banking in New York, London, Frankfurt, Tokyo, Hong Kong, and Zurich. Prior to founding Baer Capital Partners Ltd., Michael was the head of private banking and a member of the executive board at Julius Bär Group, the largest Swiss private bank.*

Baer Capital Partners Ltd. was founded in 2006 by experienced finance professionals. The broad mandate of its subsidiaries is to conduct investment management, corporate finance, and wealth advisory businesses in the Indian subcontinent and the Middle East region.

Michael graduated from TCU cum laude with a bachelor of business administration and major in marketing in 1985. He is a member of the Neeley School International Board of Visitors.

After TCU graduation, my parents wanted me to come back home to Switzerland. I wanted to stay away from home and chose Hong Kong as my first destination of a long international career. Since my parents would no longer sponsor me, I boarded a flight with two suitcases, flew to Hong Kong, and searched for a job. I found one as an analyst for Hong Kong listed shares.

With my background from TCU in accounting and marketing, I was able to research companies with names I could hardly pronounce. I assume that I did a good job, as I was promoted quickly and ended up being in charge of sales to European clients.

This first career move set the foundation for a long international career.

UNIVERSITIES IN AMERICA

I grew up in Switzerland and, like most children there, went to public school. After getting the baccalaureate degree, I wanted to study in the United States.

I went on a tour and visited several schools throughout the country. One of the institutions I visited was TCU, and it was apparent immediately that this university was different. People were very friendly, even welcoming. I did not expect this. The curriculum was designed to fit my needs, and the international center was able to introduce me to other students, who in turn told me all about TCU.

I was not sure what I wanted to do when I entered college. We had a family company, but I was not sure that I really wanted to work for the family. I hoped that a degree in business would give me enough background and understanding so that I could go out into the world anywhere, get a job, and start a career. A degree in business was a good starting point, and I was able to take advantage of it.

My major was marketing. I believed then, as I do today, that marketing is everything in life. You need to market yourself, every day, all the time. If you are looking for a job or if you are talking to clients, you always need to understand how marketing works. If you are selling or developing products, marketing is an absolute must.

John Thompson was one of the professors who had a profound impact on me and was seriously interested in my progress. He pushed me to broaden my horizons and to accept new ways of thinking; he forced me to adopt new strategies when solving problems.

I completed my master's at the Massachusetts Institute of Technology, where I was able to complete the Sloan Fellows Program, a one-year, numbers-based curriculum.

MAKING CHOICES

There were many experiences that allowed me to decide what I did not want to do. These are just as important as the ones that actually do define what you want to do! For me, one defining moment was the accumulation of negative factors that led me to leave the family business and set up my own company in India and Dubai. I figured out that if your vision, style, and risk appetite do not match that of the company or its major shareholders, it is time to move on with life.

It is a hard decision, especially if the expectations people have in you are different. Breaking away is a courageous but liberating experience.

Starting a new business is difficult and riddled with danger. Trying to work for yourself, building a sustainable enterprise, and being a good corporate citizen can all be achieved if you are the founder of the company.

ADVICE

- Enjoy your time at the university. Learn, explore, and debate. And know that going to work is much more difficult.
- Explore your passions and use your time wisely. Learn about things in which you are genuinely interested.
- One of the most important work attributes is honesty. It's not always appreciated by others, but it's always welcome to those who mean well.
- It is hard work to build a career. It can require endless hours, determination, and much high quality work to get started and stay ahead.

David Breedlove
Humanitarian Mission Drives Career.

DAVID BREEDLOVE *co-founded CrossFoot Energy LLC in 2007 with two partners. The energy firm was developed to help make underperforming and dilapidated oil wells more productive. But most important, says David, is that the founders give away 10 percent of their top-line oil revenue — not the investors' money — to humanitarian and mission work.*

Earlier in his career, David was managing director of The Private Consulting Group, assisting successful businesses and high-impact individuals with their financial planning. He is a former executive committee member of the Fellowship of Christian Athletes, has provided color commentary for the TCU/ESPN sports network, and also served as a chaplain to the TCU football team.

At TCU, he graduated with an undergraduate degree in accounting in 1992 and an MBA in 1993, while being a four-year letterman and two-year captain on the football team.

Four pivotal events shaped my life:

First, after graduation from Lee High School in Tyler, I hoped for a football or academic scholarship. I was recruited by some Ivy League schools for academic/athletic purposes, but was snubbed by most of the elite football schools. I don't blame them. I was really small for a center. Coach Jim Wacker took a chance on me. As he offered me a scholarship, he said he believed in me and that he thought I might even be a team captain one day. That moment was life-defining. I was eventually a two-year captain and a four-year letterman. I've talked to many friends who played football over the years, and they were also encouraged by Coach Wacker.

Second, my wife Kelly is an amazing woman and the great love of my life. We married in 1993 as we waited tables at Joe T's to pay for my last semester of grad school. She played a pivotal part in helping me make it through that and every other battle I have faced in my life and has always been my greatest advocate and friend. She is probably the strongest and most godly woman I have ever met. Choose your spouse carefully; your entire future will be affected by that decision.

Third, becoming a father taught me instantly how great God's love for me must be. If I can be so captivated with love for these children, how much more able must God be to love me?

Fourth, a dear friend brought me an opportunity I hoped might come across my desk once in a lifetime. With the support of eighty investors, we started CrossFoot Energy and capitalized the business with a distinctive business model.

Our management company is structured to drive a significant portion of the top-line revenue to charities in furthering Christ's love. We give away a portion of our money, not the investors'. This mandate gives a greater purpose to CrossFoot Energy than simply making money. Our bylaws pay the first of each dollar to these causes.

Specifically, we got involved in humanitarian and mission work to Muslim communities in the Himalayas of Central Asia. We build schools, hospitals, and orphanages, hoping to help people understand how much they matter to God. I take teams of men there during the summers to trek deep into the mountains and serve alongside our overseas partners.

EARLY YEARS

My first job was mowing yards, from ages 14 through 18. I drove my riding mower around the neighborhood and dragged the push mower and gas cans in a trailer behind it. I learned to budget, to satisfy customers, and to keep the equipment running. I also learned that if you don't do a good job for the neighbor, it really stinks getting fired in front of the whole neighborhood. I didn't want to do that as a career, but in hindsight I could have always fallen back on that business. I'm glad I didn't have to, and I really appreciate guys who do that for a living!

In college, I started out as a political science major but switched to accounting. I planned to get my MBA and then go to law school. I finished my undergraduate studies by taking twenty hours my last semester. Several professors said I couldn't switch majors, graduate on time with an accounting degree, and start my MBA by my fifth year.

Somehow I made it, thanks to Dr. Bill Moncrief and others for bending the rules a bit. I tried to make the most of my five-year scholarship and completed the MBA in a year and a half but was burned out on school and just went to work. Another three years for law school seemed like an eternity.

CAREER AND CORPORATE GIVING

My first job after college was as a financial advisor with a group in Dallas, where I learned about business succession planning, investment advising, and tax planning. I learned to see the difference between companies that succeeded and those that failed. I also learned to persist in meeting with folks who really don't like to talk about these issues. More importantly, I was able to see how some families created wealth while others created a lasting legacy by teaching their heirs stewardship.

Many people have been mentors.

Mike Breedlove, my dad, taught me how to handle adversity. He lovingly bailed me out of trouble when I was at my breaking point but allowed me to struggle and experience the weight of my own mistakes. He taught me that I had more strength than I imagined and that my breaking point was much further away than I realized.

Gary Randle, a former TCU basketball player and co-founder of H.O.P.E. Farm — which helps kids break away from crime and poverty — helped me through some dark times. He inspired me to look outside my own struggles and make a difference in others' lives.

Dave Stone of First Rate Investment Systems gave me a model for building a company that gives away a large portion of the top-line revenue. He proved that it can be done — so after watching him for six years, that's how we built CrossFoot Energy. I find great satisfaction that every barrel of oil we produce impacts our mission in Central Asia.

ADVICE

- Never give up, but be willing to evolve. If you're wrong, don't be a blockhead and keep doing the same thing while expecting a different result.
- No matter what happens, take responsibility for your role in the situation. There's always a role to play, and there's always a lesson.
- Live for a cause greater than yourself. If you don't have a cause, ask God to reveal the one He has for you. That's what you were designed for: to make a difference in the world.
- Money is not the end, merely a mechanism for helping others. If your focus is your own happiness, no amount of money will fill that hole in your heart.
- Your value to the world isn't what you make, it's what you give.

Jesse C. Edwards
Two Minutes
Shifted My Priorities.

JESSE C. EDWARDS *is the senior product manager for medical image interpretation and distribution systems for Philips Healthcare, the leader in North American implementations. The company develops radiology and cardiology devices as well as information and image management technology solutions for customers around the world.*

Jesse graduated with a management major from the Neeley School in 1980.

M. J. Neeley directly changed my life, but he never knew it.

He gave a talk to TCU's business fraternity sometime around 1980. After his remarks, the students drifted to one side of the room, while he stood at the other. I walked up to him and searched for an ice-breaker. He was an old man at that point, certainly in his eighties.

So I said something like, "You must be very proud of your accomplishments, given that you've been able to support TCU enough to have the business school named after you."
His response caught me off-guard.

He said something like, "No. I'm not overly proud of my life. There are two types of men in the world: men who are motivated by money and others motivated by their careers. I've always done what I needed to do to make money, and I did it well. Men who find a career doing what they enjoy make enough money to take care of their families and are happier. I should have been a career man."

This philosophy of pursuing a career instead of money has been central to my life.

TEXAS BOUND
I grew up in a suburb of Omaha, Nebraska. In high school I worked in a hospital running errands. These duties ranged from moving emergency-room patients to x-ray, getting specimens to the lab, wrapping patients for their last trip to the morgue, and taking pharmaceuticals to patient wards. That exposure to health care is what has shaped my career to this day.

After graduation, I started college part time. My best friend, who was at TCU, invited me to visit for the weekend. She set me up on a blind date with a TCU freshman. Well, it was love at first sight — for me anyway. Suddenly, I had a new goal. I wanted to leave Nebraska, attend TCU, and date this incredible woman. It worked out. We celebrated our thirtieth year of marriage in June 2011.

I think luck plays a factor in most people's lives; it has in mine. Other than that, I'm a highly analytical person who married well! As a result, the chaos I may have had in life was smoothed out by the love of a good woman.

At TCU, I majored in business with an emphasis in finance. It prepared me well. Also, I received an Army ROTC scholarship and went into the service after graduation.

Charles Becker in economics opened my eyes to the "invisible hand" first described by Adam Smith. He also gave me excellent life advice. I'm still a finance kid despite the graduate work in software engineering. Because of that, in my writing and speaking I emphasize business justifications.

CAREER FOCUS

I was an Army medical platoon leader in the 7th Infantry Division. I learned about the reality of leadership versus the theory I had been taught. I also developed a more colorful vocabulary.

As a platoon leader, I managed a significant budget, and a couple of years later, I was managing the Army health-care budget in the Republic of Korea while overseeing management studies. In Korea, I earned a master's in system management at night through a program offered by the University of Southern California in Seoul. Later I completed another master's in computer science on USC's campus in Los Angeles.

Since 1991 I've had primarily a civilian career. It's a combination of radiology and administration. Medical devices are mostly all computers, so I've been able to use my degrees to integrate the medical and computer fields.

I served in Afghanistan in 2008 training Afghan National Army combat battalions and retired from the Army Reserves in 2009 as a lieutenant colonel. I enjoyed the dual career tracks but don't miss doing mandatory physical-fitness training.

ADVICE

- My career attitude has always been: Find work that is fun.
- A business education is a great career foundation, because it provides financial perspective. Business classes benefit almost anyone.
- A career is dynamic. It's a living, breathing entity. Nobody knows where they'll end up.

FOCUS ON INTEGRITY
Dean Homer Erekson ('74) discusses business ethics in 2010 with BNSF Next Generation Leadership students, Catherine Brown ('11), Caitlin Irvin ('11), and Trevor Woods ('11).

David Glendinning
The Mysterious Case
That Arrived by Plane

DAVID R. GLENDINNING *recently retired as a special agent in charge at the U.S. Department of Justice, where he supervised nationwide criminal investigations of felony crimes against the United States. He currently works as a private consultant on legal and federal investigative matters.*

David graduated from TCU in 1974 with an undergraduate degree in management and received a law degree from SMU.

Very early on Thanksgiving morning, 1978, an FBI agent and I met the first plane as it landed at Dover AFB, Delaware, and watched as Airmen began unloading the bodies.

Dover was my first assignment as a young special agent with the Air Force Office of Special Investigations. It has the largest military mortuary on the East Coast. Just a few days earlier, U.S. Congressman Leo Ryan had been killed in Guyana in an assassination allegedly ordered by People's Temple cult leader Jim Jones, whom Rep. Ryan had been investigating. Jones and his followers were soon found dead in their compound in the dense Guyana jungle, apparently of a mass suicide that followed the congressman's murder.

As the bodies were transported to Dover, my responsibilities included gathering evidence related to Rep. Ryan's death and assisting in the forensic identification of the bodies. The first body off the plane was that of Jim Jones. There were about 100 others.

Then we heard we'd receive more remains — first estimate about 150, then 300, then 500, and finally, in only a matter of hours, more than 900. As you can imagine, plans changed rapidly. Working with base officials, we learned not only how to manage the immediate and urgent need for a huge increase in logistics, forensic support, and security resources, but to accomplish it all under the growing presence of worldwide news organizations — all while remaining focused on the primary goal of supporting the investigation of the congressman's murder.

This was certainly a powerful learning experience in crisis management: how to confront multiple situations in a rapidly changing dynamic when all the world is watching.

THE 70s LOOK
This photo of David Glendinning ('74) was taken in 1973.

NEW YORK NATIVE

I grew up in the New York City Borough of Queens. My interests included stickball, the Mets, the racetrack, and generally not getting caught!

My first job in high school was as a stock boy at a shoe store in Queens. I hated it. The job lasted about three weeks. The boss had a highly developed (in his view) inventory system. It meant that for each pair sold, an entire wall of shoes had to be rearranged like a Rubik's Cube. That job killed me. I learned that for your life's work, you should look for a job you find fun, and the rest will take care of itself.

I heard there was a recruiting push by Texas colleges in 1969 in the Nassau County area. Several guys talked about a great Fort Worth school. At the end of recruiting season, many chose TCU.

I was one of them. I'd heard it had a strong business school, and I'd be exposed to a different regional culture — and TCU offered me early admission.

I majored in management, which gave me great training for addressing situations and devising solutions in law enforcement. Dr. Quinn McKay, who taught organizational behavior, was wonderful. Literally, not a year went by over the course of my thirty-year-plus federal career when I did not think of and purposefully apply his foundational lessons in understanding the dynamics of organizational behavior and professional responsibility.

Dr. McKay's insights into corporate versus personal behavior — and the motivating forces for them — proved key in devising various proof scenarios associated with investigations I managed involving criminal fraud and corruption allegations against Fortune 500 corporations.

CAREER THOUGHTS

I graduated from SMU law school. Based on my Neeley training, I concentrated on business law and the impact of criminal and civil statutes — as well as regulatory requirements — in shaping the business environment.

My first position was as a special agent with the Air Force Office of Special Investigations. That's what brought me to Dover Air Force Base and the Jonestown investigation. We collected and processed potential evidence in support of this extremely high-visibility investigation. I learned the real meaning of crisis management and that no matter the nature of the challenge, good managers can move through seemingly overwhelming circumstances. Not much frightened me after that.

My training in business and law schools taught me to manage investigations in much the same way a business plan is developed: Focus on a goal and adopt a strategy to accomplish it. That's what we had to do in the aftermath of Jonestown. Every boss since then has trusted my judgment and allowed me the freedom to stumble, a circumstance from which I learned most of what I know.

ADVICE

- Business school is a training ground for life, not just business.
- Government needs good managers. People get promoted based on technical ability and rise as proficiency increases, but not as many as you might think have a clue how to manage people and processes.
- Your success as a manager arises from your ability to personally engage and lead people — with respect — toward clearly defined, ethically achievable goals.

Seth Hall
Airplane Parts Business
Takes Off.

SETH HALL *is president and chief executive officer of an amazing business. He started Source One Spares in 1997. In college he began working weekends at a company that repaired airplane parts. He picked the company to use as a college research project and wrote a business plan about how he'd begin a company in that field.*

"We've completed over 30,000 part sales transactions." Seth said. "With 10,000 aircraft in operation, there is a good probability we have one of our parts on most commercial aircraft flying worldwide." Total sales revenues since inception have exceeded $400 million.

Seth graduated with a double major in marketing and management from the Neeley School in 1994 and serves on the Neeley School Alumni Executive Board.

While growing up in Houston, I had a yard-mowing business. I started at a young age with our house, added the neighbors, and built it up steadily. By the time I graduated from high school, we were handling forty-five yards a week with several employees. For my first vehicle, I paid $9,000 cash for a pick-up truck when I turned 16 years old. That helped expand the business into other neighborhoods.

Mowing yards taught me several things: marketing (knocking on doors), business development (planting winter grass for free to cut year-round), management (hiring employees to grow the business), capital equipment investment (buying mowers and weed trimmers), plus the inherent entrepreneurial rewards of working hard to earn a good living.

My father Wayne, now CFO of Source One Spares, gave me enough rope — even at a young age — to go out and test the boundaries. Working with my dad and my younger brother at Source One is one of the best things in my career.

My uncle Skip Kinch, a TCU BA and MBA, helped steer me to TCU. His background in human resources helped Source One correctly navigate the inevitable employee and operational issues that have come up in our business.

KEEP 'EM FLYING
Seth Hall ('94) provides a tour through the Albuquerque Source One Spares warehouse.

PICKING A SCHOOL

In my high school senior year, we took a road trip statewide to see a bunch of different universities. TCU just felt right. Fort Worth is also a great college town.

As a private school, it was more expensive, so there were financial obligations that I took on. Working my way through school was required to help pay the way, but it gave me great work experiences to complement my education. Having just recently paid off my last TCU school loan, I can truly say it was worth every penny and then some.

At TCU, I focused on marketing and management for a good basis of skills that I still rely on. In one of Bob Greer's management classes, we role-played terminating an employee. To this day, I think back to that class when I have that unpleasant experience with one of our employees.

Because of my work experience at UPS and Wal-Mart while attending TCU, I was able to go straight into the SMU MBA program after graduation. I met my future wife Dana Haran in the TCU Library on the evening of October 5, 1991. She graduated from TCU with a nursing degree and went on to become a nurse practitioner in cardiology.

FLYING BUSINESS

My first full-time job after graduation was the company I started, Source One Spares. We stock, repair, and distribute commercial aircraft parts for Boeing and Airbus planes. Our customers are the world's airlines. During our first year in business, 1997, we did $395,000 revenue. After four years, in 2000, we did $52,000,000.

In September 2001, the terrorist incident profoundly affected the country and the aviation business. We reduced from eighty-eight employees down to twenty-five people. With airplanes parked everywhere, airlines could rob parts from their own planes rather than buying from our company.

Several major airlines filed for bankruptcy, and our company took some major receivable hits. We were forced to file for bankruptcy as well. The company reorganized and fought our way back. On the downside, it was terrible for our employees who were let go and for our vendors who were hurt. On the upside, once you've been through something like this as a business manager, it seems you can handle anything else that comes your way.

Several TCU graduates came to work at Source One Spares shortly after we started. When we downsized, most moved on and started their own companies. They are Andrew Sage, who owns Broadwing Aviation; Taylor and Michelle Reimer White, who own adWhite; Rob Hill, who owns Ranger Air; and John Rosson, who owns Import-Export Aviation. I am very proud of them all and how successful they have become as entrepreneurs.

ADVICE

- I encourage every young person interested in business to subscribe to the *Wall Street Journal*. Ten minutes every morning opens up a world of possibilities.
- Never underestimate the value of persistence. Sometimes half the battle is sticking with something until you are successful.
- If you want to start a business, spend thirty days straight working on it for ten hours a day. At the end of the thirty days, you'll be well on your way.
- You don't need an original idea. Just pick an industry you like and go for it. Out-hustle everyone else. Young people often try to think about the next Microsoft, Coca-Cola, Google, or some other great invention, when there is a world of business opportunity right in front of you in so many different niches.
- As TCU marketing professor John Thompson said over and over again in his classes, "Business is not rocket science, folks! Just go out there and do it."

J.J. Henry
Serving the Community Too

RONALD "J.J." HENRY III *is a professional golfer on the PGA Tour. While at TCU, he was the individual runner-up in the 1998 NCAA Division I Men's Golf Championship.*

He turned professional and joined the Nationwide Tour in 1999 and moved up to the PGA Tour in 2001. His first major tour win was the 2006 Buick Championship; he was the first Connecticut golfer to win the event. He also played on the 2006 Ryder Cup team.

J.J. graduated with a bachelor's degree in marketing from the Neeley School in 1998.

Playing for Team USA in the 2006 Ryder Cup has been the apex of my career thus far. It was much more than just an athletic accomplishment; it was emotional and mental as well. To be entrusted to represent your country on such a large stage in not only your play, but your demeanor, conduct, and sportsmanship as well, was a responsibility I took very seriously. I will always carry that experience with me.

American Ryder Cup team members received a grant for a charity of their choice. This gave my wife, Lee, and me the opportunity to set up the Henry House Foundation, a nonprofit organization. Its mission is to generate public awareness and to support community-based programs that focus on the health care and well-being of children in this community.

We've focused on tangible products. For instance, we helped Cook Children's Hospital build a teen room for its patients age 13-18. We call this a "needle-free" hospital zone, a place where they can relax with their family and friends. In 2009 we also began purchasing therapeutic equipment for KinderFrogs, a laboratory school for children with Down syndrome located in TCU's College of Education. This gives children there access to the best possible therapies.

Golf provided me with a great profession. It's also given me a platform to help children in my community.

HIGH SCHOOL AND COLLEGE

I grew up in Fairfield, Connecticut. That's a long way from Fort Worth, but the environment just seemed right. I loved TCU from the beginning — from the academics to the athletics to the overall atmosphere of Fort Worth. I met my wife there, and we are both proud TCU alumni.

In high school I worked as a golf caddy. This taught me some great life skills that I use in both golf and business. It also taught me about hard work and how to make thoughtful decisions.

During my middle-school years, Dick Borges was both my history teacher and the best coach I've ever had. The life lessons he shared with our basketball team made a lasting impression on me, and I recall them to this day. He always encouraged us to be better on and off the court, and he truly shaped me at such an impressionable age.

At TCU I majored in marketing. It's an integral part of my profession, because I now market myself! Whether it's corporate outings, sponsorships, or meet-and-greet events, I'm fully aware of how I'm presenting myself as a potential marketing opportunity.

ON THE TOUR

Since graduation, I've been very fortunate to play on the PGA Tour for eleven years against the best golfers in the world. To be able to live out my childhood dreams motivates me to work hard and to continue learning as each year comes. I am very fortunate to do what I've always wanted to do for a living. I've learned never to take these opportunities and experiences for granted.

My father, Ron Henry, Jr., introduced me to the game of golf. He also always made sure that I focused on my academic and personal growth as well.

Paul Kelly is a golf pro whom I knew growing up. He believed in my game and gave me the confidence to pursue golf wholeheartedly.

ADVICE

- Focus on the competitive will to succeed.
- Don't be afraid to set high goals and expectations for yourself. Think big, aim big, succeed big.
- Marketing is a valuable skill. Whatever our professions, it's helpful to be able to point out our special skills to prospective employers and clients.

MARKETING THROUGH
THE YEARS

Marketing Class, 1957

Marketing Club, 1969

Marketing Association, 1972

Marketing Association, 2011

Brian Hoesterey
Prepare to Run Through the Wall.

BRIAN HOESTEREY *is a managing director at AEA Investors LP, a private equity firm in New York City, where he focuses on investments in the specialty chemicals and value-added industrial products sectors. Before joining AEA, he was an executive with BT Capital Partners and has advised corporate management and boards of directors throughout the world on financial and strategic issues.*

He graduated from TCU in 1989 summa cum laude with a bachelor of business administration in accounting and then received his MBA at Harvard.

My first job after graduation was as a financial analyst in the Investment Banking Division of Morgan Stanley. This was a demanding but rewarding job, and I learned a lot about business and people. Given that we were working with CEOs and CFOs of major companies, I learned that perfection was the requirement in everything we did. This included no typos or mistakes in any of our presentations.

This standard of work still stays with me to this day. I picked up very strong finance skills and an understanding of process management. Perhaps more importantly, I saw many different interpersonal styles and learned that there were ways to be tough and demanding as a "boss" or leader while being fair, enjoyable to work with, and a good mentor. Adopting that type of management style leads to success, because people will want to work with you — and that results in your having the best team around you.

I had my first global exposure during my first job, because I had the opportunity to spend two years in Hong Kong. This really opened my eyes to business in the rest of the world and allowed me to have an outsider's perspective on the United States. This has been invaluable in terms of having an objective view on different business styles and practices and realizing that we can learn from many different cultures.

While at Morgan Stanley, I also learned a lot from my fellow analysts. Morgan Stanley attracted the best and the brightest from all the top universities. However, I also learned that some of the most successful analysts were hardworking smart kids from the nontraditional schools who were every bit as smart, more determined, and more personable. When I look for employees today, I look for people who have that fire in the belly and leadership personality as well as the intelligence and experience.

EARLY DAYS

Our family moved to Dallas when I was eight years old. My primary interests in high school were tennis, playing clarinet, business, and pre-law. I had an internship at a law firm during high school and decided that was not for me. My extracurricular activities were a key focus and took up a lot of time.

My first jobs in high school and college were mowing lawns and teaching swim lessons. I worked for myself in both jobs. The experience taught me that it is far better to control your own sales and business generation so that you can make more money than just being a hired hourly employee. While I have not continued to be an entrepreneur, I have looked for situations in which I could actually share in the value I've helped to create, not just be a paid worker.

Like many high school students in Texas, I did not see any point in leaving the state. However, unlike many of my friends who were going to the University of Texas, I wanted a smaller school with a more personal touch. I was looking for an undergraduate honors program and a business degree. I also wanted to go somewhere with Division 1 athletics.

ENTREPRENEURIAL SPIRIT
Matthew Burke, Neeley first-year student and the 2011 Texas Youth Entrepreneur of the Year, accepts congratulations from Brian Happel, Fort Worth Market President for BBVA Compass.

SHAPING THE FUTURE

I was an accounting major at TCU. Accounting prepared me for all sorts of jobs, as it is the basis of financial statements and its own language. It has given me a strong business base and one that is difficult to ever pick up if you don't study it in college.

Another part of my business degree at TCU that has served me well is the communications emphasis at the Neeley School. The emphasis included a business communications class focused on written communication and specific oral presentations, including videotaped sessions, which significantly improved my overall communications.

Several teachers and professors in high school and college made a lasting impression. The first was Mr. Temme, an eighth-grade social studies teacher. His primary teaching method involved using two simulation games that he had developed himself — a World War I simulation game and a world trade simulation game. He showed that you could learn more through unconventional routes when the students were excited and engaged.

Joe Steele at TCU also taught both conventionally and unconventionally. His course on board of directors and governance went well beyond the textbook and explored how companies could truly create value and how boards can be helpful in this. I currently serve on seven boards, and his guidance and thought process still serve me well today.

CHALLENGING MOMENTS

One of the least favorite parts of our job as control investors in numerous companies is the need to make changes to senior management, which often entails firing CEOs. Frequently these are accomplished, seasoned executives who have not often failed in situations and who are almost always older than I am. The memory of the first time I had to make a CEO change has remained with me.

The CEO was a very nice man, and we had a great relationship. He was hardworking, cooperative, and open to constructive feedback. But we needed more aggressive change in the business and did not think he could get it done. He was in his early sixties, and I had concerns that it would be difficult for him to find another CEO job after this one.

When we made the decision to replace him, we took all this into consideration and structured a solution that we hoped would work for all parties. We designed an orderly transition in which this CEO would stay on and help us with the search for the next. We explained that we would now be owning the business for several more years and thus needed a CEO who would lead the company for the next owners, which could be an additional five years. We invited him to stay on the board as a way to help the transition.

This solution worked out well. While I think it was still a big blow to the incumbent CEO, it allowed him to retire with his pride intact and with an explanation that would allow him to go on to something else. We got the benefit of his experience in our CEO selection and transition and maintained a very good relationship with him.

This proved to me that even in difficult situations you can seek out win-win outcomes. Also, it has been a requirement of all our management transitions that we balance the needs of the companies and shareholders with the personal aspects of hard-driving, proud individuals who are having their lives turned upside-down.

ADVICE

- It starts with a strong work ethic. There really is no substitute for determination and dedication to being successful. People notice this and want to work with someone who will "run through walls."
- Find something that you love doing and then find a way to make money and a career out of it. You will spend the rest of your life in the jobs you choose, so make sure you love them. You will be most successful and happy doing something you really enjoy.
- Find mentors along the way. Seek out and try to work for people who you believe you can learn from, who will make you better, and who are willing to help you out with your career.

Lori Lancaster
Overseas Travel
Develops New Perspectives.

LORI LANCASTER *was named managing director of the global investment bank Nomura Securities in July 2010. She focuses on oil and gas clients for the Americas. Before that, she was a managing director of Goldman Sachs, an associate in investment banking for J.P. Morgan, and an assistant vice president of Bank of America.*

She holds a 1991 bachelor's degree in finance from TCU and an MBA in finance and strategic management from the Booth School of Business at the University of Chicago.

When you see the past come alive, it can shape your future.

That's what I discovered when I signed up for the TCU at Oxford summer program in 1990. That was the year the integration of the European Market was being finalized. We had meetings in both the United Kingdom and Brussels. Then a friend and I spent a few days traveling the European mainland. The first thing I noticed was that when people my age went for coffee, they talked mostly about politics!

I quickly realized their centuries-old historical perspective. Our culture's been around a few hundred years, while theirs involves multiple centuries. In addition — because of geographic proximity — they're forced to interact with, and understand, other languages and cultures. In the U.S., we must go out of our way to leave the country. In Europe, they can just drive a few minutes!

And Europeans know much more about our history than we do about theirs. This trip awakened in me the desire to learn much more about world cultures, and it's something I think about every day.

EARLY LIFE

I was born in Texas, at the old Perrin Air Force Base near Denison, during the last years of my father's military service. Dad's subsequent career was at Tandy Corporation. We settled in Arlington when I was about ten years old.

The youngest of three children, I was the first in my immediate family to graduate from college. My father had started college in Ohio near where he grew up, but left to join the Air Force. My mother married at a young age and started a family. I viewed education as opportunity. Listening to stories from my father on his international travels while in the military instilled a desire to see more of the world.

Although I was always intent on attending college, it was still a fairly scary proposition and something I had to navigate largely on my own. While both my parents were very supportive of my goals, this was a road they hadn't exactly traveled themselves.

I wasn't ready yet to leave Texas, so I focused on in-state schools. Tandy Corporation offered a partial scholarship program to children of employees. TCU had a good reputation and made sense for geographic and financial reasons. I started TCU thinking I would complete a then-offered five-year MBA program and major in computer science. I later realized that business was going to give me a much broader career base.

I was also fairly quantitative, and my decision was cemented when I took my first finance and accounting classes and loved them.

NEELEY RANKING HIGH
Super Frog celebrates the Neeley School's undergraduate rank of no. 30 in national ranking in BusinessWeek *in 2010.*

JOBS AND CAREER

Given the cost of a TCU education, my parents and I agreed they would pay for my tuition and housing but that I would keep part-time jobs throughout school to pay for discretionary items and other living expenses.

I had a variety of jobs during college: a hostess and waitress in restaurants, working retail at the local mall (not a good choice for a clothes horse, as I may have spent more than I ever made), and a bank teller. My favorite job was in high school, when I applied to work at Texas Rangers stadium one summer. Hanging out watching the games on my break, selling a little pizza (probably eating even more), and flirting with college boys — not a bad way to make a few bucks!

On a more serious note, holding part-time jobs during school and in the summers since I was 14 years old clearly taught me about time management, professional responsibility, and the value of money.

After graduation, I joined the credit training program at NCNB, later to become Nations-Bank and ultimately merged into Bank of America. I spent a little more than two years in Fort Worth and Dallas in their credit analyst program and then was asked to move up to the D.C. area in 2004 to help with the integration of a recent acquisition of a large bank in Maryland.

I worked there for another year and a half before leaving for Chicago and graduate school. Commercial banking for me was excellent training in accounting and financial statement analysis, skills I still use regularly in my current career.

Almost every move I've made academically and professionally since high school has come with some level of fear and even self-doubt. But I've learned those are the only situations that offer potential for growth.

I believe mentors are incredibly important and think it is almost impossible to reach one's full potential without them. As a woman trying to succeed in what is often seen as a male-dominated industry, I've found it critical to find both female and male mentors. They bring different — but equally important — perspectives to situations, and their advice reflects such. Be ready to ask for what you want and justify why you think you deserve it, because the guys do this way better than we do.

ADVICE
- Learn accounting.
- The only way to expand your comfort zone is to step outside of it on a regular basis. If you're not nervous and somewhat uncomfortable, you're not challenged and need to make a change.
- Ask for feedback from others you trust to tell you the truth. Use this to increase your self-awareness and find a career that will fit well with your strengths and weaknesses. Don't force it.
- Manage your career or it will end up managing you.

Paul Lauritano
Great Books Help
Investment Career.

PAUL M. LAURITANO *is a managing director in J.P. Morgan's Global Special Opportunities Group (GSOG). GSOG is J.P. Morgan's principal investment platform, focusing on junior capital investments into corporate situations. The group is managed from Hong Kong with teams located in Beijing, Mumbai, Sydney, London, and New York.*

Paul has worked in finance in Asia for eighteen years. Prior to that, he was a member of the United States Foreign Service for six years. He speaks fluent Japanese and conversational Thai.

After receiving a bachelor's degree in Asian studies from the University of Virginia, Paul earned his MBA from TCU in 1991 with a concentration in finance.

Two books tremendously influenced my life.

As a high school senior, I read James Clavell's historical novel *Shogun* about sixteenth-century Japan. I remember thinking that Japanese culture was very different and fascinating. I knew then that I wanted to learn to speak Japanese and to work in Asia. That prompted me to major in Asian studies and to seek a job that could take me to that part of the world.

David Schwartz, author of the book *The Magic of Thinking Big,* also made a great impression on me. His book was written in the 1950s and is still in print. Although I did not know him personally, the lessons in his book conditioned my mind toward success. I read the book six months prior to attending TCU and tried to apply his lessons during my time there. I think I've re-read the book about ten times during the course of my career

DECISIVE MOVES

I chose TCU for graduate school because I had an uncle who lived in Dallas, and I'd always wanted to live in the state. TCU was one of three schools to which I applied. They offered me an academic scholarship, which made my choice much easier. I was married and had a child at the time and had limited funds.

Prior to coming to TCU, I'd worked for the U.S. Department of State as a diplomatic second secretary. I had served at the U.S. embassies in Tokyo and Manila. Working in government had been very good training. However, the higher you advanced, the more bureaucratic policies seemed to determine your further advancement. I wanted to move into a field where my own actions were the chief determinant of my success.

In my TCU MBA studies, the theoretical grounding in finance theory helped me understand a lot of underpinnings to trading. My first job after TCU was as a bond trader for Lehman Brothers. At the time an MBA in finance was almost a prerequisite for getting a job on a trading floor.

The professor whose teachings I remember most is Robert Rhodes. He taught me business law and spent a great deal of time going through the commercial code. This background allowed me to work closely with lawyers, to ask them pertinent questions while structuring deals. I always believe in reading what the statutes actually say before just blindly accepting someone else's view on what they mean.

ADVICE

- Don't spread yourself too thin.
- Take time upfront to decide where you want to go and what steps are likely to help you get there.
- Address thorny or tough issues head-on and upfront. While these issues may not be fun to raise and sort through, if left unaddressed they almost invariably lead to bigger problems at a later date. But if addressed early and in a frank manner, there's a clear road forward when issues do occur, and there are no hard feelings afterward.
- As a trader, it is important to be on the right side of the market. If your decision proves to be wrong, you have to change course and get on the winning side! In trading, it is important to make money — not to have your initial opinion proven correct.

DEDICATED PROFESSORS
Neeley professors Garry Bruton, Mo Rodriguez, and Dave Craven take a break outdoors.

Melinda Lawrence
Saying Yes to
New Career Opportunities

MELINDA LAWRENCE *is a CPA and audit partner with Ernst & Young in Dallas. She leads client engagement teams, performing accounting and advisory services for both local and global companies in various industries, primarily real estate. In addition, she provides mentoring and counseling guidance for younger staff.*

She started her career at Arthur Andersen's Dallas office, worked with Andersen's U.S. Professional Standards Group in Chicago, and worked in Paris for three years assisting French clients on their U.S. transactions and SEC filings.

Melinda graduated magna cum laude from TCU in 1992 with a major in accounting.

I walked into my first Paris meeting and didn't know what they were saying.

This was my third day in France, and I was working with a large global client for Arthur Andersen's Capital Markets Group. Everybody spoke French except me! We had 100 points to cover. The only way I kept track was by listening to when they changed number, because I understood French numerals. Afterward, I quickly found another American who worked with the client and who brought me up to speed.

In 2000 I had received the opportunity to work in France. I jumped at the chance and worked with several global, billion-dollar French companies that were implementing initial listings in the U.S. I gained new perspectives that included an appreciation for the work ethic of these people, and I discovered that "our way" in the U.S. is not always the only way. I also learned that the United States has the best customer service anywhere in the world!

Two unrelated personal events made my three years there even more memorable. When it was time for our first beautiful daughter, Sophie, to be born, we had to take the bus to the American hospital. But the experience went well, and the hospital even brought us champagne to celebrate the birth.

Another time, our dog escaped from our central Paris apartment and made it to the city's far eastern side before the police caught up with him a couple of days later. They impounded him and marked him with an identifying tattoo inside his ear. He carried this as a permanent reminder of his adventure and it's made a great story for years.

During my time in Paris, Andersen fell apart, and I had to find new employment. I knew that when we returned to the U.S., I wanted to join Ernst & Young in Dallas. This worked out great, because Andersen and EY ended up merging in France, and we were able to stay another year in Paris.

DALLAS AND RICHARDSON NATIVE
I was born and raised in Dallas and attended Richardson High School, where I was very active in my church youth group, the community, dance, and any adventure on the lake, like water skiing. Dad and Mom always encouraged my sister and me to go to college. Dad was a CPA, and Mom was a teacher. Their love for learning spilled over into our family activities. Together we traveled all over the U.S., and by college I'd visited more than forty-five of the fifty states. I also learned at an early age the importance of giving back to the community.

When I toured TCU, I fell in love with the campus and the people. I realized I could reap the same benefits at TCU as I would at a larger school. I received an early acceptance and knew that was it!

As an accounting major, I was involved in Beta Alpha Psi and other business fraternities and served as a Neeley advising associate.

Dr. Robert Vigeland, accounting department chair, was always available to provide guidance, even if it was not related to accounting. A friend and I were in a car accident on campus and missed Dr. Vigeland's class. He called to check on us to be sure we were OK. When I got pretty sick for a few weeks during my senior year and missed more than a week of classes, Dr. Vigeland took the time to personally call and talk with me. His concern made a lasting impression. To this day, we remain in contact and get together at least once a year for lunch.

CAREER

I began working for Andersen as a staff accountant in Dallas immediately after graduation. This marked a time in my career early on that I learned to say yes to just about everything. This included new assignments and working with new teams.

By saying yes, I positioned myself for growth, and it opened the door to many excellent learning opportunities that otherwise might have been missed. As a staff member, I was willing to put myself out there to gain new experiences and to try things that weren't in my comfort zone.

During my time at Andersen, Alvin Wade diligently worked with me to help me gain experience for career growth.

At Ernst & Young, I also found an amazing network of professionals willing and ready to provide support because someone at EY had faced similar circumstances.

Billie Williamson, Ernst & Young Americas Inclusiveness Officer and audit partner, helped me understand what I needed to do to become a partner after I returned to the United States. Her assistance was invaluable in helping me navigate that path. Ed Montgomery, an EY audit partner, is a mentor whose extensive experience is something that I rely on consistently.

ADVICE

- No matter what task is handed to you, anything is possible if you are part of a team.
- Don't be afraid to say yes.
- Some of your most profound learning experiences will happen as the result of trials and challenges.
- Don't have so much pride that you do not ask for help. Opening yourself up is not a weakness. This allows opportunities for growth.
- In times of challenges, I lean on the Bible, in particular, from Proverbs 3:5-6, to trust in the Lord with all my heart.
- Find amazing mentors in your professional and personal life, and they will make a difference.

Vinod Mirchandani
Technology Analyst Creates Popular Book on Innovators.

VINOD MIRCHANDANI, *founder of Deal Architect, is a former technology industry analyst (with Gartner), outsourcing executive (with PwC, now part of IBM), and entrepreneur (founder of sourcing advisory firm Jetstream Group).*

He is a thought leader on trends in software, outsourcing, and offshoring and has advised companies on IT risk management, globalization, and sourcing issues.

Vinnie recently authored the book The New Polymath. *A polymath — the Greek word for Renaissance man — is one who excels in many disciplines. In the book, Vinnie shares his varied experience as a technology advisor and market watcher to explain — in business language — the diversity of today's technology and to profile a wide range of innovations.*

Vinnie earned his MBA from TCU in 1980 and participated in the Educational Investment Fund.

I have had several mentors and major moments in my career, but I give the most credit to "Lady Serendipity" for what happened in October 1983.

I had graduated with an MBA from Neeley in the summer of 1980 and gone to work in the Fort Worth office of Price Waterhouse. Three years later, I had just received my first promotion, but I was restless. I did not really enjoy being a CPA, and I'd noticed an opening published in the firm's newsletter. They were looking for staff in the Riyadh, Saudi Arabia, office. Not a plum expatriate assignment by any definition — and the region was about to get very dangerous.

As I was getting to Saudi, the U.S. Marines' barrack was bombed in Lebanon, and the Iran-Iraq war started soon after. Because the assignment was considered a "hardship," we were allowed to leave the country every three months. It gave me a chance to see the world, and I have now been to forty countries.

Going to Saudi in 1983 was a major moment because it honed my curiosity "antennae."

BUILDING ON EXPERIENCE
My two and a half years in Saudi Arabia allowed me to diversify my skill sets in a small office. I was allowed to work on technology projects I would never have done in a U.S. office.

I came back to the Dallas office but jumped at the opportunity to go back to another assignment in Saudi. From there I spent two years in London (where I met my Irish wife, who had been to thirty countries on her own) and in the Netherlands. My passport kept filling up.

From Price Waterhouse, I moved on to Gartner, an IT research firm, and then was an entrepreneur in a dot.com that failed.

For the last five years I have been a technology strategy consultant. I also write two technology blogs, and that has led me to write a well-received book on technology-enabled innovation, *The New Polymath.*

While the career has meandered, and the start-up challenged the family's financial foundations during the technology meltdown of 2001-2003, each of these moves has brought a new set of industry contacts. People are amazed when they hear that I wrote my book — which includes interviews and profiles of more than 150 innovators — in just four months. My wide network allowed me to do so.

ADVICE
- Take every opportunity to go out and shake as many hands as you can. I am part of every social network you can name — Facebook, Twitter, Flickr, and others — but there is nothing like breaking bread with people around the world.
- Be curious about a wide range of subjects. Polymath, in my book's title, is Greek for a Renaissance person like Leonardo da Vinci or an innovator like Benjamin Franklin, people who were good at many things.
- In today's society and workplaces, we are encouraged to be specialists. You do need to specialize and be very good at what you are doing at that particular time. But there is no law that says you have to do the same specialty over and over again in the same exact location.

BEIJING ALUMNI
In 2007, Neeley alumni celebrate with Professor Nancy Nix in Beijing.

Salvador Rodriguez
Prepared to Lead
Around the World

NOTE: This selection was based largely on an interview with Salvador Rodriguez just prior to his passing on April 26, 2011.

SALVADOR RODRIGUEZ *operated an international and corporate law office in Houston, Texas starting in 1997. He was a 1967 accounting graduate of TCU and law graduate of the University of Houston. A former letterman in football, he was an active member of TCU's Frog Club and the Houston Alumni Board.*

Salvador negotiated oil service contracts with Kuwait, Saudi Arabia, and Venezuela National Oil Company; handled transfer price issues with the United States, United Kingdom, Canadian, Venezuelan, Dutch, and Norwegian tax authorities; and negotiated joint ventures with the United Kingdom, Turkmenistan, Russian, and Saudi Arabian partners of U.S. companies.

Salvador's first job in high school was as a stock boy in a department store in El Paso. The unusual element is that it was in the ladies' lingerie department. That definitely made an impression on a 16-year-old boy.

While at TCU, he worked for the company that delivered the bed sheets and towels to the dorms and picked up the dirty ones from the prior week.

Those jobs certainly taught him something about humility, among many other things.

EARLY YEARS

Salvador was born in Mexico in 1945 and immigrated to the United States, moving to El Paso in 1953. He grew up playing sports and reading a substantial amount of history, both about the U.S. and the world.

He chose to attend TCU over Wyoming, Colorado, and the Air Force Academy because he was so impressed with the campus setting, and TCU was a good place to play football.

And maybe as an inkling of what was to come, he attended law school at the University of Houston rather than the University of Texas, because he fell in love with the city of Houston. He regarded it as one of the most sophisticated and cosmopolitan cities in the world.

CAREER PATHS

Salvador had wanted to be a lawyer since he was in high school. He originally intended to major in history, even though his high school freshman coach told him to avoid history classes taught by coaches. His summer counselor during orientation at TCU, an accounting adviser, Professor Charles Foote, exposed him to the world of business and its possibilities and was instrumental in directing Salvador toward a business degree as a prelude to law school. Salvador always regarded Professor Foote as a source of wisdom.

Salvador's first job out of law school was as an international counsel for Raymond International. He later went to work at Zapata Corporation, where he learned the art of negotiation, how to value a document, and how to draft documents in the basic legal systems of the world.

Two weeks after starting employment with Raymond, he worked on his first transaction, which involved construction piers for the new airport in Qatar. It was full of what seemed to Salvador to be incredible circumstances. In working for Zapata, he traveled overseas, managed visa issues, and negotiated on his own with Qatari government officials. Then he continued to Cairo to handle a tax situation. Following that was a trip to Rotterdam for an offshore rig matter. Six weeks later, he was back at home. And that had been his first trip abroad.

Throughout his career, Salvador benefitted from mentors such as Arwin Strelow at Raymond, Bob Rickard at Arthur Andersen, and Jeff Goddard from Zapata Corporation. Salvador appreciated their advice on various matters, including career, transactional, employment, and personal issues.

ADVICE

- Succeeding in business takes determination and humility.
- Life is an adventure. Be open to what the world offers.

NEELEY NETWORKS
Students gather at Dan Rogers Hall in 1970 for study and good conversation.

Wil VanLoh
Firm Basis for Valuation

WIL VANLOH *is the president and chief executive officer of Quantum Energy Partners, which he co-founded in 1998. Quantum manages a family of energy-focused private equity funds, with more than $5.7 billion of capital under management. He is responsible for the leadership and overall management of the firm and leads the firm's investment strategy and capital allocation process, working closely with the investment team to ensure its appropriate implementation and execution. He oversees all investment activities, including origination, due diligence, transaction structuring and execution, portfolio monitoring and support, and transaction exits.*

Prior to co-founding Quantum, Wil co-founded Windrock Capital, Ltd., an energy investment banking firm specializing in providing merger, acquisition, and divestiture advice to and raising private equity for energy companies. He has worked in the energy investment banking groups of Kidder, Peabody & Co. and NationsBank.

Wil has served as a board member and treasurer of the Houston Producer's Forum and currently serves on the finance committee of the Independent Petroleum Association of America (IPAA).

He graduated cum laude from TCU in 1992 with a bachelor's degree in finance and participated in the Neeley School Educational Investment Fund.

I grew up in Temple, Texas, a small town about two hours south of Fort Worth. Growing up, I loved three things: school, sports, and figuring out creative ways to make money. I decided to go to TCU because it had a good pre-med program (my parents wanted me to be a doctor), and I wanted to play football for the Horned Frogs.

In my whole life I think I have worked for someone else for a grand total of maybe two years (that includes my time in high school, college, and after college). I've always been an entrepreneur at heart. In college I started four businesses: window washing, a fraternity/sorority telephone directory, a phone message board, and a coupon book business. What I learned in the process is that I could accomplish almost anything if I did three things: visualize what I wanted to accomplish and articulate in my mind the steps or processes necessary to do so; work harder and longer than everybody else; and when I failed (as I often would), apply the lessons I learned from my failures to trying again and again until I succeeded.

FINDING A CAREER

I started off as a pre-med major but quickly learned that medicine was not my passion. My sophomore year I switched to the business school and ended up majoring in finance. My TCU education provided a solid foundation to enter the business world, particularly the experience on the Educational Investment Fund — my first taste of investing.

Dr. Chuck Becker, my economics professor, and Dr. Stanley Block, one of my finance professors and head of the Educational Investment Fund, made the biggest impact on my education. Both of these men embraced the Graham and Dodd style of value investing and taught me how to think about the true worth of a company. They inspired within me a genuine passion and curiosity for securities analysis and taught me the core financial principles that I would need to become an investor.

LEARNING ON THE JOB

My first job after graduating from TCU was as a financial analyst with NationsBank (now Bank of America) in its energy investment banking group. I sent out twenty resumés to various investment banks my senior year at TCU, got eighteen rejection letters (which I still have, by the way), two interviews, and one job offer. From the job search process I learned that if at first I don't succeed, keep trying. Because in many respects life is a numbers game — you have to put yourself in enough situations in order to have a shot at success.

From a business skills standpoint, in the nine months I spent at NationsBank and the nine months I spent at Kidder, Peabody & Co. (my second job out of school and the last time I worked for someone else), I learned how to tear apart a company's financial statements and create complex financial models to analyze mergers, acquisitions, and various corporate finance transactions. I also learned just enough about energy investment banking in eighteen months of working for two Wall Street banks to think I was qualified to start my own investment banking firm at the ripe age of 24. Thank goodness I didn't know what I didn't know, or I would have never attempted that.

Since I have been self-employed most of my life, I haven't really been in a lot of situations to have a mentor as most people traditionally think of them. However, the two most influential persons in my business career are my business partner of eighteen years, Toby Neugebauer, and my business partner of thirteen years, A.V. Jones, Jr. Toby was in my analyst class at Kidder, Peabody & Co., where on the first night we met in New York City at analyst training, we made an agreement that one day we would start a business together. And A.V. was a legendary Texas oilman-turned-venture capitalist, who in his mid-sixties saw something (still not sure what) in two 28-year-old guys that made him lend us his credibility and checkbook and together go raise an energy-focused private equity fund in 1998.

People often describe Toby and me as the yin and the yang. We have spent tens of thousands of hours playing devil's advocate with each other's thoughts and ideas, and that process has probably in aggregate been the biggest single contributor to my success. Toby is an unconventional thinker who has pushed me to think out of the box. A huge part of our collective success also stems from the common sense and tenacity that he embodies and has helped instill in me.

As for A.V., I think it is fair to say that Quantum Energy Partners, the private equity fund that the three of us started together in 1998 and that now manages $5.7 billion in assets, would never have come into being without his ability to see through our youth and inexperience to give us a chance to prove ourselves. From A.V. I learned that picking great people to invest in is much more important than picking great assets. I also learned to be patient and to never put myself in a situation where I could run out of money and be forced to make a move out of weakness. He also modeled for me how one can achieve worldly wealth but still be humble and treat even the most junior people with whom you interact with respect and dignity.

ON FINDING TRUE WORTH
The most profound experience in my life occurred about a year or so after college when I made the decision to completely give my life to Jesus Christ. Nothing has never been the same since. Knowing that God loves me so much that He would give His Son to die for my sins and that He is in complete control of every event in the world allows me to live both my personal and business life with a sense of peace, joy, and confidence that surpasses all understanding. Christ has given me a clear sense of purpose in my life that allows me to love other people more than I love myself and to help others with the gifts and resources that God has entrusted to me.

So in the search for true value in life, keep your priorities straight: God, family, work — in that order. Be humble in your success, for no man has achieved greatness by his own accord, but rather every man's success has been enabled by God who gave them the mind, intelligence, foresight, strength, skills, personality, and drive to succeed.

ADVICE

- Figure out what it is in life that you have a passion for and that you are good at and pursue that as your career with vigor and tenacity. You will never work a day in your life. You will be happy and content, and regardless of your profession, you can genuinely make as much money as you will ever be able to spend.
- Become a great listener. Seek first to understand before you seek to be understood.
- As long as you have at least an average IQ (which everyone at TCU has), common sense and emotional intelligence (EQ) are significantly more determinative of business success.
- Treat everyone with respect and dignity. True character is built when you do this for people who can do nothing for you.

IN CHINA
EMBA students visit China in 2010.

Fehmi Zeko
Become a Specialist in a Growing Field.

FEHMI ZEKO *is senior managing director and head of U.S. media and telecommunications for Macquarie Capital (USA) Inc., based in New York City. He has more than twenty-five years of advisory experience in the media, entertainment, and telecommunications industries.*

Previously, at Deutsche Bank, he was a vice chairman of its global investment bank and chairman of global media and telecom. Prior to joining Deutsche Bank in 2006, he was group head of global media and co-head of global communications at Citigroup. Most recently, he was vice chairman at Foros Group, a boutique investment bank where he was responsible for media and communications advisory practice.

Mr. Zeko has been involved in a number of significant transactions and industry mergers in media and communications throughout his career, including GE/NBC's acquisition of the Weather Channel, Time Warner's spin-off of its cable and AOL subsidiaries, Live Nation's acquisition of Ticketmaster, the sale of Vivendi Universal to GE/NBC, and Warner Music's IPO.

He received a bachelor's degree in marketing in 1981 and an MBA in 1982, both from TCU, and he is a member of the Neeley School International Board of Visitors.

I got my first job at age 11, caddying at a country club. I quickly learned — from the inside out — that golf is an important social and business sport. I also discovered that you need to make some very important and competitive people happy in a social environment.

I was social as a high school student and a well-ranked competitive tennis player from Kansas City. Much of my time soon centered on working at the tennis club.

I chose TCU for its size and for the chance to play for the ninth-ranked men's tennis program in the country. I was academically strong and originally thought I might like to be a doctor; I changed my major to business late in my sophomore year.

Once in college, two events shaped my future:

The Educational Investment Fund experience provided a practical learning environment. It opened my eyes to Wall Street and what a career in finance would really be like. It showed me how the Street works, from buying and selling stocks to what drives valuation. Coupled with a fantastic internship working in the office of the CFO at Union Pacific Resources headquarters in Fort Worth, this gave me the entire package to move from being an undergraduate to becoming an MBA to then be fully prepared for the workplace.

MOST DEFINITELY PERSONAL!
Fehmi Zeko ('81, '82) and former Mayor Bob Bolen enjoy the festivities at the Neeley 75th anniversary kickoff celebration in 2011.

In my junior year I became president of my fraternity, Phi Kappa Sigma. My class was a part of a major push to build its presence at the school. I learned valuable leadership skills and how to run a 200-person organization. Under my watch, our chapter was runner-up as the best chapter in the country.

CAREER STEPS

In 1982 I joined Citigroup's global investment bank MBA program. I was first hired as an associate in Citigroup's global petroleum group.

At the time, Citigroup and J.P. Morgan had the best corporate finance training on Wall Street. I received great skills training, including accounting and corporate finance. My college accounting and finance training prepared me well.

In 1996, going from Bear Stearns to Salomon Brothers was a pivotal move. Salomon was recovering from the Treasury setback and needed to rebuild its investment bank. And they desperately wanted to rebuild their media and entertainment group, which had been wracked by departures. Along with a group of three other professionals, I was recruited to run the media practice. That move positioned me to eventually run all of Salomon's — then Citigroup's — global media and telecom group.

The communication industry and the clients I service have been quite dynamic over my career. When I began to bank the industry, cable TV was just starting to be a growth industry with very few channels and HBO showing just movies. The wireless telephone industry was also just beginning, and the first handsets weighed three pounds. The internet did not exist! And the Dow Jones Industrial Average was 700. Fast-forward to today, where media, telecommunications, and technology are converging at a pace that requires bankers to think differently in order to service their clients. This makes what I do continue to be very dynamic and exciting.

MENTORS GUIDING THE WAY

I have been fortunate to have several mentors to guide my thinking and to offer role models. It started with my father, who thought I had natural ability working with people and anticipated that I might be a great salesman. He pushed me to think like an entrepreneur and to take risks, to be passionate about what I did. He gave me the foundation and strength to eventually start my own advisory firm.

As a student in the Educational Investment Fund (EIF), I worked under investment fund head Bob McCann, who later rose to great prominence on Wall Street — first at Merrill and today at UBS. He was an inspirational leader who both pushed all the students in the program and made it fun.

Dr. Stan Block is one of the five most influential people in my career. He was the EIF founder, a great teacher and thinker. He opened my eyes to the excitement and challenge of financial services and pushed me to seek an early career on Wall Street. He helped clearly position the Neeley School as an important factor in business education and is just a fantastic human being!

In my business career, three people were pivotal in opening doors for me. William L. Adams, retired chairman of Union Pacific Resources (now Anadarko), introduced me to several people on Wall Street after I had served a summer internship. Fred Pickering, my first major boss at Citigroup, taught me how to deal with real clients, how to lead a top-notch professional organization, and the importance of having fun. And Eduardo Mestre, head of investment banking at Salomon/Citigroup, was a world-class strategic thinker and ultimately recruited me from Bear Stearns to head the media group.

ADVICE

- The sooner you specialize in your career, the better. Get practical experience in that specialty. That creates enormous personal equity value.
- Figure out what makes people happy and what they need. I care about my clients and want to help them succeed.
- Have a passion for what you do. Love it — or don't do it!

Index

The People and Companies of *Major Moments*

Photos contained in *Major Moments* are used with permission from the TCU Mary Couts Burnett Library Special Collections, the Neeley School of Business archives, and individual contributors.